# SQUINT

José P. Ramirez, Jr.

University Press of Mississippi
Jackson

# SQUINT

## My Journey
### with
# Leprosy

*Willie Morris Books in Memoir and Biography*

www.upress.state.ms.us

The University Press of Mississippi is a member of the Association of American University Presses.

First printing 2009

∞

Library of Congress Cataloging-in-Publication Data

Ramirez, José P., 1948–
  Squint : my journey with leprosy / José P. Ramirez, Jr.
    p. cm. — (Willie Morris books in memoir and biography)
  Includes bibliographical references.
  ISBN 978-1-60473-119-4 (cloth : alk. paper)  1. Ramirez, José P., 1948-—
Health. 2. Leprosy—Patients—Louisiana—Carville—Biography. 3. Leprosy—
Louisiana—Carville—History. I. Title.
  RC154.R36 2009
  362.196'9980092—dc22
  [B]                                                    2008024098

British Library Cataloging-in-Publication Data available

# SQUINT (*skwint*)—to peer with the eyes partly closed.

During the Middle Ages, persons suspected of having leprosy were not permitted to attend church services, but they were allowed to view the religious rituals through an opening in the back of the church. This "window," an architectural feature called a "squint," was just big enough to allow a person to press his face against protective iron bars to view the Mass.

Up through the 1960s, persons affected by leprosy faced the prospect of partially losing their sight, causing many individuals to squint in order to have a clearer view of their surroundings.

In 1968, I was transported to the hospital in Louisiana in a hearse. The 750-mile trip on mostly two-lane highways was tiring for the drivers. When they stopped at rest stops or gasoline stations, I moved, trying to shift my body. This motion caused those standing close to the hearse to squint their eyes and peek inside.

In 1972, as I nervously watched from a side door for our wedding ceremony to begin, I squinted to see my fiancée finally receive her mother's blessing on the marriage.

# CONTENTS

# FOREWORD

The story you're about to read from José Ramirez places him firmly in the Carville Hall of Fame. The combination of José's innate sense of optimism and goodness and his compelling narrative make him a model, not just for people with Hansen's disease, but for anyone who is facing challenges in his or her own life. This book represents a significant contribution to the remarkable literary tradition that is an integral part of that magnificent story which, as they say, is "known to the rest of the world simply as Carville."

Carville has seen truly magnificent scientific and human achievements. Over the years, I've heard many compelling stories about the patients and doctors at Carville: Betty Martin, Stanley Stein, Josephina Guerrero, Sister Hillary Ross, and Dr. Faget to name but a few.

Just this past spring (2008), I visited the National Museum of Health and Medicine at Walter Reed Army Medical Center for the premiere of *Triumph at Carville: A Tale of Leprosy in America* in addition to the unveiling of an exhibit on my hometown of Carville, Louisiana. So many people have been captivated by the people and stories of the Gillis W. Long Hansen's Disease Center—from the patients like José to the selfless work of the Daughters of Charity to the research community to the community of Carville itself that embraced the facility and the people.

Growing up, my daddy engrained me with the notion that Carville was the best place to live on earth. And looking back, my daddy could not have been more right.

James Carville

# ACKNOWLEDGMENTS

This story, based on my life, is for the benefit of those newly diagnosed with Hansen's disease, more commonly known as leprosy.

It is dedicated to my wife, Magdalena, to my parents, José and Rosa, and to all those persons diagnosed before me.

This book would not have been possible without the support and love of my parents, José P. Ramirez and Rosa S. Ramirez; my parents-in-law, Roberto and Josefa Santos; and my siblings, Yolanda, Raquel, Diana, Margarita, Javier, Rodolfo, Idalia, Fernando, Ramiro, Rene, Gerardo, and Rosalinda. Thanks also go to Lorenzo Garcia, Julian Garza, Roberto Ortiz, Gabriela Ramirez, Glenn Skates, Elma Ramirez, Roberto Santos, Jr., Sergio Palizo, Leticia Palizo, Marta Vergara, Rosario Ramirez, Juan Puente, and José Luis Hernandez.

Ongoing encouragement from my children, José Roberto (J. R.) and Erika Betzabe ("Princess"), and over fifty nephews and nieces has been invaluable.

My deep appreciation goes to Sister Mary DeLillis, Sister Virginia Marie, Joanna Hooe, Darryl and Mary Broussard, Vernon Bahlinger, Oscar and Sandy Diaz, and high school friends, especially Nicandro "Nicki" Villarreal and Tony Navarro. I thank Ymelda Beauchamp for allowing me to include her poem "To Carville—The Hospital."

I would also like to thank those who critically reviewed the numerous drafts of this book, including Dr. Margaret Brand, Consuelo Martinez-Elizondo, Gilberto Rendon Gonzales, Irma Guerra, Anwei Law, Don Levit, Diana Ortiz, Alana Lenz, Erika Betzabe Ramirez, Yolanda Rios, Ana Santos, Marta Santos Vergara, Nicandro Villareal, and Gloria Quintanilla.

SQUINT

# No One Told You?

"You mean to tell me that no one has told you that you have leprosy?" With this awkward question, Dr. Dickerson from the Texas Department of Health informed me of my diagnosis. His wide-open eyes made his face look circular and forced me to focus on the center of his face, at a spot right above his lips. He slowly looked to his left and then to his right, staring in amazement at the people encircling my bed—parents, siblings, Sisters of Mercy, nurses, and some people I had never seen before. But no local doctor was present.

Realizing that I had just been told that I had leprosy—"the curse of mankind"—I felt the frightening sensation of drowning.

At age thirteen, I had joined some of my friends for a swim at one of the only public pools in the small town of Laredo, Texas. My parents could not afford the fees needed for me to participate in swimming classes at the Boys Club; thus I could not swim. My friends, all excellent swimmers, did not know this and proceeded to forcefully pull me out of the shallow part of the pool and into the deep end.

I still recall my panic as I struggled to move toward the pool's edge and found myself sinking, choking on water as I gasped for air. My eyes were open as I vividly saw the flashback of my life, ending with the only piñata party I ever had. My life passed before my eyes in black and gray colors, reflecting my ashen look as I slowly stopped reaching for the pool's edge. Luckily a lifeguard saved me.

The sound of the word "leprosy" jolted my memory back to the time of my near drowning experience; however, this time I did not feel the hands of a lifeguard pushing me to safety. I could hear myself breathing but was unable to feel the comfort of air entering my lungs. I saw the blur of black and gray of those standing around my bed, and wondered why they looked so still . . . so unalive. I again saw my life flash before my eyes; it seemed possible again that I was dying. I felt I had died in the presence of my family.

Dr. M. S. Dickerson, summoned from Austin's Bureau of Communicable Disease Services to quickly come to Laredo for an epidemiological study on a "newly diagnosed leprosy patient," had walked into my room at Mercy Hospital with an air of authority. The sense of authority came from his reputation in the field of leprosy and his skill in identifying other persons who might require treatment as a result of their contact with the "primary carrier." Prior to dropping the bombshell of my diagnosis, he had quizzed me on what can be best described as my eating habits and sex life.

Many years later I found out through my readings of professional journals that in the 1950s some in the medical profession believed that food was a possible link to leprosy. The food that was seen as the primary culprit was fresh fish. At the time, the only fish my parents could afford were breaded fish sticks which had to be cooked in the oven. The closest I had come to a live fish was when the family had taken one of its vacations, a weekend visit to Dad's family in Corpus Christi, Texas. Those long trips on hot summer days would inevitably lead us to the beaches, occasionally littered with dead fish surrounded by flies.

The theory of sex being the reason for my illness simply did not match with my history. All border town natives are exposed to activities that might be perceived as illegal on the U.S. side. One of those activities is sex for sale found in "Boys' Town," one of the enclosed communities sanctioned by the Mexican government in an effort to control prostitution and diseases. As far back as I can remember, I had seen the employees of Boys' Town, especially when I would go to Nuevo Laredo, Mexico, with my parents for grocery shopping and for monthly haircuts. Boys' Town used to be located within walking distance of the main marketplace and plaza. Fortunately or unfortunately, at the time of my diagnosis the idea of buying sex was only in my imagination and from a distance.

Dr. Dickerson wanted every sordid detail of my nonexistent sex life in front of everyone. He asked a series of embarrassing questions, which I found very humiliating. I was deprived of any privacy or dignity. This was not the last time I would be embarrassed in the process of being examined by a physician.

The day before Dr. Dickerson's arrival, the United States Public Health Service Hospital (USPHS) had confirmed my diagnosis to Dr. Joaquin Cigarroa and Dr. Raul Vela, local doctors who agreed to consult on my case. Orders were quietly issued to relocate the man who was sharing my hospital room, thoroughly clean the room, and permit entrance to the room only if visitors were wearing hospital-issued caps, masks, gloves, gowns, and foot covers. My parents had refused to be shrouded in this garb, and uncharacteristically showed defiance to authority figures, entering my room with embraces and kisses, never expressing disgust with my condition.

Dr. Dickerson agreed with my parents' actions but for different reasons. He advised me that I "would be normal again some day" because medication was available for treatment of leprosy. Furthermore, he said, "There is no reason to fear leprosy" and reversed the orders to keep me in isolation.

Knowing my diagnosis was a relief, because for almost two years I had been getting progressively worse with hypersensitive pain, labored breathing, lack of concentration, poor mobility, and sores throughout my body that looked like very large pimples, and which left deep crater-like scars.

The one comment that sent chills down my spine was hearing Dr. Dickerson refer to me as a "leper," while he handed me a blue and white "Booklet for Patients with Leprosy." This term caused me incomprehensible, confusing guilt.

Growing up Catholic and going to Mass almost every Sunday during my childhood, I must have tuned in to what many have informally referred to as the "leper Mass."[1] The Bible includes the laws to be followed by priests.[2] Leviticus gives graphic detail on how Aaron the priest was to identify those affected by this disease. He would separate the "clean and unclean," including animals with cloven hoof, fish without fins or scales, birds such as vultures and bats, rodents and lizards, and humans with "whitish swelling of the skin, whitening of the hair and ulcers." People were required to cry out "unclean, unclean," as well as burn their clothes and all other belongings. Sermons referencing Leviticus usually led to topics on punishment and sin and the gruesome description of leprosy. The service was designed to have persons "identified as having leprosy" undergo a religious ritual performed by a priest. In this ritual, the person was symbolically buried: his soul was excluded from society and thereafter he was permitted to participate in religious ceremonies only by squinting at the Mass through small openings shielded by iron bars. The ceremony was intended to label him an "outcast." He would be required to wear bells and distinctive clothing and sever personal contact with other humans. At the end of the ceremony, the priest would place the person on his/her knees, saying, "Be thou dead to the world" and then recite the "Ten Commandments" for persons with leprosy.[3]

- I forbid you to enter churches . . . or into any assembly of people.
- I forbid you to wash your hands or even any of your belongings in a spring

or stream of water of any kind. If you are thirsty, you must drink water from your own cup.

- I forbid you to touch anything which you may wish to buy.
- I forbid you to enter taverns or other houses.
- I forbid you to have intercourse with any woman, except your own wife.
- I command you when on a journey not to speak to anyone without first warning them of your disease.
- I charge you if you need to use a public road, not to touch posts or anything else unless you are wearing your gloves.
- I forbid you to touch anyone or give them any of your possessions.
- I forbid you to eat or drink in any company, except of lepers, and when you die, to be buried in your own house.
- I charge you to live a pious and God-fearing life.

Thus, the term "living dead" was born.[4]

The Jewish Torah also references Aaron. Jewish law states that the punishment for committing any of the "divine sins"—criticism of others, incest, jealousy, murder, slander, theft, and vanity—is to be the infliction of leprosy, making the individual with the disease a *metzora*, or "leper."[5]

Leper, the "l" word, continues to awaken my innermost feelings. Dictionaries routinely link the term to one who is shunned for moral reasons, a pariah, a strongly disliked individual, corrupt person, someone rejected or ostracized, an outcast, an untouchable, a person in disfavor.

During my sophomore year at Martin High School, and up through my senior year at J. W. Nixon High School, I had some small sores on my legs and hands that resembled infected pimples with a thin layer of skin covering a whitish-looking bulge. These "pimples" would quickly disappear after I applied the slightest pressure, leaving a depression on my skin. Additionally, I accidentally discovered that I had loss of feeling in my pinkie and ring fingers on both of my hands and in my forearms. To this day I jokingly tell my high school football teammates that this is the reason I scored only one touchdown. I would startle my siblings by sticking needles into my skin and not flinching with pain. This insensitivity both fascinated and scared me. Is something wrong with me? Am I possessed? Is this normal? Of course, I found out later that this was not "normal."

The Vietnam War was a serious concern among us eighteen-year-olds. The fact that females our age admired the second lieutenants training at the Laredo Air Force Base (LAFB) made many of us feel envious. The military police (MP) were always present whenever any of their trainees broke the law, either on the U.S. or Mexican side. The base commander and its federal resources played an important part in the community's fiscal stability and possessed a strong influence in all decision-making processes.

During the summer of 1966, after high school graduation, I worked at the LAFB and saw firsthand the privileged life of the officers and how young women would smile at the knowledge that a future pilot was in their sight. My father, who had been on the Laredo police force, would often talk about orders for preferred treatment from the mayor's office involving alerting the MPs any time one of their people would get into trouble with the law. Privates did not count as "their people" and were expendable, but pilots were untouchable.

I continued having problems that summer with some sores on my back and legs. My father took me to the only dermatologist in town, who diagnosed my condition as "grease balls." He proceeded to squeeze some of the "grease," and, with the two of them holding me, he cut into the skin of my back to extract the "whitish-looking fat." He told my father not to worry, and added, "No me debe nada" ("You do not owe me anything"). A common practice in Laredo, bartering, obligated my dad to pay with a future favor related to his connections in law enforcement.

When the sores on my legs continued, my parents took me to see the local surgeon. After one look at my legs, he said I needed surgery because I had varicose veins like Mom, on whom he had operated years before. Within a week, I had an operation to correct my varicose veins, but the sores returned.

For the next twelve months I continued to experience decreased sensation in my arms and legs, but increased pain to my upper and lower extremities. They were hypersensitive to the slightest touch and the pain would continue for what seemed to be an eternity. Instead of my feeling an instant of pain with a gradual decrease in sharpness, the pain would actually increase in intensity.

My parents would watch in despair as I tightened all of my facial muscles in an effort to keep from crying. I had intermittent fevers and frequent congestion. Visits to doctors in Laredo continued, but the physicians could not find a cause, and one of them even suggested that my pain was only imaginary. My parents called him a quack and pursued alternative medicine for a resolution to my unknown illness.

My first year in college was very traumatic. It was hard to believe that just three months earlier, I had been on top of the world: I had been voted by my high school classmates as runner-up for most popular, had completed my senior year, was awarded a scholarship from the Laredo Classroom Teachers

Association, and had a great girlfriend, Magdalena, at our rival high school. She had also been awarded a scholarship and was voted runner-up for most popular. My parents were gloating with pride. Now in college, I was actually expected to study and complete assignments within a specified time frame without extensions on deadlines. College was definitely not high school.

The stress of college seemed to make my body more painful to the touch, and I developed more sores. On weekends, I umpired softball games played mostly by ex-high school athletes looking for camaraderie in a high-scoring league. I had learned this skill by accompanying my father while he umpired high school games in Laredo and minor league ("A" level) games in Nuevo Laredo, Mexico. At fifteen, I had found it an easy way to make money. However, now umpiring games at 10 a.m. and noon on Sundays left me physically drained, but I had gasoline and spending money without having to work during school days.

The challenge of school elevated my spirits and motivated me to do better. Study groups and joint projects with Magdalena helped me focus on school rather than on the constant pain. These distractions, however, were not available at night when I would find myself alone and in pain.

Ever since I was a child I had shared a bed with two of my brothers, Javier and Rudy. Being the oldest of the boys, I had enjoyed some perks. My sisters, for example, regardless of their age, would iron my clothes and prepare my meals if Mom was not home. Living in a house without air conditioning, I had the right to sleep by the window: the bed was pushed all the way to the corner in order to make room for another bed in the other corner for my mom's uncle, who lived with us. This perk progressively became a burden, as I had to jump in and out of bed, increasing the amount of movement of my legs and arms.

Getting up in the morning became a dreaded activity for me. Not only did I have to endure tear-producing pain, but I also had to compete with fourteen other people to get to the bathroom first. There was no trophy for the family member who was able to hold his bladder the longest. The ritual of crawling over my brothers in order to get off the bed made me feel pain of much higher intensity than any I had ever felt before. It was chronic and long-lasting, and I cried every morning for over a year. The morning crying was done silently and in secret, because I once overheard Dad say, "Se está haciendo para no trabajar" ("He is faking the pain to avoid work"). Considering that the doctors could not find anything wrong with me, I wondered if maybe Dad was right, that my pain was psychological and not physical.

We lived in a small community where Dad was very well known and respected. He was affectionately known as *Kinnin*, an obsolete Spanish term meaning oldest or only male in a family. He possessed the "power" of playing the guitar and singing like Pedro Infante (a deceased Clark Gable–type actor and singer from Mexico); he possessed "power" in a community where figures of authority were revered. Being a "junior" made comparison inevitable and caused me to feel that I could not possibly live up to expectations.

I forced myself to hide the pain from everyone except Mom. She knew that I was not feeling well. Since she washed my clothing, she would regularly find small blood stains in my boxer shorts and white socks from the never-ending eruption of sores. Magdalena would usually wait for me to initiate a plan to go dancing, but my silence inevitably led her to ask on more than one occasion, "Why don't we go dancing anymore?"

Dancing had been a family tradition which I valued. It was a way to escape problems and find solace. To this day, I can recall the ambience and hear the sounds of moving feet (slower though) as my sister Diana was teaching me how to slow dance. A waltz is required dancing at the *Quinceañera* (coming-out party for fifteen-year-old Hispanic girls). The onset of the disease had curtailed my dancing with Magdalena.

Mom eventually convinced Dad that I needed some medical attention. Since we had exhausted almost all of the medical resources in Laredo, I was taken to *espiritualistas* (spiritualists), *yerberos* (herbalists), and *curanderos* (folk healers) in Laredo, Texas, and Nuevo Laredo and Monterrey, Mexico.

My parents, who were both born during the twenties and were survivors of the patronage system in south Texas, the Great Depression, World War II, the Korean War, floods, unemployment, and hard labor, were firm believers in alternative medicine.

Alternative medicine, or *curanderismo*—folk healing—has been in existence since Aztec times.[6] There has always been an emphasis on prayer and on special, some say magical, activities that force bad spirits out of the body and allow it to function in the manner intended by nature. The introduction of Catholicism by the Spaniards to my ancestors (mix of Spanish, Aztec, and African genes) served as a link for my parents to the importance of prayer, worship of saints, and to the ultimate goal of eventually going to heaven. The route to hell is to be avoided at all costs. The rituals of confession and spiritual cleansing can help in at least pointing the way to heaven, but not paving the way to get there. In an effort to attain success in healing, *curanderos* have utilized religious paraphernalia such as crosses, pictures of Christ and selected saints, and candles.

One such saint revered by Catholics of Mexican descent is Our Lady of Guadalupe. Our Lady of Guadalupe is reported to have first appeared in 1531 to Juan Diego. Upon hearing of the Lady's apparition, a priest demanded proof. The Lady filled Juan Diego's cloak with roses, which he carried to the local priest. When Juan Diego released the roses, her image appeared on his cloak, which is on display at the great Metropolitan Cathedral in Mexico City.[7]

The canonization of Juan Diego in 2002 opened up a debate among scholars on whether he actually had existed or not. Myth or fact, Juan Diego has had a tremendous impact on how people of Aztec, now Mexican, ancestry have overcome great challenges throughout the centuries.

I had seen the magical powers of faith and the resulting cures. Whenever I had a stomach ache or constipation, Mom would cleanse my body with a stomach massage. Using the same lard that was always available at home for use in making flour tortillas, she would liberally apply it to my stomach. This lubricated the skin and lessened the pain created when she pressed her thumbs on my stomach. She would slowly go from my rib cage downward, stopping immediately above my crotch.

She repeated the process until she "felt the large intestine releasing the stool from the inner walls." She would then turn me over, place her left hand flat on my back and with her right hand, clenched in a fist, aggressively hit my back. She would move her hand around my back in a circular motion. She would do this a number of times, ending with the painful pinching and lifting of the skin on my back. She also pinched up and down my spine until she could hear a cracking sound, signifying that the treatment was effective. Within hours I would have a bowel movement, leaving my body drained. This cleansing was always done in the evening, allowing me to sleep soundly and wake up in the morning without any unpleasant side effects.

Mom also had other treatments for earaches, fright, or "*susto,*" resulting from a traumatic experience, fevers, and headaches. For burns, the treatment was the liberal application of the sticky sap of the aloe vera plant.

I recall Mom and her mother having conversations about how to live healthy lives, regularly walking out to the backyard to compare notes on the best ways to "*curar*"—cure.

Three plants that were always readily available to us, regardless of where we lived, were the *nopal* (prickly pear cactus), *hierbabuena* (mint), and *limón* (key lime). These were essential for quick access to traditional medicine.

Mom would describe how *nopal,* a plant credited with producing the trophy white tail bucks in south Texas, mixed with scrambled eggs would make a good breakfast. According to Laredo's "Medicine Man," Tony Ramirez (no relation), the *nopal* was "*muy bueno*" for the heart and controlling diet.[8] *Hierbabuena* was made into a tea and we drank it constantly whenever flu-like symptoms appeared, speeding our recovery. And the ever-present *limón* was used to freshen up the house after a cleaning, for gargling when a sore throat appeared, for making a mixed salad taste better, and for tenderizing the cheap and tough cut of meat called flank steak.

Altogether, my parents took me to six individuals with varying degrees of compassion and knowledge. One of the visits was in February of 1967 to a lady in Nuevo Laredo, Mexico, who lived in a house surrounded by a wrought-iron fence. The property had two brick houses, separated by a narrow alleyway. One house, belonging to the lady we were visiting, had the main entry towards the rear. I recall my parents' using old newspaper to cover my head, as it was drizzling and cold. Going inside the house did not make my body feel warm, but rather made me shiver. The darkness of the house and the large two-room multipurpose structure saddened me because it was a reminder of my deceased grandparents' adobe house.

The lady we went to see was probably in her late twenties, but her obesity made her look older. There were many babies or small children on her bed when we arrived. They were moved to another corner of the room as I was ushered to a stiff wooden chair next to her bed.

My mother took the initiative with the discussion. She gave the lady my medical details of the past year. Her name has since been erased from my memory, but my mother addressed her with a great deal of respect, "Doña." The Doña, surrounded by velvet portraits of Jesus Christ with a crown of thorns and tears of blood, was lying on the bed. She apologized for her appearance because, unbeknownst to me, our appointment had been scheduled two hours earlier. The traffic crossing the international bridge had been very heavy, delaying our plans.

The Doña delicately touched my hand and quickly concluded that I was in great pain, caused by emotional rejection by a girl at the age of fifteen. I glanced at my parents who were nodding their heads in agreement, as both knew I had had a "girlfriend" for all of two months at age fifteen. However, I had felt neither loss nor ongoing emotional pain. I recalled being disappointed, but an older friend who had also dated this girl consoled me by simply saying, "Don't worry, in high school there are many more girls to choose from."

Trying very hard not to disagree with the Doña in front of my parents, I also nodded. The lady asked my parents to wait while she escorted me to an adjoining room. She indicated that the rejection by my old girlfriend was making my body "bleed." She added that this girl probably put a curse on me and we both needed to pray. The praying, however, had to be done in the nude. I reluctantly agreed, primarily to please my parents. After all, they continued to pool their emotional and financial resources to find a cure for what ailed me. In addition to my father's contributions, all the money earned by Mom in selling Avon products was hers, but she also used most of her earnings to make donations to the church and to *curanderos* to assist in finding the right prayer to cure my unexplained illness.

The room where we were with the *Doña* was made of cinder blocks, had a cement floor, and resembled a small shrine. It had hundreds of lit candles in clear and colored glasses and a small altar with a portrait of Our Lady of Guadalupe. The odor of incense permeated the room.

The cold weather always seemed to heighten my pain, so the *Doña* helped me undress. My poor health numbed my sense of shyness in being naked in front of her, but I felt very uncomfortable with her gentle touch of my body, starting with my head and ending with my toes. She explained her treatment as a way to transfer "the curse" to her. She was startled by my comment, "Won't the curse hurt you?" Her eyes opened wide and her mouth gasped. She seemed insulted by my apparent disbelief in her treatment. She then asked me to pray with her so I could be forgiven for my rudeness and continued her touching of my body, but not so delicately now. Considering my young age and high testosterone level, I was surprised that her touch didn't arouse me.

After a few more sweeps of my body she ordered me to get dressed and left the room. Once I returned to the "bedroom," I could hear her explaining to my parents that the cleansing would allow the "romantic curse" to transfer to her. For effect and possibly to gain my trust, she gently touched my hand and said, "Don't worry, my mind and body will combine to destroy the curse without hurting me." I saw Mom in tears and Dad sighing approvingly. I left feeling no better than when we had arrived.

Another visit was to a *yerbero*, or herbalist. This visit was also made during the winter, as I still remember the chills I felt. Several years later I found out that nerve endings buried deep in my body would swell, as the Hansen's disease (HD) bacilli multiplied. The swelling was caused by the illness, with the HD bacilli attacking the cooler areas of the body—face, earlobes, hands, arms, legs, and feet. The swelling would also make me hypersensitive to pain, very sharp, long-lasting, tear-producing, and incapacitating pain. I recall dreading to be touched in a manner that could place pressure on my skin. This was counter to the way Magdalena expressed her affection toward me, gently moving her hand up and down my back. This was a clue to how she felt about me, loving and trusting. This massaging continues to be very soothing for my children and me.

Learning by trial and error, I realized that I could "self-medicate" by using my environment, the sun, to lessen the pain during the winter months. Laredo regularly records the hottest temperatures in the United States. Rarely has this town, composed of mostly Spanish-speaking persons of Mexican and Indian ancestry, experienced long stretches of cold weather. But when the temperature gets into the sixties or dips into the fifties, natives immediately feel "the cold." In a way, I was the exception.

Anyway, I could anticipate the change in weather by how intense my pain was, especially in my hands and feet. I learned to go outside my parents' home and squat against the south wall of the house, letting the rays of the sun warm my body. Mom found my behavior odd but she would not question it as long as it made me feel better. Many years later she shared with me her thoughts on my "treatment." Considering that I would usually stay outside long enough to slowly pray a rosary, she believed that I was praying to find relief from the pain. I guess in my own way, with my head tilted towards heaven (to enhance rays from the sun), I was praying and seeking solace.

The *yerbero* in the Mexican culture is a person with great knowledge about plants. These persons are equivalent to the modern-day researcher who travels deep into the rain forest searching for cures for HIV, cancer, and other diseases. The *yerberos* may not have much formal education, but they are highly educated in herbal medicine and in communication with their clientele—mostly poor laborers and their families in low-paying jobs unable to afford visits to a doctor or prescriptions and medications.

The *yerbero* we went to visit was unlike any I had ever seen. He was young, probably in his thirties, and his "office" was in a house, not at the marketplace or a rundown hut. The man did not fit my perception of a *yerbero*; thus, my trust in this thin man with a thick, black mustache dramatically decreased. He had many green shrubs in his front and back yards, but I did not recognize any of them as "*yerbas*." The shrubs appeared to be mostly weeds.

The house of the *yerbero* was in obvious need of some painting and was surrounded by vacant lots. It was situated on an unpaved street with potholes of varying depths. My parents and I sensed that this might be the wrong address and after what happened on the visit, I wish it had been only a dream. Dad softly whispered to Mom, "Are you sure this is the place?" Mother shrugged and said, "Sólo Dios sabe" ("Only God knows").

We got out of Dad's '64 Chevy and climbed the stairs to the front door. The *yerbero* seemed like a snake oil salesman, a con man, especially when he requested payment before the "treatment." My parents complied and then stared with their mouths wide open as the *yerbero* took off his two-inch-thick belt and ordered me to take off my shirt. My parents remained silent as I was hit on my back with the belt. The pain startled me, but I did not make a sound and prayed that my parents knew what they were doing.

The alleged *yerbero* quietly told me that the "evil spirits would soon be beaten out of my body." He continued to hit me on the back, and each whack weakened my knees until I was leaning over the dining room table.

"¡Ya Basta!" ("Enough!") my father finally screamed. My mother rushed to hug me and tend to my bleeding back. My father, who was on the Laredo police force, was carrying his .38 with silver chrome and placed the barrel of the gun against the man's temple, saying, "Te mato si le pegas una vez más" ("I will kill you if you strike him one more time").

The man tried to explain his actions, but we were in no mood to listen and departed swiftly. My parents could not apologize to me enough, saying they would do a better job on referrals next time. My mother cried and my father cursed. Then, to make a bad situation worse, Dad could not shift gears. The Chevy had gears on the floor and the mechanism to shift gears occasionally locked into position. Thus I had to get under the car to manually unlock the gears. The apologies continued all the way home until I finally screamed, "¡Ya Basta!"—and the three of us laughed uncontrollably. We never spoke about the visit to the "*yerbero*" again.

Sensing that alternative medicine might not be the answer to determining an explanation for my deteriorating condition, my parents decided to return to "modern" medicine.

On a day when I was feeling so low, my parents' spirits were up. They had made a decision to take me to San Antonio, Texas, for a visit with a "world-renowned dermatologist." The term "dermatologist" made me cringe, as I recalled the last time I had visited a skin specialist. But, being the obedient son, I complied with their plans.

We left for San Antonio early on a Friday morning. My father believed that getting early starts whenever we traveled would mean avoiding traffic. Dad also enjoyed stopping for breakfast on the road, giving Mom some respite from the tedious task of making tortillas for breakfast.

Back in the sixties, a trip from Laredo to San Antonio, Del Rio, Corpus Christi, or Monterrey, Mexico, meant traveling 150 miles and a minimum of four hours on a narrow two-lane road.

With a stop for breakfast in Encinal, a small town seventy miles north of Laredo and the site of President Lyndon Johnson's first job as a schoolteacher, we arrived at the dermatologist's at approximately 9:30 a.m. His office was in the middle of downtown, just blocks from the Alamo.

The dermatologist was a thin man with gray hair and glasses. His nurse took a history of my illness and put me through the now-routine paces of height, weight, blood pressure, and temperature. The doctor did not actually examine me until almost noon. He said little but seemed intrigued with my sores and collected blood and puss on cotton swabs, saying he wanted a culture. He impressed my parents by saying his experience probably made him one of the best dermatologists in the country. What he neglected to mention was that what I needed was a biopsy, not a culture—leprosy bacillus does not grow on a petri dish.

He had us wait until late in the afternoon, and, after examining the culture, he determined that a diagnosis was not imminent and suggested follow-up visits. He also concluded that I needed medication to relieve my constant pain. He gave my parents a prescription for codeine. We filled the prescription in the same building where the doctor's office was located and left to visit with the Lozano family, long-time friends of my parents. I took the medicine as soon as we arrived at the Lozano home, and I fell asleep.

I slept pain free until awoken at 11 p.m. by my parents. Dad had to work the next day, and we had a four-hour drive back to Laredo. My parents and I were both surprised with my ability to get up from the bed without any apparent discomfort. Obviously the codeine had been effective; however, the doctor had prescribed only enough for the weekend. On Monday, the pain returned.

By Thanksgiving of 1967, I had managed to work part time, had finished my freshman year at Laredo Junior College (LJC), and was doing well with my grades during the first semester of my sophomore year. By then I knew that I did not want to be a high school teacher, and had set my goals on pursuing a master's degree, but had not selected a specialty.

I was able to successfully complete my third semester of college and endured much sadness during the winter break due to lengthy bouts with fevers and pain. Counter to my bleak disposition, the Ramirez tradition of gift exchanges continued. Dad would sit in his favorite chair next to the well-lit Christmas tree and pass out presents to everyone. There were always aahhs and oohhhs and wows and thank yous throughout a ceremony that would last for hours. Pictures were taken of the whole event.

The constant pain I felt in December of 1967 was equivalent to a finger being crushed in a door. I also experienced difficulty breathing due to congestion and had an increased number of sores. These bouts with poor health forced me to curtail most of my activities. Additionally, I was always tired and had to relinquish my right to sleep by the window, as my knees could not tolerate the pressure placed on them as I climbed over my brothers. For many years thereafter, I would feel despondent during the holidays, subconsciously reminiscing about this difficult time.

More of my friends were either drafted or volunteered for one of the armed services. Within a very short period of time, after completing basic training, they were on a plane overseas—"to Vietnam." I had lost my desire to join the service, but wondered if I would be drafted if I could not continue my education. Not wanting to test the system, I preregistered for my fourth semester of college.

My condition continued to deteriorate and I struggled to simply get up in the morning. One day in late December Mom received a call from Amparo Meza, a family friend whom we had first met when we were neighbors at the Guadalupe Housing Project.

We had been in a two-story complex, which had an unusual design. At one end sat our unit. Without the walls, it would have looked like an inverted L. Next to us lived "*Comadre* Amparo," also in an inverted-looking, L-shaped, four-bedroom unit. Squeezed between us was a two-bedroom ground-floor unit. Thus, three families could live in each complex. "*Comadre*" means female godparent, but my mother and many women of her era used the term as meaning good friend/neighbor.

*Comadre* Amparo, who had four children the same ages as four of my siblings, had always been accepting of the Ramirez family as neighbors. Her tiny yard was always well manicured. She had a vineyard (unheard of in dry and hot Laredo) that yielded large amounts of green and juicy grapes. Every Sunday afternoon she served as host of the community *lotería*, a type of bingo using forty-eight characters commonly found in the Mexican culture. *Lotería* had been created at the turn of the century in Mexico, was an educational tool, and it was indeed a lesson in money management for all of us. As many as twenty-five adults and children would spend hours paying five cents per game with the final pot for ten cents.

*Comadre* Amparo also used this opportunity to bring her oldest child, three years older than I, from his bedroom and sit him on the floor to "play" *lotería*. Her son, with severe mental retardation and many physical disabilities, would socialize with everyone. *Comadre* Amparo would often say how, when he was born, doctors and nurses had admonished her for not placing her son in an institution. Her response had always been that God had brought him into this world as a member of the Meza family and Laredo community, not as a "freak" destined to die in an institution. Her compassionate and loving demeanor made her one of the most popular ladies in the 250-unit complex. This unyielding love for her son made a lasting impression on the way I communicate with persons different from me. Today, as a social worker addressing the needs of persons with intellectual and developmental disabilities, I think of the story of the Meza family and it helps me stay focused on emphasizing community inclusion, not institutionalization.

The call from *Comadre* Amparo was actually a special invitation to my parents. This invitation was for the *comadre* to serve as sponsor, all expenses paid, to take me to Monterrey, Mexico, to seek help from "the best *curandero* in Mexico." Mom wanted to accept the invitation but she also knew how disillusioned I had become with anyone professing to have some knowledge of how to diagnose my illness. My parents allowed me to decide on whether to accept the offer or not. I reluctantly agreed.

Within days after Christmas, *Comadre* Amparo, my parents, and I traveled in Dad's '64 Chevy Impala to Monterrey.

We went to a very poor section of Monterrey, located in one of the hills surrounding this beautiful city. The Sierra Madre mountain range embraces the city, shrouded by snow- covered peaks. The home of the *curandero* was a small hut, poorly protected from the elements. The inside walls were covered with all types of herbs, reminding me of a cool spring day flourishing with a fresh growth of flowers and weeds. He appeared to be very old and wise, with the crevices on his face and hands indicating a life of physical hardship. He spoke in an authoritative tone.

The visit to the *curandero* lasted less than five minutes. My parents were impressed with his sagacious appearance and sincere honesty. He refused to accept any type of payment, saying, "Yo no le he ayudado" ("I have not helped"). We were, however, confused by his comments—"Esta enfermedad se encuentra en la biblia" ("This disease is found in the Bible"). Was this a riddle? Did he mean an illness that could be cured or one that was fatal?[9]

After a cursory look at my sores, he informed my parents and *Comadre* Amparo that I needed to be seen by a specialist, someone knowledgeable about diseases found in the Bible. He could not help me. "Yo no lo puedo ayudar," he said.

The *curandero* politely asked that we leave and handed my mother a "prescription." In Mexico, issuance of prescriptions is not regulated in the same manner as in the U.S. The "prescription" ended up being prednisone in liquid form, and, almost instantly after Mrs. Meza injected it into my body, I felt alive and energetic. Everyone was impressed with my "miraculous recovery," but this good feeling had greatly diminished by the time we returned to Laredo six hours later. My faith in the medical profession, both modern and alternative, was completely shattered, so I tried to ignore the pain and continued with my studies.

The second semester of my sophomore year started smoothly. I again had registered for fifteen hours, a full load. It included the usual array of required courses—history, math, English, biology, biology lab, and speech. Considering that the usual distractions were missing in my life, like weekend parties, dancing with Magdalena, and drinking beer with my buddies, I did not procrastinate in completing my homework.

I would usually spend enough time at LJC to attend classes and walk to the library, holding hands with Magdalena. Soon after escorting her to the library, I would leave for home, struggling just to shift gears in my '57

Plymouth, which was my pride and joy, bought with money earned in 1964 doing migrant work in Montana and Wisconsin.

Having such a large family, my parents needed three vehicles just to keep up with everyone's busy schedule. Dad needed a car to go to work and collect payment for services rendered through his new business, Kinnin Security. Mom was still an Avon cosmetics salesperson and cleaned offices at a law firm to supplement the family income, so a car was essential for her. I used a vehicle not only to go to school myself, but also served as a "taxi driver," taking my siblings to and from school.

I was enjoying school. I was learning to appreciate Greek mythology in Mrs. Garza's English class and about the pros and cons of escalation and de-escalation of the war in Vietnam in Mr. Daly's (a World War II veteran who had lost his left leg during combat) history class. I was learning the significance of the circulatory system (in frogs) in Mr. Salazar's biology class. My unknown illness had ironically opened up opportunities for me to spend more time studying. I continued, though, to feel very tired.

I was losing the battle of blocking out the constant pain, and the weakness in my body also affected my ability to concentrate on my studies. So on a Friday morning during the first week in February, I simply stayed in bed and asked my mother to call Magdalena and request that she take notes for me in class.

Mom realized that I was too weak to get out of bed, went to buy a small portable bedpan for me, and tried, without success, to arrange for a doctor to make a home visit. By this time, I could not see any benefit in spending time or money on doctors and rudely told Mom that I was glad she failed. Obviously startled by my behavior, Mom made several efforts to influence my way of thinking. So, I had a procession of people coming to "talk some sense" into my "stubborn head," starting with my father, progressing through my siblings and neighbors, and ending with Magdalena. All of their combined efforts could not shake the anger and distrust I had regarding the medical profession.

Two of my younger brothers, Javier and Rudy, who had shared my bed since we were children, stopped sleeping in the same bed with me. Years later Javier told me that he could not stand my moans and groans of pain whenever he would move the bed; thus both of them had decided to sleep on the floor.

Approximately one week passed, with me completely bedridden, when my sister Raquel came to my room to beg me to consider a "new plan." She came to my room in the early evening, and in the dark I could not see her face, but I could sense her urgency in convincing me to seek treatment.

As she discussed her plan, she silently cried, holding my hand. "Manito" ("little brother"), she would say with almost every sentence, "por favor oyeme" ("please hear me out"). I listened attentively to the plan and instantly rejected it. She pressed me for a specific reason for my turning down her offer, and I said, "Porque no tienes compromiso de nadie" ("Because you do not have a commitment from anyone").

In Raquel's plan, supported by all of my family, a team of doctors, Dr. Vela (family doctor) and Dr. Joaquin Cigarroa, were to work cooperatively, conducting all types of tests in an effort to find a cause for my illness. In my mind, the idea was not plausible because of my biased perception of doctors. I did not believe that Laredo doctors could work as a team. Additionally, the plan required hospitalization—an expense my parents could not afford. Of course, my reasoning was clouded by the negative experiences I had been having for two years.

Raquel manipulated my distorted view of all doctors by getting me to agree to the plan if she could get a commitment from the doctors to work together. What she neglected to tell me was that she had already broached the subject with the doctors and both were willing to explore this option. They were aware of the seriousness of my condition and sincerely felt they could help. She made a few telephone calls and within half an hour came to me and said, "Bueno, vengo a colectar" ("Well, I came to collect").

My parents wanted to call an ambulance as I was in too much pain to walk, with sores on the bottoms of my feet. With my usual stubbornness, I refused. This proved to be a mistake. The distance from my bed to the car was approximately thirty feet, but I needed help just to stand upright, and any touch to my body caused me unbearable pain. With the assistance of two of my brothers-in-law, Julian and Juan, and my brother Javier, I eventually managed to make it to the car.

The trip to the hospital was uneventful and done in complete silence, with Dad driving and Mom praying in the back seat. My sisters Yolanda, Raquel, and Diana had driven ahead and were waiting for me by the emergency room with a wheelchair. The sight of the wheelchair made me realize that I was pretty sick.

Being hospitalized, I thought, meant having to drop out of school. With the negative reputation of the Selective Service Board, I expected to be drafted regardless of my medical condition. How wrong I was.

Immediately upon being admitted to the hospital, the tests started, with blood being drawn every fifteen minutes, or at least that's how it seemed to me.

My three older sisters, my parents, and Magdalena came to see me regularly during the three days I was at Mercy Hospital. At the time, the administrators had a strict rule which forbade visits by any children. I therefore did not see some of my siblings for many months.

During my brief stay at the hospital, I was introduced to two beautiful ladies who epitomized love and compassion, Sister Mary DeLillis and Sister Virginia Marie. Sister DeLillis was Raquel's supervisor. Raquel worked in the lab and was primarily responsible for drawing blood. Sister Virginia Marie was one of the hospital administrators and provided emotional support to my soul mate to be, Magdalena.

Sister Virginia Marie had very light skin, was taller than me, and had a sweet smile, a gentle hand, and a very soothing voice. She was like a drill sergeant, orchestrating every move made by the hospital staff. The sister's smile and friendly manner were inconsistent with the stern and stoic personalities of the sisters I had known as I was growing up. It was difficult for me to comprehend that they were real people.

My earliest recollection of contact with nuns was when I was approximately four years old. Dad was concerned that my role models were primarily my three older sisters, Mom, my aunts, and my grandmother. Dad was usually at work so he felt that his influence was missing.

Dad convinced Mom that I needed to be exposed to a harsher life than I was experiencing with so many "*mujeres*" (women) around. His solution was to place me in an orphanage for a short period of time. The rationale for this action was based on his life as an illegitimate child. He believed that facing the harsh realities of life would make me "*fuerte*" (strong) like him.

So, one day, over the loud objections of my sisters, I was taken to an orphanage located close to where my maternal grandparents lived. I recall the unsmiling faces of nuns. I remember the strict rules and the painful consequences for not following them. Kids my age were using curse words when adults were not present. Other kids encouraged me to cry when being hit with a twig by nuns so that the beating would stop, but not to cry when lonely or alone.

The stay at the orphanage probably lasted no more than two months, but for me it was a lifetime. I recall telling Dad after leaving the orphanage, "Yo soy hombre y no lloro" ("I am a man and I do not cry"). He was so proud of me.

During my training to complete my first communion, the nuns would emphasize strict discipline and were quick to punish whenever we allegedly misbehaved or were slow in learning our prayers. This training was supposed to be our first hurdle on the road to heaven. Many of us emulated our teachers, after class, of course, and would pinch each other, hit each other on the head with a closed fist, and yell, "Son animales" ("You are animals"). Privately, we wondered if heaven would offer us protection from the angry nuns.

How, then, was it that a beautiful person like Sister Virginia Marie could be a nun? Another nun who made a dramatic impact on how I interacted with nuns was Sister Mary DeLillis. Sister DeLillis, active until her death in 2007, worked with Laredo's large population affected by poverty. She was so loved and respected that the owners of the newly built Mercy Hospital placed a life-size statue of her by the front entrance in 1999.

Raquel daily updated her boss, Sister DeLillis, on the status of my condition. Sister DeLillis kept up with the progress of the doctors' attempts to find a diagnosis for my condition. Sister DeLillis also assisted Raquel with convincing Dr. Vela and Dr. Cigarroa to work cooperatively and arranged for my admission to Mercy Hospital.

My brief stay at Mercy Hospital offered me the opportunity to reevaluate my cynical view of Catholicism and again get on the road to faith, spirituality, and love.

The day of my diagnosis was a very sad time for my parents, siblings, and Magdalena. Their recollection was a mixture of anger ("Why, God?"), fear ("Will he die?"), confusion ("Is this treatable?"), and hopelessness.

Raquel was the first to find out about my diagnosis. She recalls feeling faint, glancing at the report over and over again, looking for a sign that this was a mistake. The report, sent by the U.S. Public Health Service Hospital in Carville, Louisiana, confirmed the diagnosis of leprosy two days after Dr. Vela performed a biopsy on my left hand. She went to Sister DeLillis, handed her the report, and cried on her shoulder. Without much time to comfort Raquel, Sister DeLillis called Dr. Vela, who offered to visit my family that evening and attempt to explain what this diagnosis meant.

Raquel and Sister DeLillis went to get Mom, who was in the hospital chapel praying. Mom, according to Raquel, immediately started to cry and angrily looked at Jesus on the crucifix and asked, "¿Por que? ¿Por que?" ("Why? Why?") Both then left the hospital to look for Dad at the B-29, Laredo's pool hall, where he was trying to earn some food money playing eight ball. He remembered realizing that something must be terribly wrong for Mom and Raquel to show up at this predominately men's hangout. All he could say was "Dios nos va ayudar" ("God will help us").

Mom, Dad, and Raquel returned to the hospital and found Yolanda, Diana, and Magdalena waiting for them. Raquel spoke, saying, "Nuestro manito tiene lepra" ("Our little brother has leprosy"). No one seems to recall what else was said except that the next thing they remember was being at Guadalupe Church, crying and praying. Magdalena went home sobbing, seeking comfort in the arms of her mother. Her family was silent, speechless. Her older sister, Marta, remembers thinking that I would soon be dead and Magdalena would be left behind to grieve forever.

Diana and Yolanda went home to research leprosy in the 1959 edition of the *World Book Encyclopedia*, purchased by my parents nine years earlier as an investment in our education. Under the section "leprosy," my siblings read about the "biblical lepers" and the incidence of the disease worldwide (at that time over twelve million). They also read the technical name for the disease (Hansen's—the bacilli having been discovered by Dr. Gerhard Henrik Armauer Hansen of Norway in 1873), the location in Louisiana of the only leprosarium in the continental United States, and the effects of the disease if left untreated. They read about the types of leprosy (tuberculoid and lepromatous) and the common treatment at the time (dapsone), and saw the picture of a black child with nodules on his face prior to treatment and a second photo showing the effects of treatment. This young man ended up being one of my best friends.

Many years later I found out that the man who discovered the existence of *Mycobacterium leprae*, Dr. Hansen, did so at the expense of publicly disagreeing with the most respected "leper specialist" of the 1870s. This man was Dr. Danielssen, his mentor and future father-in-law, who claimed that "leprosy is hereditary" (proven to be false). Another ironic twist to Dr. Hansen's history is that the man known to have identified the gonorrhea bacterium, Dr. Albert Neisser, also incorrectly claimed to have been the first to identify the bacillus of leprosy. This may partially explain the ongoing existence of the myth that leprosy is a sexually transmitted disease.[10]

Norway's Ministry of Justice also admonished Dr. Hansen for conducting an operation on one of his leprosy patients without securing her consent. He publicly acknowledged that he erred and proceeded to become a strong advocate for patient rights and against experiments on human subjects.

My siblings have told me that they all cried as Diana sat at our small dining room table reading the encyclopedia over and over again, not finding any hope for a "quick recovery" as stated by Dr. Dickerson. Hope was rapidly diminished because, even though I was hospitalized, there was no sign of improvement in my condition. We had all been indoctrinated to believe that hospitals were built to make people feel better. If hospitals were for treatments, and I was to get medication in Louisiana, how come I could not get the medication in Laredo? If leprosy was not to be feared, why was a doctor from Austin, a place foreign to us, in Laredo, examining my siblings and me? If leprosy was not communicable, why was I being sent so far away? My siblings and Magdalena feared the worst and were inconsolable.

As promised, Dr. Vela arrived at the house. According to Diana, his look of great sadness and his tears did not keep him from attempting to paint a bright picture of my future. Dr. Vela tried to explain my diagnosis not as an illness, but rather as a temporary detour in my life. He encouraged everyone to see my leaving Laredo as they would a brief stay in the army. With so many young men being killed in Vietnam, his analogy, though well meaning, was not well received.

My three older siblings and parents devised a plan—"*un plan*"—to keep my diagnosis a secret from everyone except the immediate family. Their decision was based on the belief that the family was being punished by God, the limited and depressing information in the encyclopedia, and vague assurances from Dr. Dickerson. Luckily for me, they abandoned this plan prior to my lengthy trip to Carville, Louisiana.

Magdalena's mother, unbeknownst to her, had called her brother in Monterrey, Mexico. He was a "doctor" who strongly urged that Magdalena abandon any plans she might have to continue an extended relationship with me. "If he does not die," Magdalena's uncle explained to her mother, "and Magdalena remains with him she too will eventually contract the terrible disease." Not until twenty-two years later, when my wife, Magdalena, and I, along with two children, visited *Tio* Pedro (Uncle Pedro) in Monterrey did I realize that he was not a general practitioner but rather an ophthalmologist. We realized his limited "knowledge" of leprosy was based, as with the rest of us, on ignorance and hearsay.

Dr. Dickerson kept trying to reassure me and the rest of the family that the hospital I would be going to was considered the best in the world for the treatment of leprosy. When he first mentioned the location of the hospital, Carville, I thought he was referring to Kerrville, Texas, a town I had visited in high school to play a football game.

Dr. Dickerson corrected me and said Carville was in Louisiana. But he continued to pique my interest as he said that my diagnosis made me eligible for funding from Texas Vocational Rehabilitation (now the Texas Department of Assistive and Rehabilitative Services, or DARS) to attend college at Louisiana State University (LSU). "Don't worry," he said over and over. "You may not even make it to LSU because you can be cured in six months and be back in Laredo by September."

My parents were not interested in whether I could continue my education but in how I was going to get to Louisiana. Dr. Dickerson offered to transport me, free of charge, in a Texas health department station wagon driven by an ex-Carville resident. Considering that I could barely sit up and that the trip would be approximately eighteen hours long, my parents did not approve. They instead suggested that the state transport me by ground or air ambulance. Dr. Dickerson did not agree.

Sister DeLillis and Sister Virginia Marie then suggested transport by local ambulance, paid for by Mercy Hospital. My parents reluctantly agreed and went home to figure out how they could accompany me on the trip and pay for their expenses.

The visit by Dr. Dickerson and all the planning occurred on February 22, George Washington's birthday. Laredo, the Mecca for those with Hispanic roots, has been celebrating the birthday of our first president since 1898. This celebration has been an important part of the Ramirez family for decades, as most of my sisters and many nieces have been in the annual parade's procession.

My parents wanted to follow the ambulance to Louisiana and see firsthand my new home. Dad had a history of pawning his guitar, gun, hats, and jewelry whenever he needed money. Mom told me that this is exactly what he was planning on doing for the drive to Louisiana.

Luckily, Dad did not have to pawn his precious few belongings. Instead, he found upon arriving at home that he had won five hundred dollars in the national lottery of Mexico. They quickly made plans to follow me to Louisiana and invited Magdalena to go along. She immediately accepted. Raquel, without hesitation, said she would also go "as the nurse."

The next day, February 23, was a busy time for my family. My parents worked hard on getting the '64 Chevy ready for a 750-mile trip, buying food for my siblings, and washing clothes for the long journey. Up to that day in 1968, Raquel and Magdalena had never traveled outside of Texas.

The day for me was unusually long. I hoped for visitors, but with everyone so busy getting ready for the trip, only Yolanda, my oldest sister, was able to come by. She visited during her break, asked if I needed anything, and I immediately said "Sí." Could she stay with me on my last night in Laredo? I did not want to sound melodramatic, but the previous night had been very lonely. The fear of being away from my family, so far away, so alone, brought tears to my eyes. The pain, which I had so successfully blocked out of my mind, had suddenly become real, and something I could no longer ignore.

Severe depression and pain had finally caught up to me the previous evening. I had pressed the button to call the nurse and did not get a response. I continued to press the button, crying like a baby, wanting someone, anyone, to be close by, holding my hand. I felt confused, yet happy that I finally had a diagnosis, but afraid—like everyone else—of the unknown. What was leprosy? How was it treated? Who will be my fellow patients? Would Magdalena leave me? Would I ever be healthy, and normal, again?

The loneliness was unbearable and I continued to press the button. Finally, the door opened and, with only the light in the hallway striking her back, I could see the silhouette of the nurse. She had pushed the door open with her right arm but she did not move into the room. "Are you all right, sir?"

This respectful "sir" gave me dignity, but it did not lessen my new fear or old pain. So, I requested a pain pill and a sleeping pill. I suspected that the nurse knew I had been crying, but she did not embarrass me by turning on the light. She quietly complied with my request, and when she handed me the medicine and glass of water, I could see in the moonlight entering my room that she was wearing surgical gloves. This practice is expected nowadays, but it was not common in 1968.

On the afternoon of February 23, Magdalena came to visit. With teary eyes, she kissed me on the lips, embraced me, and whispered that she had accepted my parents' invitation to accompany me to Louisiana. I was elated and suddenly felt so special. My girlfriend was so compassionate. We briefly talked about her discussions with her parents, school friends, and professors, all wishing me luck and prayers, before my parents came in to discuss the next day's travel plans. We were scheduled to leave by 4 a.m. and hoped to get to the hospital in Louisiana by early evening.

There was an aura of excitement and nervousness. Mom apologized that my younger siblings could not visit. She asked everyone to leave the room so she could pray with me. When everyone left, she came close to me, gave me a bear hug and sobbed on my chest. I awkwardly stroked her hair and cried with her. She lightly caressed my face and apologized for being such a bad mother, "*una pecadora*," a sinner, wondering aloud what she ever did to be punished by God through me. With so many saints credited as "protectors" of persons with leprosy, Mom could not be consoled by any of them.[12] She left the room sobbing, leaving me perplexed about her comments.

Mom was very traditional. She could control our behavior with an evil eye ("*curar nuestro mal de ojo*"), paralyze us with a wicked pinch, yet push us to do our best. She would curse when angered, yet religiously light a candle at church. She gave us life with her breast milk, yet found it difficult for us to leave her bosom. She would routinely save the last tortillas for Dad, but never let us go hungry. She never said much, but always got her wishes across to us; she never said no to Dad, but knew when to say no to us.

Mom became an only child after her twin sister died at birth. However, she spent a lifetime caring for her parents, uncles, husband, and thirteen children. The family has often joked that she prepared approximately 21,240 breakfasts and over 1.2 million handmade flour tortillas by the time my youngest sibling turned eighteen. So I wondered: how could she possibly feel that she was not a good mother? I was very confused.

Within minutes after Mom departed, Dad walked into the room. By now it was getting dark outside but he did not turn on the lights. He started to cry and asked for forgiveness. I felt frightened by his behavior because the only other time I had seen him cry was at Raquel's wedding. Of course, he had been drinking at that event and the emotions of the occasion had probably contributed to his tears. However, he had not been drinking prior to his visit with me so I could not understand his crying.

I was also confused about his asking for forgiveness. He said that God was punishing him, through me, for some dreadful sin he had committed as a young man. He could not describe the sin, but, whatever it was, he regretted having committed it. The Catholic faith, with an emphasis on pain and suffering in order to cleanse one's soul of sins, had again had an impact on my life. This time I felt frightened and helpless. It was not something I could simply attribute to our Mexican culture. He cried for what seemed like an eternity, but I could not console him. He had never taught me how to handle such an unusual situation. There was no one to model after, so I cried with him and said nothing.

Dad was an illegitimate child, rejected by his natural parents and not acknowledged by his mother until she lay on her deathbed. His stepparents forced him to survive in the world of adults at a young age. He wanted to make me strong, "*fuerte.*" He believed that by isolating me from feminine influence he could force me to be immune to the harsh realities of life. He wanted to keep me from becoming a "*maricón*"—a sissy.

My parents were devout Catholics and grew up in what may have been the oldest neighborhood in Laredo, "el barrio Azteca."[13] The Azteca neighborhood had streets so narrow that cars crossing paths would be only inches apart as they moved in opposite directions. The homes were primarily of adobe, with ornate Mexican wrought-iron fences. Azteca, described in 1992 by the *Laredo Times* as a "diamond in the rough," was not tolerant of any resident who deviated from the teachings of the Bible. My parents felt torn between the shame of possibly having violated some unknown rule of the church and the expectation for parents to love their children blindly, regardless of their weaknesses. Being ill with leprosy was perceived as a sign of weakness, possibly conceived through sin.

Felipe Ramirez and Margarita Peña bore a child, who became my father. His parents married other individuals and his maternal grandparents brought him up. He learned to survive by turning heartless as soon as he walked into a pool hall and drained friends and foes of their money. He also learned to play the guitar and sing, mesmerizing the girls with his melodies and then charging his friends for getting their girlfriends *"en un modo romántico"* (in a romantic mood) with his elegant voice.

As a result of his natural parents never being legally married, he had twenty-two half brothers and sisters with the family names of Ramirez, Peña, and Perez. His complete family history would probably encompass several volumes.

Dad, a traditional authoritarian father, always tried to impress his children by stating that he knew the most and had done the most. His body was full of experience and his mind full of knowledge, yet oftentimes he allowed his children to learn things the hard way—on their own, rather than by example, just as he had learned. As a result, few of us can sing, no one can play the guitar, all the males can shoot pool, and everybody likes sports.

Dad was a very proud man, trying never to show fear, rarely saying *"no sé,"* on occasion allowing others to see tears of joy, always working to have food on the table. Dad reluctantly shared two of the most frightening moments of his life. One was when he feared losing his mother to God before she could whisper to him words he longed to hear—"Hijo, te quiero mucho" ("Son, I love you very much"). He finally heard those words at her deathbed when he was in his thirties.

Another frightening moment occurred during his twenties when he was in the U.S. Navy. His job on the ship he served on was simple: "gofer and cleaner . . . go for this and that . . . clean this and that." On one occasion, while his ship was in the Pacific, the infamous Japanese Zeros attacked them with pilots trained as kamikaze.

Dad, in describing this experience, said, "Me cagué cuándo vi el avión!" He soiled himself when he saw the Zero and then ran inside the ship after seeing one of his shipmates cut in two from bullets fired by the Zero. The next thing he remembered was hearing a gun cocked to his temple by one of the officers, who said, "Son, I know you are scared, but you either return to the deck and help man the machine gun or else you die here like a coward." He slowly got up and, still shaking, returned to the deck.

Dad eventually regained his composure and turned on the lights, asking Mom to come back into the room. In unison both started to sing "Happy Birthday." I was startled by their quick shift from sadness to happiness. They placed a ten-inch, ten-karat gold chain with a religious medal (Virgin of Guadalupe and San Juan) around my neck. Their explanation was that they had been so overwhelmed with my illness that they had overlooked my twentieth birthday on February 9. *"Ya que eres un hombre"* ("Now that you are a man") they said that I deserved a saint to watch over me.

For over thirty-four years, Mom would regularly tell me that St. Peter would never accept her into heaven because she had made me unclean—"*sucio*." After I was diagnosed with leprosy, we often talked about having the medal blessed and, symbolically, also her soul.

Yolanda's unselfish acceptance of my invitation to stay in my hospital room helped me sleep better that night. I still cried silently but did not feel alone.

## chapter 2

# The Journey

One of the first things that I found out about this strange and biblical disease was that what is described in the Old Testament—"T'sarath"—meant that people were "stricken by God." Translations of the Bible from Hebrew to Greek have caused much confusion throughout the ages and continue to fuel the myths about leprosy. This fear has transcended all religious faiths, possibly because it is the disease mentioned most often in the Bible.[1] The fear and resulting ostracism cross all cultures worldwide.

Leprosy is mistakenly referred to as the "oldest of diseases." This is possibly due to its association with humans, who are the only living creatures capable of sin; i.e., persons with leprosy are being punished for their sins.[2]

Archaeologists have been able to date leprosy to ancient times by examining human skeletal remains with "claw-like digits and the loss of the front two incisors." Over long periods of time, the HD bacillus can damage the cartilage which gives the nose its shape. This damage can cause the nose to collapse. In advanced stages, leprosy can affect the gum area that holds the incisors in place.

The earliest documented evidence of leprosy dates back to 600 BC when written records in India and Egypt accurately described leprosy and its accompanying disabilities of deformities and blindness. The leprosy bacillus next spread to China and Japan in 500 BC. Records from the time focused on damage to the eye, due, it was believed, to sexual promiscuity and sleeping on the ground (association with soil).

The conquests of Alexander the Great in 300 BC brought riches—and leprosy—to Greece. Alexander, realizing the fear that the populace had of this illness, ordered that traitors have their noses and ears cut off so as to resemble those with the disease and thus be forever labeled.

Between AD 1000 and 1400, leprosy was spread throughout Europe. After 1492, travels by the Spanish, Portuguese, Chinese, and others into the Americas and importation of slaves from different countries made it possible for the leprosy bacillus to flourish.[3]

The night before my journey east, I was recalling that several weeks earlier, I had read an article in the *Laredo Times*. The story was about a Mexican American woman from "the valley" (south Texas) who was attending college after having been hospitalized for years for the treatment of leprosy. How odd that I would recall reading this story. How lucky I was to eventually meet such an inspirational person, one who had conquered her fear of being rejected after being diagnosed with HD. She became a role model for me and many others in speaking out against ignorance and fear. Her name was Julia Rivera, later Elwood, and she was the first ex-resident to be hired at the hospital in Carville.

I had overheard Dr. Dickerson's attempt to explain to my parents that the incubation period for leprosy could be as long as twenty years, thus I might have had the bacilli in my body as a child.[4] Dr. Dickerson was interested in finding out my family's medical history. He was attempting to determine the source of the bacilli that had infected my body. He eventually concluded that my maternal grandfather, who had, according to his death certificate, died of cirrhosis of the liver, "probably had the disease." He reached this conclusion by looking at a photo of my grandfather and noting that he appeared not to have any hair on his eyebrows. This was a side effect of having HD. When I interrupted his conversation with my parents, and noted facetiously that my grandfather also did not have any hair on his head, he restated his comments to say that he "might" have had leprosy. There is no medical record or recollection by Mother to substantiate Dr. Dickerson's theory.

A second thing that I learned about the disease was that it is impossible to diagnose without conducting a biopsy. Leprosy is a bacterium that can remain dormant in the peripheral and ulnar nerves and under the skin. For unexplained reasons, the bacteria can then either slowly or rapidly begin to multiply, making cool areas of the body more susceptible to the growth. The immune system weakens and the toxicity results in open sores that then can cause secondary infections. At the time of my diagnosis, the most effective medication to temporarily slow down the growth of the virus was prednisone. How interesting that a poor *curandero* from Mexico had so much insight into the diagnostic process and how quickly he could attack a problem with a possible solution, prescribing prednisone yet emphasizing ongoing treatment from "a specialist."

According to Laredo's "Medicine Man," Tony Ramirez, the curandero's ancestors probably treated the *lepra* brought by the Spaniards to the New

World with a variety of plants. For example, the masked pods of the prickly pear cactus, *nopal*, were generously applied to open sores. The juice of the key lime, *limón*, could have been used as a tea to soothe the throat infections that accompany the growth of HD bacilli. And the bark of the guazuma and mangle trees might have been used to ease the pain caused by open sores and infections.

It takes faith, a belief, in order for alternative medicine to be effective. It was this same faith in a greater being that first made my parents believe that I might have a chance at recovery.

Having been poor all of their lives, my parents always thought *mañana* would be a better day. The Mexican movies that they so dearly loved and that I learned to appreciate always seemed to have themes of complacency, suffering, and prayer and of starting a new day, a la Scarlett in *Gone With the Wind*.

The day of my diagnosis proved to be one of their new mornings, *una mañana nueva*. My parents were constantly looking for ways to make more money, and one of these ways was taking chances. My mother's way of taking chances was to play bingo at the local churches and the American Legion Post #59. The latter is located on prime land next to the Rio Grande River one block from St. Augustine Church, the oldest church in Laredo. On one special bingo night in 1962, my parents did choose a lucky card. They won the thousand-dollar grand prize. Many of our neighbors, frequent cohorts at bingo, came by the house to congratulate us on our newfound wealth.

Dad, on the other hand, used to make extra money by umpiring high school and Mexican League baseball games, playing eight ball, or *bolita*, at the local pool hall, or betting on the Mexican lottery. In Laredo, many individuals perpetuate the constant desire to get rich quickly by having *palomitas*. *Paloma* literally translates to pigeon, or dove, and *palomita* is a baby pigeon or dove. The *palomita* is like money—once you bet you either never see it again (have you ever seen a baby pigeon or dove?) or it flies away (is spent) quickly. The *palomita* is a gambling game whereby one person sells a series of numbers to one individual or a group of people. Based on how closely matched the numbers are in relation to the numbers drawn from the Mexican lottery, the "winner" gets a full or partial share of the total amount bet.

On the eve of my diagnosis, Dad won a partial share of the *palomita* he had bought that morning—five hundred dollars. He did not find out about his winnings until approximately 9 p.m., and he quickly went to collect. That winning was their *mañana*—a sign from God—that their praying and patience and desire to be better parents, *mejores padres*, would pay off in my recovery. Their priority was to get me to Carville.

The day before my departure to Louisiana, my parents had again asserted themselves by demanding that the Texas Department of Health or some other governmental entity fly me to the hospital in Louisiana. Dr. Dickerson was adamant in refusing their demand and instead offered a Texas Department of Health station wagon driven by an ex-patient. He emphasized what a good driver he was and that other "lepers" would accompany me on the ride. My parents objected to Dr. Dickerson's use of the "l" word by firming their lips. I did not hear him use this term again.

Realizing that it would be weeks before I could be transported to Carville, both my parents and Dr. Cigarroa strongly objected. Dr. Dickerson shrugged his shoulders, looked at Dr. Cigarroa and said, "You decide," and walked away.

What happened next I would not find out about for almost ten years. Dr. Joaquin Cigarroa emphasized to my parents the urgency of getting me to Carville for treatment, implying that my condition could worsen, hindering the chances for recovery. Therefore, calls were made to the local funeral homes that provided both ambulance and burial services. From the mid sixties until the early seventies, funeral homes focused their money- making activities on quickly arriving at accidents to transport the injured and dead. By arriving first at the scene of an accident, the ambulance drivers and owners could get a quick payback of up to forty dollars per delivery to the emergency room. Laredo was no different from other communities throughout the country. With three funeral homes competing for the opportunity to transport the injured, none was willing to have their vehicles out of service for an hour, much less for an out-of-state trip.

With continued pressure from the only source of emergency medical care, one of the funeral homes suggested using a hearse to transport me to Carville. After all, "the dead can still travel in comfort" and they would not lose money, as the Sisters of Mercy offered to pay for the trip. Mom sobbed when she shared with me years later that the funeral director also added, "Ambulances are for the living, hearses for the dead." Due to the severe pain I was in, and the rapid decision to take me on a long journey, I did not find out that my transport to Carville was in a hearse until December 1978.

The next challenge was to find two people who would drive me to Carville. Luckily, two men named Francisco Almeida and Tololo Casso knew my family. Francisco had had a crush on my two older sisters, Yolanda and Raquel, since they were in elementary school. My sisters had repelled his advances by throwing rocks at him and inflicting a scalp wound resulting in a scar. Fortunately, he was forgiving. Dad had coached Tololo when he played Little League, and my sister Diana had cheered him on when he was the basketball star in high school and she was a cheerleader.

The trip started like any other planned by my father, at 4 a.m. My parents, older sister Raquel, Magdalena, and the two drivers came into my room, waking Yolanda and me in spite of their whispering. They all surrounded my bed, and at the count of three, gently lifted me onto a gurney for a short ride to the emergency room.

On the way from my room to the first floor, I glanced up at the ceiling. I was surprised to see that the lights were as bright at 4 a.m. as they were at 4 p.m. I expected them to be dim so that the other patients would not be disturbed. It was difficult to comprehend that others were actually awake, working. "Who are these people?" I asked myself. As quickly as I mentally asked the question "do they know that I have leprosy?" I had it answered. The answer was "yes." For being so early in the morning, there was a large number of people hugging the hall walls. The people were wearing different colored scrubs and many had surgical masks on. I could hear their breathing as they stared at my body in a horizontal position covered by sheets and blankets. There was also a priest who came into my sight and then moved to the back of the procession, clutching his Bible and praying silently. I still do not know if the priest was asked by Mom to join us or if it was coincidental that he was on the floor at that hour of the morning. Either way, he had a deathlike pale look, was tightly pressing his lips together, and to me it felt as if he were saying the last rites.

The silence from the passengers on the elevator was unbearable. We could all hear the cables and pulleys working as we slowly descended to the first floor. Dad had his look of authority, totally in charge of his surroundings. Mom was teary-eyed, holding her rosary and silently praying. Magdalena also was crying, but looked strong and confident, and her presence gave me comfort. Raquel was quiet and staring at the numbers over the elevator doors indicating the floors. Sister Virginia Marie was gently patting my mother's shoulder, comforting her. Francisco and Tololo were nervously holding the side of the gurney as if they were moving a cargo made of glass. The silence was finally broken as the elevator bell rang to let us know we had reached our desired floor, and Mom said, "Ya nos vamos hijo" ("We are now leaving, son").

The eerie silence continued as we exited the elevator and slowly moved towards the emergency room. I again was lifted up and gently placed on the stretcher and covered with heavy blankets. This time, sobbing broke the silence. It seemed to me that everyone was crying, but I could not see my siblings. My parents had decided that it was best they not witness my departure in a hearse.

The attendants appeared to be in shock, possibly because they had not dealt with such a cargo before.

As soon as I was pushed into the ambulance entrance area, I felt the cold wind slapping my face. From my horizontal position, I was unable to see that my mode of transportation was not an ambulance, but the only thing that mattered at the time was that the inside was warm. Raquel positioned herself next to me and gave me an injection of morphine to lessen my pain and discomfort. The back door was slammed shut, the vehicle thrown into first gear, and off we went toward Highway 59 on our way to Freer, the first town we would pass on the route to Louisiana. I again felt alone, but fell asleep before I was able to dwell on my loneliness.

I next woke up in George West, Texas, approximately one hundred miles from Laredo and two hundred from Houston. We had stopped for breakfast and some rest for the drivers. My parents and Magdalena came to check on me almost as soon as they parked in front of a restaurant. I told them that I was not hungry, but Mom insisted that I eat a taco. Magdalena volunteered to stay with me as people walked by the hearse and squinted in an effort to peek inside.

As Magdalena sat next to me, she grabbed my hand, gently massaged my fingers, and looked at me with tears in her eyes. She showed me a smile that soothed the pain and slowly moved her lips to form the words "I love you." We did not say much in the warm confines of the hearse, but I knew she was concerned about something other than my comfort. I found out what it was when my parents returned with tacos for both of us. She had limited funds, but still demanded to pay her way.

Besides being an early riser when traveling, Dad also complied with the speed limit. Actually, he would normally drive slower than the speed limit. As a police officer for almost twenty years, he had seen many auto accidents resulting in permanent injury or death. He would often talk about his fear of death in an automobile accident and would exhibit stern anger whenever my siblings or I exceeded the speed limit. It was this fear that resulted in our arriving at George West almost three hours after leaving Laredo's city limits at 8:30 a.m.

It was 9:45 a.m. by the time we departed George West. The next town, Beeville, only fifty miles away, seemed to never come into view. The two drivers kept telling me that Beeville was very similar to Laredo—air base (training base for military pilots), predominantly Mexican American population, and "*muchas muchachas bonitas*" ("many beautiful young women"). Our arrival in Beeville was a disappointment, as all I could see through the small windows was a small but elegant courthouse with a sandstone exterior situated in what appeared to be the middle of the road. The vehicles meandered to the left, making a half-moon turn in order to continue on our way.

The roads in 1968 were mostly two lanes, with few expressways. Therefore, we had to travel through every small town on the way to what seemed to be the other side of the world. The next small town was Victoria, also requiring a snakelike maneuver to get to the other side of the city limits. We made another stop in Victoria to allow Dad to stretch, snack, and sip coffee. What he really needed was sleep. The others bought gas, soda pop, and greasy burgers. Raquel helped me again by administering an injection of morphine to ease the pain. What we really wanted was to get this trip over with. We departed Victoria, my sister reflected years later, with the service station attendants scratching their heads as to why my parents had delivered food to the back of a hearse.

Approaching Houston, we passed the small communities of Richmond, Rosenberg, and Missouri City. The drive through Houston was on Highway 90, leading directly to the middle of downtown. Mom was riding in the hearse with me, and she could not resist the temptation to open the small curtains so we could peer up at the tall buildings, at least taller than the twelve-story Hamilton Hotel in Laredo. Similar to all other times when the curtains were opened and strangers noticed the movement inside, they were drawn to peek inside the hearse. The people in downtown Houston were easily startled, I thought.

By the time we reached Houston, the natural light that had embraced us all day started to fade. Raquel had never traveled farther than Houston, and Magdalena had gone to Monterrey, Mexico, as a child to visit relatives. Mom and I had gone as far as Helena, Montana, to do migrant work and Dad had traveled the world during World War II. However, this cold ride into the dark of night made us fearful. We were riding into the unknown.

The ride continued into Beaumont, and then Orange, Texas, and then the state line came into view as we crossed the bridge over the Sabine River. We all celebrated with a yell on crossing the border, and Raquel gave me another injection. There was an even louder yell as we approached Lake Charles, and we crossed the majestic bridge over the lake. It felt exhilarating being so high.

The road veered toward Alexandria and then curved toward Baton Rouge. As we approached Baton Rouge, we could see a high steel structure that was the bridge into West Baton Rouge Parish. When we were on the middle of the bridge, we could see the beautiful capitol building on the left and LSU's Tiger Stadium, with its lights on, to the right. We all had a sense of excitement and confidence.

It was almost 9 p.m. when we drove through Baton Rouge and started on our way to Highway 61 going toward New Orleans. Francisco finally acknowledged that he was lost and low on fuel, so he pulled into a service station in Gonzales, Louisiana, not knowing that we were approximately ten miles from Carville.

After both vehicles were filled, the hearse would not start. It seemed to be objecting to the lengthy and tiring trip. The service station had a mechanic who diagnosed the problem as a bad battery. Francisco and Tololo barely had enough money for gasoline and a burger for the return trip, so Dad paid for the battery. The mechanic, a large black man with the body of a professional wrestler, offered to accompany us to Carville provided that he was returned to the station. Realizing that we would never be able to find the hospital on our own, Dad accepted this offer.

Louisiana's state roads are notoriously narrow with deep ditches on either side. This area also had tall pines embedded in swamps that hugged the roads. There were no streetlights, so having a guide in Louisiana's wilderness was a godsend. The gentleman rode with my parents while we followed close behind. My parents described the young man as being very talkative, saying that the hospital had some "good people" working there and indicating that he did not fear the disease.

Within twenty minutes, after numerous twists and turns on the road, we arrived at the gate—an open space protected by a security guard. My parents went to the enclosed area where the security guard was safely protected from the elements, received verbal instructions on getting to the ambulance ramp, and signed a form admitting me "voluntarily" to the hospital. The hearse was driven to the ramp where a large man in a white uniform waited for the delivery. His name was John and he was known to the other residents as Big John. He was to become my friend, sounding board, counselor, and jokester during the many nights that I was in the hospital's infirmary.

The "voluntary" admission system was a way to mask the practice by states of transporting persons diagnosed with Hansen's disease to the only hospital of its kind, a leprosarium, in the continental U.S. The Texas Department of Health would acknowledge proudly that the state had a station wagon and driver to bring people back home "on pass" from Carville. The "pass" was an irony, as persons with leprosy had to sign a form to be admitted for treatment, but were not authorized to leave unless their assigned physician gave formal written permission.[5]

My parents, Raquel, and Magdalena seemed apprehensive about what to do next after the hearse backed up to the loading dock. The night was as cold as in Laredo earlier that day. I was pulled out and transferred onto a gurney. Everyone was trying to ensure that the gray wool army blankets did not allow any of the cold wind to seep in.

It must have been weeks before I saw Big John's face, but I could immediately identify his silhouette: tall and round. His walk was slow and deliberate, his steps rarely making a sound as he moved. His feet always pointed outward as if to clear the path for this large man. After I was lifted onto the gurney, the limited talking that occurred was done in whispers. Since I was on my back with people walking beside me, all I could see was the ceiling of the long hallway as we headed to the infirmary.

The squeaky sound made by the wheels as I was pushed to my room, the cold wind in my face, the arching bare walls which secured the window screens, the pinkish ceiling with peeling paint, the round glass covers on the light bulbs embraced by large cobwebs, and the silence of the place reminded me of the movies of the twenties and the thirties and how this scene could resemble the set of a movie titled *Life Inside a Tomb*. As we continued our travel down the concrete hallway, I wondered if the inside of a morgue would feel as cold or as lonely. Was I going to be strong enough to tolerate the treatment? Would tonight be the last time I saw Magdalena? My parents? Raquel? How would I handle the night? Would I be alive to see sunlight again the next day? How strange, I thought, that I could feel so alone even though nine people surrounded me.

At some point the gurney came to an abrupt stop, two doors to my left swung open, and the ride resumed. This time we were away from the cold, inside the infirmary. Questions were racing through my mind, too fast to attempt a response to each one. One very odd question was, if I was in a hospital, why was I then in an infirmary? I had envisioned the hospital as one large building as was the case in Laredo.

Little did I know that the "hospital" was composed of 350 acres and many buildings creating the infrastructure of a small community. It even had its own jail and cemetery. The communication system was similar to that of a small town; it was called gossip.[6] All of the residents, I found out later, knew I would be the newest resident even before my travel arrangements had been finalized. The "infirmary" was a small but very important part of the larger infrastructure. This two-story building provided 24/7 care for new admissions and those experiencing a "reaction"—incapacitating growth of the HD bacilli.

The infirmary's hallway led directly to the nurse's station. I overheard Big John telling my parents, in his deep and commanding voice, that we were passing the "women's infirmary" and "everyone was asleep." Women, I thought, must greatly outnumber the men if they had a whole floor for themselves. Later, I learned the disease attacks twice as many men as it does women.[7] The older residents would often joke that this was because men have traditionally committed more sins than women. No one has been able to determine why the frequency of diagnosis is greater for men than women.

Big John commanded that the gurney stop in front of the nurse's station, where out came a large nun with short, round hands and cheeks that seemed to be full of food. Was I destined to be surrounded by nuns all of my life? How could I escape them?

Sister Victoria sounded very harsh and quickly enumerated the rules: quiet, people are sleeping; no questions, she was not the doctor; no one would be allowed to spend the night with me; parents would need to sign more papers in the morning. She was tough and curt, and after such a lengthy drive from Laredo, my parents were equally testy and had some rules of their own: they expected me to be treated fairly, and I should receive morphine for pain. From my vantage point, I had a great view of Big John, who was standing at the end of the gurney facing me, between Sister Victoria and my parents. He smiled and nodded, acknowledging that my parents' support for me would not waver.

We next went into a small elevator with steel doors that collapsed and expanded like an accordion. The elevator, of very old vintage, moved slowly, allowing Sister Victoria and my parents to collect their thoughts and diffuse the rising tension.

Big John was obviously in charge by now, as he alone pushed the gurney, exiting to the left of the elevator. My room was halfway down the hall. The eight-foot-by-ten-foot room had, of course, a hospital bed and was painted white. My parents unpacked my small suitcase. Then Big John and my father lifted me onto my new bed.

Almost as soon as I was placed on the bed, I had a tremendous urge to have a bowel movement. Big John and Dad helped with the pan, and Mom, always a believer in prayer, concluded that since my internal plumbing was working, this was a sign from God that I would do well with the treatment.

Sister Victoria did give me an injection of morphine and prednisone. Magdalena and my family reluctantly left for Baton Rouge to look for a hotel and promised to return in the morning. Francisco and Tololo bid their farewells and made the sign of the cross as they left, implying that they would never see me again. Sister Victoria became a different person as soon as my family left and showed that she was not the heartless nun she had projected to my family. She came close to my face, kissed my forehead, gently caressed my hair, and sweetly whispered, "Son, you're gonna be okay." With that, I closed my eyes and quickly fell asleep. It was now almost midnight—nineteen hours since I was last in a different hospital bed approximately 750 miles away in a familiar world. Adjusting to Louisiana and to a journey with leprosy would not be an easy transition.

My official admission to Carville, the only hospital of its kind in the continental United States, was documented in my record as 10:30 p.m., February 24, 1968, and I was assigned the patient number 2855. My official discharge would not come for another 3,476 days.

# Treatment at Last

Before daylight the next day, Big John came by to empty the bedpan and check my vital signs. He again introduced himself, perhaps sensing that I had been disoriented upon my arrival in the middle of the night.

The light, illuminating his white shirt from the back, made him look saintly. His soothing voice and reassurance that I would be "okay" enhanced that perception in my mind. Unfortunately, because he worked the graveyard shift, 11 p.m.–7 a.m., I wasn't able to speak to him during the daylight hours, nor did I get to enjoy his company outside of the men's infirmary on the second floor. He had the right personality not only for the new arrivals like me, but also for the "old-timers" who had been residents at Carville longer than Big John had been alive. He knew all of the residents, and his calming demeanor made us vulnerable to sharing our fears with him and to gossiping of others in the large complex. To my knowledge, he never violated the trust we placed in him.

Sister Victoria followed Big John into my room and reported that I still had a fever, but that "we'll get that back to normal in no time." She administered two injections, one for pain and the other to "start killing that booger inside your skinny body." I had lost weight during the last two years, but the regular shots of prednisone would eventually double my weight, and also send me into bouts of depression, two serious side effects of steroids.

This wonderful sister, so intimidating to my family just hours earlier, was funny, serious, and compassionate all at once. She cautioned me against relying too much on the "pain medicine, especially the pink and grays. Other patients," she said, "have become too dependent on short-term cures" for their pains.

Later I realized what she meant, as I witnessed dependency on Darvon, sometimes swallowed with easy-to-purchase alcohol. This used to soften the physical and emotional pain that came with this disease. Over the course of time, I trained my mind to block out the pain of cuts, falls, injections, and visits to the dentist.

I saw the indulgence of drugs and alcohol by some residents and staff. I used to believe that only Mexican Americans and blacks growing up poor and in crowded housing projects were susceptible to this habit, a stereotype perpetuated by society at the time. The hospital had people from all over the world, and many were behaving in the same manner. Gradually, I came to realize that the great stresses and the stigma imposed upon people diagnosed with leprosy, compounded by living in a closed environment, could result in dysfunctional behavior and attitudes. I had worked hard to avoid falling into this trap as I grew up at *La Colonia* Guadalupe—the Guadalupe Housing Project in Laredo, Texas.

Sister Victoria said she wanted to get me ready for my family's return visit. She expressed her regret because she would not be able to see their "surprise." Her shift was ending at 7:00 a.m.

In her slow, right and left swinging motion, she gave orders to the day staff to clean my room, make my bed, help me shower and change, and bring me a "man's breakfast." With all the rapid action activities, I put aside my feelings of self-pity and physical discomfort, and joined the team to help me get ready to face the forthcoming challenge.

Two other orderlies working the day shift picked up where Big John had left off. Robert Sanchez, "not Mexican, Cajun all the way," and Vicky, "not Mexican, just black all over," were with me each time I was admitted to the infirmary.

They liked to play good cop, bad cop. Robert was the disciplinarian, a gruff type who ordered others to stop feeling sorry for themselves and learn how to take care of their disabilities—some real, some imagined. Vicky was the compassionate person, always reassuring and taking us on wheelchair rides throughout the hospital.

I found myself being able to sit pain free for the first time in months. The staff brought in a tray of food loaded with juices, milk, coffee, water, scrambled and boiled eggs, toast, oatmeal, and grits. I had never eaten grits before, and did not know if someone had left the applesauce to rot, turning it white, or if it was a simple mistake of bringing me the wrong tray. As I was contemplating what to do, a short man with an unshaven face, a cigarette in his mouth, and a raspy voice with a Cajun accent walked into my room. "Don't worry about the grits now," he said, "you'll love to eat 'em." The man with a never-ending smile, Jimmy from New Orleans, was my next-door neighbor, and he knew I was coming. Knowing that "you Mexicans love hot peppers," he handed me some freshly cut green peppers from his garden. I stared at his hands, hard with slightly twisted fingers and burns between his index and primary fingers. He laughed heartily, said, "Don't let this happen to you, kid," and walked away waving before I was able to thank him.

I had difficulty picking up the fork or spoon, so Sister Victoria had one of the staff tie the fork to my hand for easier manipulation. Almost as soon as I started eating, I sensed that someone was watching me. It was my family and everyone was in awe over my "miraculous recovery." Mom held her rosary and immediately raised both hands to her mouth, followed by a quick sign of the cross. I noticed she was crying, and as I looked at Magdalena, Raquel, and Dad, I noted that they too were crying. Their tears, of course, also made me cry, and slowly they moved toward me and we all embraced.

As we continued to cry and embrace, Sister Frances Louviere walked in and said, "Well, this is a lovely sight, can I join in?" And she did. She introduced herself and gave some instructions as to where to go to sign consent forms, meet patients, tour the facility and pray (she noticed Mom's rosary and told her about the Sacred Heart Catholic Chapel). She added that as soon as I finished with my breakfast I would be taken by "Pete" (Peterson, or Dr. Pete, as I liked to call him, from the Virgin Islands) to the foot clinic for treatment. "Don't worry," she said with her toothy smile. "Your son is not going anywhere until he can walk on his own."

Before the family was able to quiz me on my first night at Carville, a slightly built elderly Mexican American man with an armful of the *Baton Rouge Morning Advocate*, sunglasses, and cane walked into the room. He introduced himself in Spanish: "Me llamo Nacho" ("My name is Nacho"). Mom was overwhelmed, not only at realizing that "some of our own" lived at the hospital, but also because the gentleman's name so closely resembled her father's, as did his appearance—Tacho vs. Nacho, strong arms and hands, and baldness with graying hair on the sides.

What omens! Mom could barely contain herself and kept saying *"gracias"* as she looked upward—thank you, Lord. She would often relay these stories to my siblings and family friends, but few would believe in such a rapid, and what appeared to be a miraculous, recovery, especially after seeing me bedridden and then put inside a hearse. Their disbelief continued until my first visit home and people actually touched me. Magdalena experienced similar reactions of disbelief when she described my overnight response to the proper medication to our friends.

Nachito, as everyone knew him, had been a resident at the hospital for decades. He was originally from Mexico and had done migrant work in the U.S. He was diagnosed with HD as a young man, and was forced to go to Carville where he eventually lost his sight to the disease. He had become a businessman, as the only seller of the Baton Rouge newspaper at the hospital. He also had become the best source of reliable information, as he personally delivered the paper to staff and residents every morning. He delivered the news in more ways than one.

Nachito was a shrewd businessman and had come to give me a complimentary copy of the paper, but I would have to pay for future editions. Dad paid him in advance for a month's supply, and then Nachito gave them a partial tour of the hospital, introducing them to key residents, e.g., the president of the Patients' Federation, president of the Lions Club, president of the Mexican Club, manager of the patients' canteen, and the manager of the patients' post office. These introductions proved to be both valuable and detrimental to me, as I became a member of the Carville community. The immediate benefit was that these people—all men—became like surrogate fathers and would regularly provide unsolicited guidance and advice. The drawback was that they would threaten to send written reports to my parents and Magdalena if I "got out of line."

I learned that being admitted to the facility at Carville would also mean being labeled a "patient" forty years after being admitted for treatment. The word "leper" strips away our human identity and "patient" legitimizes the modern-day separation of those of us diagnosed with leprosy. For over thirty centuries, this illness has displaced people from their roots and families, branding the HD bacillus carrier as a "patient" and a "leper." The experience of those of us affected by leprosy is that we are routinely referred to as "patient" by the medical profession, media, researchers, and society in general even decades after having been cured.

I chose to at least soften the painful labeling by referring to myself as a "resident" while hospitalized at Carville. The word "resident" gave me a more familiar feeling of being one of millions living in a community, not one of millions in the world segregated because of archaic beliefs. My stand on this matter is usually ignored by most dealing with leprosy-related issues. My preference, and that of many of my "brothers and sisters" who live in the community, is to be referred to as a person affected by leprosy or, more specifically, by my name.

While my family was touring the facility, Dr. Pete took me by wheelchair to the foot clinic. This was simply a large room with different types of chairs to accommodate residents with various levels of disabilities. Sister Gabriella Richard and Sister Laboure Kennedy were in charge.

At the time of my arrival at Carville, there were over four hundred persons receiving treatment, and many had foot injuries or sores like I did. Therefore, the sisters had arranged for groups of ten to fifteen to come by the clinic every thirty minutes, sometimes starting before 6:30 a.m. and lasting past 10:30 a.m. Anyone arriving late would not be denied treatment, but they would be forced to wait until the last group was treated. While the sisters were simply trying to run a tight ship in order to serve everyone in need, I soon realized that public humiliation could be the result of noncompliance regarding both written and unwritten rules. Conformity, unfortunately, would destroy or at least keep individuality in check.

It is generally accepted in the field of leprosy that there are three major types of HD: lepromatus—many lesions; tuberculoid—few lesions; indeterminate—no lesions. I had the first, and all three can cause severe damage to nerves in the body. There is also a fourth type that is very rare and is called Lucio. During my time at Carville, I met three persons with the Lucio type of leprosy.

Lucio, found primarily in the Mexican state of Chihuahua, is extremely toxic to the skin. Lucio spreads so rapidly that large open sores, down to the bone, occur before diagnosis is confirmed. Treatment requires total isolation in a sterile environment, similar to isolation of burn victims. With the open lesions, severe infection can easily occur, resulting in complications that can cause death. Two of the three persons I knew with Lucio died.

The treatment at the foot clinic was remarkably simple. Everyone's legs were placed in a large bucket filled with warm water and Alpha Keri lotion for approximately fifteen minutes. Then, the legs were lightly patted dry and petroleum jelly generously applied to them. The legs were wrapped in gauze (especially those of us with open sores), firmed up with support hose, or simply left uncovered. Others, of course, needed more delicate treatment for their toenails, calluses, or ulcers.

As I stared deeply into the buckets where many of the residents had inserted severely damaged feet, I wondered if my ability to walk would become a part of my past. I looked in amazement at hands damaged by the disease and silently pondered if I would lose the ability to hold Magdalena's hand by interlocking our pinkie fingers. I looked at the many in the room whose noses had collapsed, and tried to imagine looking at myself in the mirror to see what seemed like a partial face.

Foot care was essential because leprosy would cause anesthesia and nerve damage. The nerve damage could also lead to a condition called drop foot. Drop foot would result in one's inability to raise the front of the foot; thus the leg would have to be lifted high enough to flop the foot forward. This condition also affects many retired professional football players with damaged nerves after years of violent hits, as well as persons with diabetes.

The staff and residents provided me with a unique education: limbs and noses do not fall off, but chronic injury and infection due to loss of sensitivity in fingers, toes, and nose cartilage can result in disfigurement. This process of disfigurement, of course, takes years and can never be corrected. I have had my share of injuries to toes and fingers, including accidentally burning my fingers with a cigarette, because they are insensitive to pain. Dispelling this myth of toes, fingers, and noses "falling off" is one of the biggest challenges facing those of us diagnosed with HD. And those diagnosed with the disease today who receive early treatment need *never* have any of the disabilities traditionally associated with leprosy.

Leprosy can easily be misdiagnosed and thus not treated, or ignored by persons who cannot find a physician to make the appropriate diagnosis. Therefore, with so many of my "brothers and sisters" at Carville having gone for years without proper treatment, the HD bacillus did its damage.

Leprosy causes chronic inflammation of the skin, resulting in lesions. These can occur anywhere in the body, leaving a series of indentions in the skin. This inflammation can also leave discoloration of the skin, scarring, poor circulation, and insensitivity to pain. The latter is what causes the most damage to hands and feet, as injury can lead to secondary infections. Similar destruction can occur to the larynx, where the slow progression of lesions results in hoarseness.[1]

The residents made me feel special and at home. At the time, I was the youngest person at Carville receiving treatment; thus, many called me "son." Some shared their stories with me, in particular the trauma of becoming pregnant, and then having their children taken away for adoption. Others had their kids brought up by relatives. Still others had their sperm count dramatically reduced with "reactions"—*erythema nodosum leprosum* (ENL)—explosive growth of bacilli limiting their chances for parenthood. A reaction could be caused for any number of reasons, such as stress or attempts by the body to adjust to the introduction of dapsone. The high fevers and severe pain resulting from a reaction usually meant admission to the infirmary.

The foot clinic was in the same building as the infirmary. The infirmary is a two-story building completed in 1937 and connected to eighteen other buildings. The connection was made through two miles of walkways wide enough to allow someone in a wheelchair and another person on a bicycle to pass while going in different directions, and still have elbow room for signaling a silent hello with the wave of a hand. The walkways, or corridors, have arcade and rectangular windows with three two-by-fours, two vertical and one horizontal, serving as supports for screens that keep the mosquitoes out at night.

The foot clinic was a beehive of activity. I learned as much from the residents about caring for my legs as I did from the sisters, whose training was in nursing. I learned that this disease is similar to diabetes in the impairment of blood circulation. I learned that because of poor circulation, wounds can take longer than usual to heal. They can easily result in ulcers and sometimes amputation. I learned that because of poor circulation, the skin is not as thick as skin not affected by leprosy; thus cuts and scrapes can occur frequently, take much longer to heal, and require special care for healing to occur without scarring.

I learned that because of the toxic effect of the leprosy bacilli on dry skin, the application of petroleum jelly would become a daily ritual for the rest of my life. Failure to do this would result in skin that would crack like dry mud and cause severe itching. The itching could lead to uncontrollable scratching, resulting in bleeding and infection. To this day, I try to avoid areas with dry and/or cold climates. Unfortunately my hometown, Laredo, is very dry, so after a two-week visit, my legs react painfully to the weather, and I return to my current home in Houston with its more humid weather.

After my legs were soaked in warm water, I received my first application of petroleum jelly. Sister Gabriella generously, but gently, applied the jelly, being careful not to put any on the open sores. The open sores were treated with antibodies or special powder that, I was told, was sometimes used on burn patients. Gauze was delicately wrapped around my legs and then secured with paper tape. I was helped off my feet and eased into the wheelchair, and as if on cue, Dr. Pete walked in and with his fragile feet and damaged hands returned me to my room.

Dr. Pete, a man of slight build, wore shoes made by staff at the hospital that were specially tailored for his feet. He liked wearing hats, especially white hats. On this cold day though, he was wearing a felt hat, making him appear very distinguished.

As we entered the elevator, Oscar, a gentleman as short as Dr. Pete and wearing a cowboy hat that appeared to be two sizes too small, jokingly asked, "Which floor, please?" We all laughed even though Dr. Pete would hear this same comment dozens of times each day. Oscar, also wearing custom-made shoes and construction worker–type gloves, worked as the "elevator operator." He knew who I was and welcomed me to Carville, adding that he had met my family in the canteen. Shaking his hand in midair, he also commented that I had "a very pretty girlfriend . . . hopefully it'll last." The second part of his comment was the first clue that many of the current residents had previously had girlfriends and boyfriends who abandoned the relationship when their mates were diagnosed with HD.

As soon as I returned to my hospital room, Dr. Robert Jacobson, a tall balding man with a square jaw and horn-rimmed glasses, arrived. At the time he was clinical director and later became the director of the Gillis W. Long Hansen's Disease Center. He conducted a thorough medical examination. He carefully explained leprosy in meticulous detail, referencing my fevers, excruciating pain, sores, and loneliness, comparing these with the experiences of others.

He said I was very lucky in not having any facial or hand deformities, but each case was different, and he could not speculate on how long I would be at Carville. He said that length of stay was the first question asked by new arrivals. "And the ability to have sex is probably the second," I halfheartedly joked. He looked at me rather seriously and said, "Yes, that's correct." His solemn response and my depressed demeanor were directly related to the swelling of my testicles brought about by the high level of bacilli in my body. He also emphasized that the ability to have children would not be lost due to such swelling.

Dr. Jacobson said he would probably see me every day for a month or at least until "the reaction"—high level of bacilli growth—stabilized. "This," he said, "would be done with a gradual increase of prednisone and then introduction of DDS." DDS, I found out, was dapsone, a drug used by the U.S. military during the Vietnam War to prevent malaria. This was the same "miracle" drug introduced on March 10, 1941, at Carville.[2] Millions have been cured since then, but not before disfigurement, social isolation, ostracism and stigma and mental trauma had affected their lives. Millions of others throughout the world did not benefit from promin and dapsone until the 1960s, due, in part, to politics and jealousies among professionals in the medical field specializing in HD research.

Ironically, dapsone, used to treat cows for breast infections resulting in sour milk, was originally identified as a "possible treatment" for HD in 1909, at the Second International Leprosy Congress in Bergen, Norway. This idea lay dormant for thirty-two years.[3]

Dr. Jacobson was fair and honest with me, and I have always credited him with being the one person I try to emulate when discussing the effects of mental or cognitive disabilities, my professional specialty.

Dr. Jacobson informed me that my body "might not like" the introduction of prednisone and DDS on a long-term basis. Therefore, I needed to be prepared to try some "experimental medications" in order to "really reap the benefits" of DDS.

As he glanced at my chart—now in three-inch binders—he noted that my parents had signed admission consent forms and realized that I was twenty years old. He mumbled that it was "ridiculous that a grown man" had to be twenty-one before being allowed to sign consent forms. He looked at me and, with a forced smile, said, "Doesn't anybody know that eighteen-year-olds are being killed in Vietnam?"

Dr. Jacobson stood up from his chair and said, "Don't take this the wrong way, but welcome to Carville." From my horizontal position, as I looked up at him in his pristine white public health service uniform, his head appeared to be touching the ten-foot ceiling. He cautioned against relying on "painkillers and bad company" for support and gently shook my hand. His long fingers were jokingly referred to as "Jacobson's weapons" when he was conducting prostate exams. He closed the door as he left. I snuggled up to the cool pillow, covering my body with a white bed sheet. The weight of army-type wool blankets would cause pain, so I avoided these gray coverings. I fell quietly asleep.

At approximately 11:30 a.m., I was awakened by a gentle caressing of my forehead. I saw my parents, Raquel, and Magdalena, all beaming and saying that they had seen the hospital. It was lunchtime and they had wanted to pull my tray next to me so I could eat. They were going to the lunchroom and planned to return to Laredo that afternoon.

After lunch, my family returned to my room and explained in great detail their tour of Carville. They talked about Nachito, the canteen, the residents, and the post office. Mom described how they had signed many consent forms. However, she was puzzled as to why she and Dad were asked if they wanted to assign me a different name. Their response was no, but they still felt confused. Residents were encouraged, but not forced, to change their names in order to protect families. Regrettably, many residents are buried at Carville's cemetery with their assumed names.

The hospital's cemetery was originally situated in the quadrangle surrounded by buildings 25–29 to the north, the power plant to the south, and enclosed corridors on the east and west sides. A total of 173 persons were buried there between 1894 and 1920. In 1921 the cemetery, under federal jurisdiction, was moved to the west side of the complex. As of July 2007, an additional 743 were buried at this site.[4]

In my mind, all I could see in Magdalena and my family was the familiarity of Laredo, which would soon disappear. I tried, unsuccessfully, to smile and be strong—"ser fuerte"—as Mom kept saying over and over. My mother met the Catholic priest, Father Kelly, praying at the chapel, and he calmed her fears that I might not be close to the hands of God—"en las manos de Dios."

My parents had purchased pens and self-stamped envelopes so I could write to all my friends. Who, I thought, would want to write to me? Magdalena, reading my thoughts, said, "I'll write to you. Every day." And she did.

So, with many hugs, kisses, and tears, my parents, Raquel, and Magdalena left my room. My dad slipped me a twenty-dollar bill, which would go untouched for months.

# Learning about Carville

I recall being in a sugar beet field outside Helena, Montana, in the summer of 1964. Some of the family had traveled north—*al norte*—to do migrant work. The moment in 1964 was so crisp in my mind because of my recollection of silence, silence so great that the crawl of a caterpillar on a dry leaf would have gotten my attention. I remember looking at the sun's rays as it rapidly sank beyond the mountains that surround Helena. I remember that the wind, usually blowing lightly and keeping it cool during the late afternoon, was now nonexistent. I remember the home of the farm's owner in the distance ahead of me, and the barnlike building with an outhouse for twenty people in back of me that was our home, but no sight of people or animals. I remember how alone I felt for an instant and wondered if I would ever feel this removed from life again. That was answered for me four years later when I was admitted to Carville.

Like an old Ansel Adams photograph, void of human life, the hallways of the hospital appeared to become frozen in time at approximately 6 p.m. every day in 1968. By this time, the 3 p.m. shift change had occurred. Staff started their departure from the grounds at 4 p.m. even though their work schedule ended at 4:30 p.m. and dinner was usually served in the cafeteria by 4:20 p.m. With the exception of Tuesdays, Thursdays, and Saturday evenings, when movies were shown in the theatre at 7 p.m., the residents scattered to their rooms or cottages, not to be seen again until very early the next day. My second night at Carville was no different. The rigid routine of staff and residents forced me to move back in time to the summer of '64, and resurrected the empty feeling of being alone.

Only a few residents in the infirmary had televisions in their rooms, and my neighbors and I were not in that group, thus no noise from next door.

The nurse's station was at least ninety feet away in an enclosed cubicle, thus no hall noise.

The silence on my second night at Carville was finally broken when I took short, deep breaths as I wept. The nightly tears eventually subsided as I learned more about HD, especially that it is usually not fatal. Even though I had heard this before, the reassurance came in realizing that many of the residents were diagnosed at a young age—the average age of the residents at the time of my admission was fifty-five.[1] Conversely, this reassurance also caused me to have some sleepless nights, wondering if I would also grow old at Carville, forever separated from my family and Magdalena. As of 1968, the earliest recorded diagnosis was for someone three months old in Martinique and the latest was for someone seventy years old in California.[2]

During my first month at Carville, I spent much time reading and learned a great deal about the history of the hospital and the injustices that most of the residents had experienced as a result of being diagnosed with leprosy.

The facility at Carville is older than many of the better-known structures throughout the United States, such as the Empire State Building, the Golden Gate Bridge, and Hoover Dam.

Those with leprosy had initially been kept in a "Pest House" in New Orleans in the general vicinity where the current airport is located.[3] Louisiana, as well as other coastal areas, had historically had a number of persons diagnosed with or suspected of having leprosy. Thus, areas of isolation had been established, unbeknownst to the general population, to house these individuals. The Pest House was far from the city and located next to the local garbage dump.

By the early 1890s, the Pest House had become overcrowded, and state officials started to look for other accommodations. An ideal location was found, rented by the state in 1894, and named the Louisiana Leper Home. The site, known as the Indian Camp Plantation, long ago abandoned by Colonel Camp, a veteran of the Civil War, was easily accessible by barge, allowing officials the opportunity to transport the residents at night. The Mississippi River meandered around the property, and swamps hugged the land, giving the impression that it was an island. In fact, most of the leprosaria built around this time and later were either on an island or some other place difficult to access—away from the community, "protecting society from the unclean."

The original admission manuscript lists the first eight people who arrived in December 1894, ranging in age from twenty-one to fifty-two, with six identified as Louisiana-born, one from France, and one from Peru. With harsh living conditions, poorly built and crumbling old slave cabins, and limited food supplies, three died within one year, and one "escaped," but they were replaced with eighteen new admissions in 1895.[4]

In 1896, the board, which had control over the Leper Home, unsuccessfully sought funding for medical personnel. Their efforts to seek volunteers proved more successful when they negotiated with the Daughters of Charity of St. Vincent de Paul to "treat and love the lepers." Similar to the "Ten Commandments" for persons with leprosy, "Rules for the Inmate" enumerated ten forbidden actions, e.g., touch, assembly, travel.[5]

Prior to selecting Carville as the site for a national leprosy center in 1921, the federal government had explored the possibility of purchasing other sites. These sites included Penikese Island off the Massachusetts coast, Angel and Alcatraz islands in San Francisco Bay, Galveston Island in Texas, Golden Island off the coast of Seattle, Washington, and Molokai Island in Hawaii. The most famous island used as a leprosarium, better known as the home for those who opposed apartheid, is Robben Island, South Africa, which was home for Nelson Mandela and others for decades.

In 1904, Boston was the site for the "largest public hearing ever held in Massachusetts" as angry and frightened residents gathered to protest the purchase of Cape Cod for a "leper colony." The attempt to purchase the land came after the department of health, pressured by staff and local residents, rejected a plan to place some persons with leprosy at the Tewksbury Home of the Insane. State officials instead purchased Penikese Island for the "colony." State officials ordered the burning of all the buildings in 1921 when the residents were relocated to Carville.[6]

In 1905, four years before Pearl Harbor was selected for a new U.S. naval base, Congress approved legislation to build and operate the U.S. Leprosy Investigation Station on Molokai Island for the "purpose of studying leprosy." This was the first congressional funding for research on a specific disease. In spite of having the most modern medical facility in the world at the time, only nine residents of the Kalawao Settlement, made famous by Father Damien, volunteered for admission. Within four years, the facility was closed because the administrators, the highest paid in the U.S. government during this era, far exceeding the annual average income of one thousand dollars per year, did not accept the Hawaiian culture—food, customs, language. In addition, there was no known cure for leprosy, so why would any of the residents want to be confined in this federal facility with its strict rules? Living free to roam around the 2 1/2-acre peninsula was understandably far more desirable.

Today, this place, twenty minutes by air from Honolulu, is one of the most beautiful places in the world, as if frozen in time when the land was not occupied by humans. This area, declared by King Kaamehamoha V in 1865 as the "place to isolate lepers," condemned many Hawaiians to an early death.

The area, surrounded by cliffs exceeding three thousand feet, was created hundreds of thousands of years ago when the northern sector of Molokai Island experienced a tremendous volcanic explosion, and a segment literally sank into the Pacific Ocean. Later, a fissure poured lava onto the coast, forming a peninsula that branches out like a giant tongue from the cliffs. The peninsula, without any natural place for anchorage and dangerous cliffs with numerous crevices and caves, was a natural prison for its early inhabitants.

Many of the "leprosy hospitals" have been started or staffed by groups, usually missionaries, affiliated with various religious organizations. These groups were seen as meeting a need most "leprosy endemic" countries were unwilling to publicly recognize. As a result, countries like Japan and China gave missionaries unofficial welcomes to their land decades before inroads were made through diplomacy and sanctioned trade.

One of these missionary groups, started in 1906, was the American Leprosy Mission (ALM), currently headquartered in Greenville, South Carolina. The ALM provided funding for research and for the building of the protestant chapel at Carville.

The site of Galveston Island was explored after the Texas legislature approved Senate Bill 69, during the thirty-first session, and allocated forty thousand dollars to build and operate the State Home for Lepers. The home had to be more than one mile from any residence and more than five miles from the town of Galveston. The law authorized the sheriff to arrest "persons diagnosed with leprosy" and transport them to the home where they would be "confined (for) life. . . ." Senate Bill 69, to "confine people with leprosy," became law on April 21, 1909. April 21 is now recognized as San Jacinto Day (a celebration of Texas's independence).

The community leaders requested, then declined, funding for a "leper home." As Galveston was recovering from the Great Storm of 1900 and attracting tourists, the building of such a home would affect the image of the community. Thus, the home was never built.[7]

The state of Louisiana operated the hospital until 1921 when the federal government took control of the facility and renamed it Marine Hospital #61; it was later changed to the U.S. Public Health Service Hospital, then to the Gillis W. Long Hansen's Disease Center, and, in 1999, to the Gillis W. Long Center.

The state and federal governments in the U.S. had similar philosophies about persons diagnosed with leprosy, involving isolation, segregation, and denial of basic civil rights, but they exercised different practices. Texas developed procedures for treatment of HD ("commitment" to Carville). This protocol after 1921 was copied by every state. Noncompliance with expected behaviors for those hospitalized at Carville meant placement in the detention room or jail for unspecified lengths of time. The federal government encouraged actions of commitment and detention through its silence.

This silence, though, had its price as more and more money was poured into the "reservation," as some journalists have referred to Carville. The 350-acre facility became totally self-sufficient within a short period of time as several buildings essential to an independent infrastructure were erected.

The main hospital buildings are elevated, approximately three feet off the ground. Considering the level of moisture in Louisiana, this was a blessing. However, the covering that the building provided also served as protective hiding places for many cats, dogs, raccoons, and armadillos.

There was an administration building, a home for nuns, a training building, dining rooms, colonial-style cottages, a man-made lake, quonset huts, water treatment plant, carpentry and paint shops, a recreation building, dormitories, two chapels, a power plant, livestock and silos for storing their feed, softball grandstand, incinerator, school, guard tower, print shop, water tower, and two golf courses (one for residents and another for staff). The cemetery is filled with many souls who never experienced the serenity of acceptance, similar to cemeteries at other leprosaria throughout the world. Simply because a person was diagnosed with leprosy, his or her body was not accepted in community cemeteries. Therefore, ostracism continued even in death.

The culture of Carville had its own unique flavor. Residents and staff I met during my first month were from almost every state in the U.S., South America, Central America, Guam, England, Greenland, Greece, Mexico, Philippines, Samoa, China, Japan, Vietnam, Thailand, Germany, Italy, Cuba, Puerto Rico, Canada, France, Korea, Ethiopia, Ireland, India, Indonesia, Australia, and Spain. One-fourth of the residents were from Texas.[8] I was constantly trying to learn a little bit about each culture, each language. Each individual would share with me, whenever I asked, how he/she was diagnosed and the manner in which his/her life had changed. Some would get misty-eyed when reminiscing about lost dreams, but most were cold and distant when discussing their past, as if they were talking about someone else.

Many of the women of Carville, most of whom were much older than I, were very guarded when discussing their history because a spouse or boyfriend had rejected almost all of them when they were diagnosed, and their memories were too painful to put into words.

I learned that basic rights had been denied to millions diagnosed before I was, including due process, choice of treatment, voting, ability to use their country's monetary system, segregation by disease and sex, and many more. Governments throughout the world approved large allocations of funds up through the 1950s to build and maintain hospitals away from the general population. As more buildings were constructed, the probability increased that rights of persons diagnosed with leprosy were denied. After the 1950s, when medication became more readily available, the building of leprosaria dramatically decreased, and minor efforts to restore rights were initiated.

Men and women told me about instances of public health officials showing up with sheriff's deputies for forced transport to Carville. Others talked about how all of their belongings, including their desks at school and their textbooks, were publicly burned as a way of showing the public that it was being protected. Still others talked about the length of time it had taken to be properly diagnosed, resulting in disabilities that affected their ability to earn a living.

A common experience was ostracism from family and friends, some forced and some self-imposed. The latter occurred reluctantly when people heard how leprosy would adversely affect their families, and the former when they were encouraged to change their names upon admission to Carville. Even when families went to great effort to either educate their friends or keep the diagnosis a secret, siblings or children would regularly suffer the consequences of rejection and labeling.

In my instance, Dad placed a one-inch notice in the local paper, the *Laredo Times*, indicating that I had been hospitalized for treatment at a Louisiana facility and listing the address. While this action proved to be invaluable to my recovery, as I received over one hundred cards and letters within a four-week period, a retired police officer harshly criticized Dad. His friend stated that publicity would destroy the whole family and me since "leprosy is a damn curse and this torch never dies."

Dad explained to me that he was crushed by this criticism from such a good friend, but when the friend explained his reasons for this bizarre behavior, Dad understood and respected his intentions. His friend, the police officer, had been a resident at Carville for many years until he "escaped" via the infamous hole in the fence dug by residents. He kept the secret of his diagnosis from his family and friends. Dad never violated his secret, but his friend must have felt unbearable pain, keeping his diagnosis and an important part of his life hidden.

One of the harshest injustices resulting from being diagnosed with HD occurred when women who became pregnant had their children taken away for adoption or saw them given to an outside family (very few had this luxury) to care for them. Two women shared with me that their baby was "declared dead at childbirth." The Carville cemetery has a gravestone inscribed, "Mary Buie, Died 1933, Stillborn Baby."

In other parts of the world, persons diagnosed with leprosy were routinely sterilized. In other extreme cases outside the U.S., women who became pregnant before sterilization could be initiated were forced to carry their pregnancy until the eighth month and then the fetus aborted. This indescribable pain was designed to force women to "voluntarily" request sterilization. I do not know which was more painful, involuntary sterilization or involuntarily losing a child.

One of my life-changing experiences occurred after a Laredo Junior College administrator notified the Selective Service Board that I had dropped out of school. I was classified 1-A—ready for immediate military service. Soon after my father notified the board of my illness, I was reclassified 4-F—forever ineligible for military service. My secret desire to join the service and "become a man" had died with my diagnosis of Hansen's disease.

## chapter 5

# Life at Carville

The hospital grounds at Carville were divided into two worlds. One was to the left of the main entrance past the administration building, "the Big House," and staff dining room. This area, which had over twenty buildings, mostly cottages for public health service staff and visitors, was off limits to us residents of the "other" world. I was able to meet only a few of the children who lived on the station, but I always wondered what their thoughts were about growing up in Louisiana where segregation by race was a common practice, and then residing on the hospital grounds where segregation due to illness was commonly accepted.

To the right of the main road, now called Stanley Stein Drive, was where we, the residents, and the nuns lived. The "patient side" was composed of eighteen two-story dormitories elevated from the ground by five-foot pillars. An aerial view of the facility shows a flat oval design, with two parallel rows of dormitories lined up next to each other, joined at the middle by the infirmary, resident dining room, and recreation building. The oval design, according to the National Register of Historic Places, mimicked the "footprint that the former slave cabins once occupied" on the Indian Camp Plantation.

The dormitories were connected by a long, wide, covered walkway, protected from the ever-present mosquitoes by window screens. Accidents sometimes occurred in the walkways, as Louisiana's humidity made the concrete floors, always in need of repair or painting, slippery and difficult to maneuver early in the morning and during rainstorms, which came frequently. With the traffic from almost four hundred residents and twice that number of staff, and with the structures in constant need of repair, it seemed that sandblasting was an ever-present activity in the hallways.

The recreation building, which was equivalent to the courthouse of a small Texas town, was always bursting with activity, as it housed the auditorium, theater, banquet hall, pool tables, library, TV room, post office, and canteen. The canteen was under the control of the Patients' Federation and was operated by a contracted manager, who was always a resident. It was open from 8 a.m. until 8 p.m., with brief closings for lunch and dinner.

The canteen, approximately five hundred square feet, had a tiny office with an even smaller kitchen, a bar with stools, and tables with chairs. In the back, there was a room where toiletries, breads, cookies, fresh fruits, canned goods and meats, and sometimes ethnically diverse foods were also on display. The staff and residents were usually lined up before 8 a.m., waiting to get their java, nicotine, or alcohol (no restrictions on when beer was sold). The presence of customers continued all day long, making the canteen a very profitable venture and creating traffic jams for delivery trucks. The position of canteen manager was the highest paid "patient job" (three hundred dollars a month). I once aspired to have this job, but eventually changed my mind after realizing the demands of the work. The job required having control of thousands of dollars in order to cash checks; forever smiling at customers; conducting monthly manual inventories of all merchandise; having no accrued vacation time; being open seven days a week; constantly training new workers, as the turnover rate was very high; and refusing service to those who became physically aggressive or intoxicated.

Drinking appeared to be a problem for some, including staff that would sneak through the back entrance of the manager's office and drink beers or their own whiskey. This behavior was considered a secret only by those who were in denial of their drinking problems.

According to some of the older residents, a different kind of drinking with a happy ending had occurred many years earlier. As the government initiated practices to make Carville self-sufficient, the canteen grew in popularity. As a result, there was a great demand for soda pop, i.e. Coke and Pepsi. The local distributor of Coca-Cola became very concerned that recyclable bottles brought back from Carville might "contaminate" other customers and thus decided to stop delivering their merchandise to the canteen or even pick up hundreds of empty bottles.

The residents decided that they too could play the game of exclusion and informally banned the purchase of any Coca-Cola products, escalating the demand for Pepsi. The empty Coke bottles were used to decorate a garden. The Coke distributor finally changed his mind when he realized the gold mine inherited by Pepsi. I always thought this story would be a wonderful addition to Coca-Cola's museum in Atlanta as a way to educate the public about leprosy and to show the world that a management error demonstrated that they could still learn and initiate positive change.

A man named Charles Sude is buried in the hospital's cemetery. It is not known if this was a Carville name or his given name. The gravesite and footstone are made of empty Coke bottles. No one knows if this was one final snub at the Coca-Cola Company for their action against the residents.

Connected to the canteen by a common entrance was the post office. The post office was seven feet by eleven feet, making it one of the smallest in the U.S. According to James Carville, it was the only one created exclusively for use by persons with a disease. This small room was our main link to the "outside" world, as many of us would receive correspondence from faraway places. Additionally, we could chat about what we had heard on the news, read in the paper, or heard in the hallways (rumors). Also, it was where people could place bets, collect winnings, and cry over lost bets. Bets on just about any sport or political race could be made while one was buying an envelope or stamp. This was also the place to collect a crisp new five-dollar bill for voting "the right way."

In Laredo, I had seen the practice of candidates or their supporters donating five-dollar bills for consideration for a vote, but I had never viewed it being done as blatantly as at Carville.

In Louisiana, politics has its own unique flavor. Many of the residents were personal friends of Iberville Parish's sheriff, Jessel Ourso, a large man popular with everyone and known for his pot luck drawings of TVs, refrigerators, and stoves. With his flair for hosting giveaways, none of us could resist the temptation to vote for him.

During my stay at Carville I met Louisiana's governor, John ("Big John") McKeithan. At the time, my knowledge of governors was limited to Texas. Big John served two terms as governor and passed away in 1999. He was an advocate for us at Carville and would walk the halls shaking everybody's hand as burly members of the state police followed him everywhere. He used to joke that Chester Carville, postmaster for the Pt. Clair Branch Post Office, owner of the general store, and son of the founder of the town of Carville, would have been in his shoes if he were not so interested in helping others. I recall seeing his sons, Billy and James, at the store handling sales or coming by the hospital to greet people they knew. In fact, the Carville boys introduced me to capitalism when Mr. Carville convinced me to apply for my first credit card, Esso, once I purchased my first car. He, of course, operated an Esso filling station.

Chester taught his children about unyielding loyalty to friends. He did this by example. He found his best friend, Darryl Broussard, among the hundreds of residents who were ostracized by society. Darryl was as tall as "Big John" and they bonded well. Both loved the underdog and they knew how to play the odds. Darryl introduced me to Governor McKeithan as "my son, but he'll accept a donation anyway." Their laughter traveled throughout the recreation building and became contagious.

Sheriff Ourso, Big John, and many other politicians regularly visited Carville's busy ward 5, precinct 2.

Wasey Daigle, who was born in the small town of Lafayette, Louisiana, had good looks, a quick wit, a bright mind, and a strong desire to enter politics. His road to success appeared to be custom built for him. His dreams, he would reminisce, were to play football at LSU and to become governor of Louisiana by age forty. His dreams turned into a nightmare when, as a teenager, he was diagnosed with Hansen's disease. He was quickly removed from his family and taken to the only leprosarium in the continental United States, fifty miles from his home, in Carville. The hospital could have been located thousands of miles away, because he never entered his parents' home again. In order to protect his family, he changed his name to Darryl Broussard. Sadly, his family never witnessed his many successes: role model to his peers, devoted husband, fatherlike figure to many of the younger residents, reader during Mass for the hospital's Catholic Church, advocate for dignity and respect, president of numerous organizations (Patients' Federation, Lions Club, Golf Club), eloquent speaker, and postmaster for the hospital's post office. His dreams were partially achieved when he became a season ticket holder for LSU Tiger football games, and when he was personally recognized by Big John McKeithan for helping him get elected governor of Louisiana. He used a famous quote to describe himself: "I am a small man in an imperfect world." Mr. Daigle lived to be a perfect friend for many.

Darryl was married to Mary Ruth, a short Mexican American beauty from San Antonio, Texas. They had met at the hospital after Mary joined her sister, Kitty, at Carville. Her parents told her that Kitty had gone away to college in Louisiana, but she did not see her during the holidays or during semester breaks. They were reunited under sad circumstances after Mary was also diagnosed with leprosy.

Mary described her emotions upon being told of the diagnosis, saying that it was a "terrible shock." She recalled being picked up at her home at age twenty by a sheriff's deputy who kept her distance and said, "I was told not to touch so I can't handcuff you either." With the exception of some sensory loss in her foot, she did not have any visible signs of the disease, but the deputy kept referring to her by the "l" word. She was escorted to the train station and placed, alone, in a diner car for the long trip to Carville. At the end of her trip, she was ordered to get into an ambulance and, with deputies driving with their red lights flashing, she was transported to her "new home."

With Dad and Magdalena notifying my friends of my trip to Louisiana, I started to receive daily letters. Darryl Broussard, the hospital's postmaster, ran a one-person operation, and had to deliver mail to the infirmary. We would see each other daily, and gradually he and his wife, Mary, started inviting me to their home for meals and allowed me the use of the telephone for long distance calls to Laredo. Eventually, they started calling me their "son," especially after they met Magdalena. I vowed that I would not get involved in any stupid activities. Well, like any son, I did do some dumb things. However, they gave me a lecture whenever I strayed and relayed briefings of my activities to my parents.

The letters from home came at a fast clip. Friends and teachers wrote words of concern, and always closed with a positive message of "we miss you . . . a lot." I read the letters and cards over and over again, relishing the thought that I could be magically transported to my hometown with words.[1]

My siblings regularly used humor in their letters, intuitively knowing that this was both therapeutic and informative for me. Yolanda, my oldest sister, who had volunteered to spend my last night in Laredo with me at Mercy Hospital, usually kept her cards short, embarrassed about misspellings. Raquel would go into great detail but consistently emphasized that everyone was "fine" and "okay," even when she was in a bad accident and was left without transportation. Raquel would go on about how many of my male friends would send their regards via her husband, Julian. They would reminisce about my macho attempt at age eighteen to drink a quart of rum, how I passed out and was delivered to Julian's front steps—I slept for fifteen hours and woke up not knowing where I was. Raquel also elaborated on her daughter Pat's developmental milestones, proudly telling me how intelligent and beautiful she was (and still is as an adult). In candor, admittedly embarrassed, she also explained that her perfect first child had a *nido de piojos* (nest full of lice). This line brought me great joy, not about poor Pat's situation, but for my sister's sharing such a delicate moment, which made my heart ache for home.

Diana, one year older than I, would usually be the last one in the family to go to bed while we were both attending high school. She would stay up until 11 p.m. listening to *"Serenata Nocturna"* ("Nightly Serenade") on the radio, when old Mexican songs were played, making both of us nostalgic for when we were younger and Dad would sing and play the guitar. These times were very special for us, as she would give me advice on how to be a better boyfriend to Magdalena, always describing her as "sweet, smart, and probably too good for you"; i.e., I should be respectful of her.

Diana would keep me informed about the activities of *los salvajes* (the little savages), four brothers and three nephews, between the ages of five and ten. She also sent me the small newspaper clipping about my hospitalization, expressing shock because it was so much unlike my father to show such affection. She said, "Si no te mueres de susto con esto, nunca te mueres" ("If you don't die of shock from this [article], you will never die").

Javier, the football and track star of the family, would proudly send me cards enumerating his accomplishments, such as trying out for quarterback at high school and placing sixteenth (field of twenty) on the 880 at the Border Olympics. Rudy would keep me abreast of all other sports events in Laredo and seek advice on how to become a better driver. Margarita and Idalia would write about the daily routine of helping to make rice and beans for lunch and refried leftover beans for supper, with plenty of flour tortillas. They would also make sure that their good grades were included in the correspondence. I was still their big brother, even though we were separated by a great distance.

My parents received a lot of support and regular visits from their relatives and childhood friends and from my friends as well. They all knew how my illness had dramatically affected their lives and even their faith in God. Everyone would say, "Vengo a darles apoyo" ("I've come to give you my support"). My maternal grandfather, though he never learned to read, would like to say, "Arriba, marchar para arriba" ("Forward, always march forward"). He wanted us to learn from our past, and I would often remind Mom of this. Hoping that they would not sense my loneliness, I would write her and Dad long letters. Their letters, some with only a few sentences, would arrive daily, sometimes two or three on the same day. My parents and I felt the pain that so many others at Carville had felt, and we could not find the right prescription to alleviate the sleepless nights . . . wondering why we were affected by the illness . . . praying for some relief . . . hoping for a quick recovery.

My precious Magdalena, barely making enough money working at the Laredo Junior College library to financially help her parents, sacrificed buying zippers for unfinished dresses to purchase envelopes and stamps to send me words of encouragement on a daily basis. Her unselfish expressions of love reminded me of what Diana used to say: "Magdalena is probably too good for you." I wondered if maybe she was right.

Magdalena would always encourage me to "learn from yesterday, look and smell the flowers today . . . and look forward to your education *mañana*." She encouraged me to think about continuing my education. "After all," she would write, "I want to marry a good, strong and smart man." Collectively, all of my family, relatives, friends, staff, and fellow residents helped me recover, but individually, Magdalena was the one who ultimately helped me to reach a successful plateau.

Magdalena, during her brief visit to Carville on February 24–25, 1968, had been introduced to many residents as my girlfriend. Her friendly personality and custom of acknowledging an introduction with a handshake had generated much surprise from the residents. She, Raquel, and my parents had chosen to eat on the patient side, instead of the visitor side, of the cafeteria. Visitors were allowed to eat at the patient cafeteria, but patients were not allowed to eat in the staff cafeteria. This simple action had endeared all four to the hospital population as word spread about their generosity and lack of fear of the disease.

As my sores started to heal, the pain decreased and the fevers became less frequent. I was offered more opportunities to be wheeled to the canteen, Catholic chapel, library, recreation hall, and the terrace of the infirmary. This, of course, opened up chances for meeting more staff and residents. As a result of increased contacts with the community, I started to receive unsolicited advice.

One of the most startling pieces of advice from almost everyone, especially staff, was that I should keep my diagnosis a secret. I was really confused. Why would I hear that I could "easily integrate back into the real community," as emphasized by Frank Kanatani of the training branch, yet at the same time be told "you will regret telling anyone" as emphasized by the special services officer (SSO).

Kanatani, a career public health service officer, primarily focused on the training and education of visiting professionals. The SSO, on the other hand, was the enforcer of policies and practices of the hospital, so his words were considered gospel. Fellow residents told me that he controlled the assignment of dormitory rooms, jobs, and dining privileges.

The SSO was addressed by everyone in a formal manner, with people always emphasizing the "Mr." before stating his surname. He may not have had total control, but he possessed a great deal of influence, serving on committees that addressed resident- and staff-related activities. He reminded me of a southern plantation owner with his air of authority, snow-white hair, natty white clothing, and white plantation hats. When he was angry his face turned red as a beet. He also wore a shorter version of a Salvadore Dali–style moustache. So, for anyone to talk the talk and walk the walk, he or she had to first look in the direction of the SSO in order to do it right. Thus, I was strongly encouraged to "keep it a secret."

I felt publicly humiliated when I broke this rule through my actions. In 1970, Magdalena had flown in to visit me, and I decided to treat her to a nice dinner and dance at a Baton Rouge restaurant that I could not visit unless it was a special occasion. Having Magdalena's company for a few days was very special.

As we were being led to our table, I spotted the SSO with his wife and some friends, all enjoying an evening out. After ordering drinks, I decided to go and say "hi," hoping to have an opportunity to show off my girlfriend. The SSO noticed me as I walked toward his table, correctly guessing that I was about to greet him and his party. He quickly stood up, and like a stiff guard at Arlington National Cemetery, walked in my direction, communicating with his glare—you do not belong here. He firmly grabbed my coat and sternly demanded to know what I was doing there, as if he owned the restaurant and I was not welcome.

His message was twofold: first, that I was not his equal, and second, that an introduction would mean violating *his* rule of keeping my diagnosis a secret. His behavior should not have been a surprise to me, but it was extremely painful to be treated in such a condescending manner. I was in too much shock to utter a word, so I returned to the table. After reluctantly describing to Magdalena what had happened, she stood up, grabbed my hand, escorted me to the middle of the dance floor, and defiantly stared back at the SSO.

The residents were almost universally in favor of keeping my diagnosis a secret. Many had experienced a painful moment when their diagnosis was exposed. They feared having an unpleasant experience with rejection if their diagnosis were revealed, or they were reluctant to find out the consequences from the SSO and others if at any time they said anything about the HD bacillus being in their bodies. For years I too followed suit.

Some other advice I received was: "Don't make waves, don't challenge the system, don't squeal on anyone, and don't be disrespectful to the female patients." I never violated the latter two don'ts, but I quietly changed my thinking on the first two.

Yet another piece of advice was to either marry or maintain a relationship only with another person currently or previously treated for leprosy. "For the good of someone else" was a powerful and convincing argument for those of us with a significant other upon diagnosis. Most had this issue resolved for them via divorce, since many states granted divorces based on diagnosis, denial by family of their existence, or self-imposed exile.

This advice and pressure to marry within the community led me to stupidly attempt to break off my relationship with Magdalena. Luckily, she showed me her stubborn streak, refused to accept my "Dear John" comments, and again showed her strength. Eventually, I realized how absolutely dumb the advice was, especially after I witnessed love affairs that resulted in marriage among some residents and staff, residents and adult children of staff, residents and Carville "outsiders." Residents who married people who did not have the disease were forced to either live "outside," or have two homes. People without the disease were not allowed to live with a resident at the facility. Of course, many others found their soul mates among the resident population and lived happily together until their deaths.

Within three weeks of my arrival at Carville, I was asked to participate in a training session. The hospital's training branch regularly had large groups of individuals visit for the most current updates on the diagnosis and treatment of HD. These groups included laymen from the 40 and 8 posts (part of the American Legion composed of veterans and strong supporters of *The Star*, a patient-published magazine started in the late 1930s), leprologists, researchers, nurses, dermatologists, clergy, Job Corps volunteers, etc. I was told that my recent diagnosis and lack of physical disabilities would make a perfect situation for educating others about the disease. I accepted the invitation.

I recall Dr. Pete coming to the infirmary and transporting me to the training building in a wheelchair. He was in a friendly mood as usual and reminded me "not to show too much or say too much. They don't care how we feel." I did not understand his comments, and we arrived in the training room before I could ask for an explanation.

The room was like any other conference room with chairs and tables for an audience of approximately twenty individuals, all males, in white shirts and dark ties. At the front was a large screen for viewing films, slides, or transparencies. There was also a small stage, five to seven inches above the ground, with a long table used by presenters or panel members.

I was not provided much information other than to "not worry about clothes, just come in your hospital pajamas and robe." Upon arriving, I heard one of the facility's physicians, a man with horn-rimmed glasses and a very round figure say, "Oh, there he is." The doctor was not popular among the residents.

The doctor said, "Hi," and maneuvered my wheelchair up onto the small stage, directed someone to dim the lights except for those on the stage, and proceeded to talk about *me*. I felt like a slab of meat on display. "This is a twenty-year-old Mexican from Texas recently diagnosed . . ." His cold demeanor and the hot lights made me feel nauseous.

As he continued to talk, I blocked out his voice. He then grabbed my arm and with one swoop had me standing. He proceeded to remove my robe and pulled my pajama bottoms and boxer shorts down to my ankles. He was showing the audience open sores, emphasizing the damage that leprosy could do to the body if left untreated. He neglected to mention my embarrassment.

I recalled the time with the *Doña* in Nuevo Laredo, Mexico, and Dr. Dickerson in my room at Mercy Hospital.

After his presentation, he asked me to pull my pants up, and I was wheeled to the hallway and left alone for approximately an hour waiting for Dr. Pete to take me back to the infirmary. I was angry and recall thinking that this could be the type of pain a person feels after having been raped—alone, silently contemplating a quick death, unable to articulate innermost thoughts, sensing an empty soul drifting out of the body, and experiencing great difficulty in crying to lessen the pain. I vowed never to participate in "training" again unless I saw a written agenda, was briefed on the type of audience present, was assured there would be no display of anatomy, especially private parts, and was properly introduced by my full name. Since that day, I have trained many individuals on terminology, diagnosis, and psychosocial issues related to HD. Regrettably, I never confronted the doctor on the proper manner for conducting a training session.

By becoming a teaching hospital, Carville made a major contribution to the field of education, helping many to become better informed about diagnosis, treatment, and reconstructive surgery of persons affected by leprosy. Unfortunately, it also contributed to physically stripping us of our dignity, just as society in general stripped us of our emotional dignity.

The library, operated by a resident, had newspapers from all over the country, some in Spanish. It also had books written by current residents. *Alone No Longer*, written by Stanley Stein, gave me an opportunity to reflect on how I too could overcome loneliness. This gentleman gave life to some of the stories I had heard from the residents and staff, including the fact that not all hospital directors had been advocates for the residents, but rather had spent their time enforcing and creating rules and regulations that focused on exclusion and incarceration. Mr. Stein was, and continues to be, an inspiration to all of us challenged by HD throughout the world. His hands became a powerful weapon whenever he grabbed a pen and wrote about dignity and respect.

Stanley, whose real name was Sidney Levyson, liked to jokingly describe himself as a "wannabe actor and real life Texan."[2] As an aspiring actor in San Antonio, Texas, and a licensed pharmacist, Sidney had accurately described himself. What he did not realize about himself was the strength he possessed when confronted with the unexpected challenges of life. As with many of the Jewish faith like himself, he experienced a holocaust of rejection, labeling, ostracism, fear, hatred, and loss of identity. Unlike others in Europe who were sent to the gas chamber, he was sent to a place of isolation for simply being diagnosed with Hansen's disease. When Sidney was a young man, his life of success and happiness turned into an unexpected life of sadness as his name was changed to Stanley Stein and his sight was lost to the HD bacillus. However, unwilling to comply with society's expectation of isolation, he championed a cause to "radiate the truth about HD."[3]

He became the best-known advocate for the elimination of myths related to HD and the restoration of basic human rights for those affected by leprosy. He educated and enlightened us with his experiences, warmth, skill with words, and strong desire to initiate positive change.

A person who regularly came to the library, even when he lived "outside," was Harry Martin. Harry was a handsome, soft-spoken man. He would patiently sit and tell me Carville stories, but each had a happy ending, e.g., "cured, found love, saw the light, changed my ways, forgave, worked hard." Harry never identified himself in these stories, but I found out many years later that they were his personal stories.

Harry turned out to be the soul mate of Betty Martin. Betty, whom I first met through Harry's stories, gave the world a special peek into life at Carville. As a young debutante, she gave New Orleans residents a touch of class. As a scared young resident at Carville, she gave Harry a hope and desire to never give up. As a young, prolific writer, she educated the world with her book *Miracle at Carville*. On March 10, 1941, the day that promin (injected) and later diasone (oral) were introduced at Carville, she was one of the first volunteers to take the medication, opening the road to recovery for millions with HD. Numerous visitors to the hospital have shared with me how her book became required reading for many elementary school students throughout the 1950s. When I served as a tour guide at the hospital, visitors would inevitably ask if Betty and Harry still lived on the station, hoping to get a glimpse of this famous couple whom they had "met" as children.

A favorite place for me was the second floor of the recreation building. This area had a spacious ballroom with beautifully kept wooden floors. A large stage leaned against a high wall. On the opposite side of the room, large windows admitted natural light. The doors opened onto a terrace. From this location, we had a view of the residents' golf course and, approximately one and a half miles away, there was a majestic oak tree in the middle of a huge open field.

In one of the corners of the ballroom, two regulation-size pool tables sat side by side. This was a wonderful place to spend my time fantasizing about being a champion pool player and a fancy dancer. For brief moments, I could escape the routine of institutional living and painful reactions.

I was not the only one who used fantasy as an escape from reality. Sam, a crusty sixty-year-old with strong hands molded from years of hard work, went fishing in Lake Johansen and talked daily about "the one that got away." Lucio, a gentle man from Mexico, talked about his cooking, with vegetables and herbs from his garden, as if he were a blue ribbon gourmet chef. Salvador, a sixty-year-old laborer hired to mow the golf course greens, reminisced about doing the same at the U.S. Open. Jose A. from Cuba fantasized about his beautifully chiseled body being on the cover of *Ring Boxing Magazine*. Pasquale from Italy boasted about his ability to win any type of ballroom dance contest. Junior thought about marrying a Miss America beauty. Tonia wanted to own and operate a restaurant. Nong wished he could regain his status as an officer in the Vietnamese army. Tetko dreamed about her return to Japan . . . and her daughters. Hiran wanted Minnesota Fats to come to Carville and get a whipping at the pool table. Vicenta wanted to regain her semblance of family. And Jose Ro., from Mexico, talked about so many alleged conquests of beautiful women that I nicknamed him *"Mil Amores"* ("Thousand Loves"). I dreamed the impossible dream of being invited to spend the night at the White House and instantly eliminating the stigma associated with leprosy.

Of course, not everyone fantasized. Instead they acted on their dreams. Father Germain LaFontaine from Canada would maneuver his electric wheelchair to the Catholic chapel to assist Father Kelley. He was the first resident to conduct Mass at the hospital's chapel. Manuel, the last person isolated at Penikese Island in Massachussettes before being transferred to Carville, created several species of orchids in a tiny greenhouse, and sold them to florists. Amelia, who had lost both her legs, established a reputation as a seamstress and also picked up clothing for washing and ironing. Ray, admitted as a teenager, became the first resident to receive his high school diploma while at Carville. He learned about the complexities of operating the print shop and became the manager of *The Star*. Linda worked hard to become an assistant in the physical therapy department. Lupita practiced her wonderful people skills by being a messenger, notifying residents of scheduled appointments. Sal used his carpenter skills and strong hands to design and build jewelry boxes from discarded colored plastic, a skill he taught me. Justa's vocal interpretation of "Ave Maria" mesmerized many of us attending Mass. Zela overcame the challenges of being arrested at her home just miles from the hospital after her diagnosis with HD and still managed to befriend everyone she met.

The knowledge I gained during my first four weeks at Carville was enormous. However, I continued to have conflicting thoughts about secrecy and protecting one's family. This conflict was, regrettably, far too common among other residents. I felt that the best way to protect my family, and especially Magdalena, was to tell them that they should see me as a potential danger in transmitting the disease. My parents and Magdalena appeared to be in shock with my cold demeanor during their visit. They could see that physically I was much better, but there was something wrong with my *mente*, my mind.

Their first visit on March 30, 1968, five weeks after my admission, was no doubt an emotional moment. The sacrifice my parents made in terms of cost, time, and planning was huge. Coming in a borrowed car packed with six people (my parents, Magdalena, Diana, Raquel, and her daughter Pat) had exhausted the group, but they were still excited about our reunion. They came straight to my room, ignoring the protocol of checking in at the reception/visitors desk and nurse's station first, which caused quite a commotion about violation of the rules. "How dare they," I recall one of the nurses saying in the hall, loud enough to deliver the message to my parents, but they simply ignored the insult and gave me huge hugs and kisses.

Vernon Bahlinger assisted my parents in getting a room at the Travel Lodge in Baton Rouge and arranged for free meals while they visited me at Carville. Mr. Bahlinger, whom I eventually tried to emulate as I started my training in social work, had briefly met with me on several occasions prior to my family's visit. He delicately tried to explain to me that my family would probably think I was ready for discharge and consider the issue of treatment resolved. I, on the other hand, "might feel sad upon their arrival," not because I would not be happy to see them, but rather because of how much I had missed them.

Well, of course, he was right. None of us, however, expected the distance I placed between us. Tears were flowing everywhere, but the more I touched them through hugs and kisses, the more I felt compelled to push them away, telling them to run away and never look back. I could not bear the thought that they too might become ill, and then end up lonely and alone, like me and many others.

Magdalena and I would not kiss in front of my parents, and I wondered if she would even be receptive to passionate kissing if we were to have some privacy. Well, that moment came in the stairway of the Travel Lodge after we had gone to the car to pick up some film. We literally melted in each other's arms, but I was still concerned about what her future would be like with me. She intuitively read my thoughts and said, "I will always be here for you, no matter how long your treatment takes." In an instant, she was able to break down the barrier created in my mind.

Their two-day visit ended in a flash, and before I knew it, they were waving goodbye. Upon their arrival back in Laredo, they excitedly wrote that they were telling everyone about my progress. Magdalena returned to her studies, my parents started going to see minor league baseball and wrestling matches in Nuevo Laredo, and Diana explained how she tried to climb a large magnolia tree at a rest stop in Louisiana just to yell out, "Thank you, God!"

I fell asleep crying, again, but not feeling as lonely as the previous time my family had departed Carville.

# Four Months and Counting

Carville had a great diversity of cultures from all over the world. However, the residents had much in common, including awareness of the fear that society had of leprosy, the label imposed on us which stigmatized us as "worthless" and resulted in many having a strong urge to keep our diagnosis a secret.

The fear of leprosy goes back at least to the time of Ramses II (1250 BC), who allegedly ordered that eighty thousand persons suspected of having leprosy be arrested and "resettled" at the edge of the Sahara Desert.[1] As recently as 1978, many state health departments were encouraging, "without coercing," persons newly diagnosed with leprosy to seek admission and thus resettlement at Carville. This practice was so common in Texas that approximately 90 percent of those diagnosed ended up, like me, in Carville.

It is generally accepted among epidemiologists, researchers, medical groups, and government entities that leprosy was introduced into the U.S. by immigrants from Africa, France, Norway, Spain, and China who entered the United States through New York, California, Hawaii, Arizona, Massachusetts, Texas, Louisiana, and Florida. This conclusion was based on data from the National Hansen's Disease Outpatient Program, which has identified that most of the over seven thousand diagnosed with leprosy in the U.S. during the last thirty years have lived in these "endemic states." Residing in areas where poor living conditions might exist usually results in more physical contact, as less clothing is needed. In reality, the HD bacillus does not discriminate, and almost every ethnic group in the United States has been affected. According to Dr. Robert Jacobson, the last hospital director at Carville, the only group never to have had someone diagnosed with HD is Native Americans, a mystery that remains unsolved.

Having the knowledge that Hansen's disease is not kin to the leprosy mentioned in the Bible and probably included many other disorders can be a great step towards the elimination of the stigma associated with HD. Leprosy can be cured, and approximately 96 percent of the world's population has a natural immunity to the disease. Unfortunately, this is not common knowledge. In very rare cases, a severe case of leprosy causing swelling of the larynx can result in death.

There are many theories about how leprosy is transmitted. While none of the theories has been proven by researchers, it is generally believed that the skin and upper respiratory tracts are the primary "portals of entry."[2]

Theories on mechanism of transmission include: physical contact with someone already infected with the bacillus; inhalation of the bacillus because of the large amounts of bacilli usually found in nasal passages; ingestion or diet, primarily fish; bites from insects (which insects not known); cockroaches; and dirt.

My belief is that I contracted the disease from dirt. I was in contact with soil for most of my first twenty years when I played in sandy dry creeks close to our home and when I was working in the fields (onion, melons, carrots, cotton) around Laredo with my grandfather and later in Montana and Wisconsin. The discovery by Carville's researcher, Dr. Kirchheimer, in 1971 of the nine-banded armadillo (a burrowing animal) as a carrier convinced me of this belief.[3] The discovery gave me and others an opportunity to capture the armadillos and sell them to the research center for five dollars a head. The armadillo is now affectionately known as part of my extended family.

Unfortunately, the armadillo is not found in other parts of the world. Additionally, the incubation period for the HD bacillus can be as long as twenty years, opening up the possibility that someone in my life could have been infected by HD.

Neither my parents, siblings, nor Magdalena ever received an invitation from the Texas public health officials or from the Carville staff to sit down and talk about the disease. Even though doctors never explained the possible cause of my illness, Mom firmly believed in God's will. "Quisiera mejor yo estar enferma . . . no debes perder la fe en Dios . . . Él nos tiene que oír y ayudarnos con los sufrimientos . . . que nos tenga destinado a cada uno." ("I would prefer to be the one who is sick . . . do not lose faith in God . . . He must hear and help us through our sufferings . . . that have been destined for each of us").

Family and friends continued to send me letters until the volume became too much for Darryl Broussard, and he assigned me one of the post office boxes, #235. This honor was usually reserved for residents who had been at the hospital for a long time, but Darryl made an exception for me because it was convenient for him. He explained his action to the ever-observant residents and staff by saying, "If Carville is indeed serious about sending this boy to LSU, then he needs his own mail box when he returns to the station from school." Darryl wrote down his exact words so that our stories would not be in conflict. Surprisingly, no one complained.

The hospital at Carville was a tax-supported institution, although few U.S. citizens have ever understood the significance of the facility. The creation of this unique institution gave birth to a community that practiced the principle of separate and sometimes equal. The residents and PHS staff lived at opposite ends of this small community.

On one side of the facility, PHS officers and Daughters of Charity resided. The PHS commissioned officers and the nuns rode to work on bicycles. The children of staff members attended private or public schools within a twenty-mile radius, and most of their weekend or recreational time was spent off station. Contact with residents came during working hours, Sunday services at the Protestant or Catholic chapels, or at special events held on the hospital grounds, such as the celebration of Mardi Gras, golf tournaments, or crawfish/fishing festivals.

Most of us lived in college-like dormitories once the growth of the HD bacillus was under control. The rooms were just big enough for a small closet, tiny sink, twin-size bed, medical desk and matching chair, rotating fan on the wall, and built-in heater by the window. Everyone had a window. The window allowed the natural light to brighten the room and remind us that another day had arrived. Unlike the society reluctant to embrace those of us with HD, the sunlight would embrace us and warm our bodies.

Some of the residents were allowed to work for "rehabilitation purposes," even though once a person was diagnosed with HD he/she was labeled as "disabled" and forbidden to work in the community in any job that required handling food or having physical contact with others. Additionally, work experience gained while in "rehabilitation" at Carville was not something that residents were willing to put on their job applications or resumes.

The hospital had other residential facilities. These were assigned based on various factors: marital status, length of time at the hospital, severity of disability, and compliance with rules and regulations. The latter was composed primarily of unwritten expectations.

Those with the least status, like me, lived in rooms with communal bathrooms. A second group lived in House 16, a building remodeled to include private baths and larger bedrooms. The third group included married couples, who lived in House 20, which had apartment-style rooms. Another group of ten lived in Cottage Grove, ranch-style, one-bedroom homes with a living room and kitchen for married couples. Still another group lived in House 19, designed to provide twenty-four-hour attendant care for those who had severe physical disabilities, were blind, had mental disabilities, or were too old or fragile to care for themselves.

The longer a person had been at the hospital, the greater the probability that, given a choice, he or she would want to remain at the hospital indefinitely. This behavior occurred primarily for two reasons: level of comfort that developed through having basic needs met and the long separation from families, which increased the level of rejection. There was limited preparation for families of discharged residents on how to address bouts of depression, how to care for insensitive hands and feet, and how to deal with rejection (real or imagined) by other family members and the community. The status of the hospital as a "special treatment center" obviously did not indicate education of residents or their families, which resulted in some myths about the disease being perpetuated even by some residents. I was guilty of this as well, especially during my first visit to Laredo.

Residents exerted some control over their lives by occasionally being defiant toward the hospital's rules, such as leaving the hospital grounds without proper authorization, "forgetting" about appointments, and not taking their medications. Many others were not in defiance of the bureaucracy, but rather, unknowingly, were probably experiencing bouts of what I believe were symptoms of post-traumatic stress disorder. The pain of being told of the diagnosis, followed by a sense of rapidly and uncontrollably falling into a form of purgatory, made many of us regress to infancy, feeling helpless and soiled. Behaviors deemed unacceptable, feelings of rejection and loneliness, and pessimism were signs routinely addressed not via professional help, but via loss of privileges, such as the denial or loss of one's job or assignment to an undesired living situation. These actions simply perpetuated inappropriate behaviors.

I did not become familiar with post-traumatic stress disorder in a clinical sense until I was in graduate school. However, at Carville I saw it all around me on a daily basis. It first became evident to me when a Hispanic male my age was admitted after being diagnosed with HD while in Vietnam. When he arrived at Carville, he was distrustful, depressed, restless, and abusing alcohol. He blended in very well with some of us. It is possible, based on data from the World Health Organization, that this young man flown to Carville from Vietnam was the last of the 102 diagnosed with HD while in the middle of a war involving the U.S. military since the Spanish-American War. There is no documentation of the diagnosis of HD of a person in the military when stationed exclusively in the continental U.S.

Without the aid of a structured support group to address our feelings of inadequacy, we informally sought support from each other. While in the infirmary, I would play dominoes, listen to stories of lost dreams and heartbreak, smoke cigarettes without being judged, cry and laugh, and "read" *Playboy* magazines provided by two veterans of Carville who told tales of southern belles. One of the veterans, Jimmy, was from New Orleans and the other, Butch, was from Houma, a small coastal town that served as a base for many helicopter companies transporting roughnecks to the oil rigs anchored in the Gulf of Mexico.

I would cautiously share some of my feelings and fears, and when it came too close to their own suppressed feelings, they would tell me to stop or simply walk away from me. I spent so much time with these two men, both thirty years older than I, that my parents and Magdalena would usually ask in their letters, "¿Cómo están Jimmy y Butch?" ("How are Jimmy and Butch?").

I attempted to visit with as many people in the infirmary as I could, and posed so many questions about the illness and their own histories that I was jokingly compared with the hospital teacher, Joan Hastings, wife of one of the physician/researchers, Dr. Robert Hastings. People who attended her classes would be quizzed about almost everything in life—she taught by asking questions about life, instead of lecturing out of a book. Because of my inquisitive nature, opportunities would later open up for me to work as a "teacher" and tour guide.

When fellow residents tired of my questions, I would escape to the roof of the infirmary and admire the beauty of Lake Johansen in the distance, embraced by varying shades of oranges and purples as the sun began to set. This roof was a spot that the older residents had found serene and beautiful when it was used as an open rooftop patio for those requiring admission to the infirmary. Some of the nuns informed me that the view, especially during moonless nights, was "breathtaking." The sight would almost always awaken memories of home. Who has not grown up without experiencing at least once the beauty of a black sky with twinkling stars?

Unfortunately, in 1968 some of these same residents who had stared at the skies in years past were now having to squint for better vision, or were wearing dark glasses.

One of the first appointments I had at the hospital was with Dr. Margaret Brand, chief of ophthalmology. Dr. Brand was a slim, soft-spoken person with a flair for detail and punctuality. Sister Laboure, who served as her assistant, scheduling appointments and providing support with routine procedures, was a perfect match for Dr. Brand, because she, too, was a practitioner of military-style precision. Additionally, both treated all of their "eye patients" with a great deal of affection and dignity. Their style was so effective that even those residents who routinely forgot other appointments would promptly arrive to see the eye doctor.

I was in total awe of Dr. Brand not only because she would give me her undivided attention, but also because she had an accent I had never heard before, except in movies. Dr. Brand was from England, had received her training in London and lived in India for decades, so of course she had a British accent. She patiently described how the loss of sensation to pain could result in secondary infections from cuts, burns, and severe bruises. This same principle applied to loss of sensitivity in the eyes. Additionally, a serious, relatively common complication of HD is the presence of lagophthalmos, or the inability to close the eyelids. Once this natural protection ceases to exist, injuries and infections can occur, resulting in the ulceration of the corneas and possible blindness.[4]

The loss of corneal sensation and lagophthalmos are the result of nerve damage, comparable to the insensitivity and paralysis in the hands and feet. Persons who had no resistance to the germ *Mycobacterium leprae* could develop additional serious skin lesions, damage to the lining of the nose or to the front of the eye.

Some would get severe inflammation. In the "old days" when there was no treatment for the disease and no effective drugs to treat inflammation, pain and redness of the eye came to be regarded as the beginning of the end. "Red eye" was greatly feared, as blindness was inevitable.

The disease caused severe dryness in my eyes, but it did minimal damage to my sight. Blindness occurred in another fashion, as the stigma of HD forced me to lose sight of those close to me. The more I saw, the more I read, the more I learned, the more I fell prey to the roller coaster ride of depression and self-pity. I would forget that the diagnosis had not only changed my life, but also the lives of almost everyone I knew, and some who knew me only through my family.

Magdalena, while overjoyed that many of our peers were asking about my health, would regularly feel "alone and down." She was concerned about both my physical and mental health and at times neglected her own emotional needs. Magdalena had a very traditional Mexican upbringing, which caused considerable pain when opportunities for personal growth evolved. The very things that attracted me to her—loyalty, strength to hold onto her values, sincerity, love of family, willingness to work hard today for a better tomorrow, and honesty—were at times a hindrance to her during our lengthy separation.

Magdalena, because of her loyalty to me, did not want to be put in a position of confronting "temptations of the flesh" as she religiously described her feelings. She was guarded with her words, usually focusing on my dilemma instead. In April of 1968 she was chosen to participate in a Mexico-Texas Symposium on Government Issues in Edinburg, Texas, and, while elated with this recognition, she feared that others might judge her for "having fun" while I was "restricted to the hospital." She decided not to attend the junior college's spring formal even though her brother had offered to be her escort. She was reluctant to go to the movies with mixed gender groups, because she might be perceived as looking for a boyfriend. "No pienses mal de mí" ("Don't think badly of me, if I decide to attend"). This dance represented the end-of-the-year event for those graduating after a two-year stint at the Laredo Junior College campus, formerly known as Fort McIntosh, the training base for famous military men such as Robert E. Lee and Philip Sheridan, according to literature available at the Nuevo Santander Museum.[5]

We wrote lengthy letters that basically projected our happy and depressive moods, but we both acknowledged that this type of romance would help us in our later years with each other. Magdalena would always compliment me on my "patience" and not pushing her to "do anything we could both regret." She would talk about how her parents had met while they were in their thirties, went on dates with escorts, and fell in love via letters—she was in Monterrey, Mexico, and he in Laredo, Texas.

Conversely, my parents married very young, and, according to my dad, "No aprendí del amor hasta años después del matrimoño" ("I did not learn to love [your mom] until many years after we were married"). We made a pact not to consider marriage until at least one of us had a master's degree, because neither of us wanted to experience the financial hardships that obviously had tested our parents' commitment to marriage.

Occasionally we could talk via telephone. This special event became increasingly difficult to do, since I had to call collect from the one-seat telephone booth located on the second floor of the infirmary. Expressing our thoughts and love for each other was impossible to do in three minutes. Both of our fathers were unemployed at the time, and therefore we had to find the means to pay for the call. Her parents, apologetic, requested that I "please—por favor," not call collect. Unfortunately, e-mail was decades away.

My parents' faith in God finding a way to cure—curar—me of this curse—maldito—never wavered. They regularly met with the father of a childhood friend of mine, Señor Vargas. Mr. Vargas was actively involved in the ministry of the Catholic Church and was in charge of a group of cursillistas, members who sang and performed special prayers upon request. The cursillistas, fifteen strong, acknowledged my parents' request for prayer and decided to conduct a daily vigil on my behalf for a week, something never done before, according to Mr. Vargas. Mom proudly wrote to tell me of *la oración especial para ti* (the special prayer for you). This, she wrote, *"vale más que dinero"* (is much more valuable than money). I sobbed as I read the letter and immediately requested a wheelchair ride from Dr. Pete to go to the Catholic chapel. As soon as he heard where I wanted to go, he quickly, but without speaking a word, took me on my ride.

The next day, God was mentioned in seven of the letters I received—from Magdalena, Mom, and five friends. Not long after receiving these letters, I received terrible news about my siblings. Dr. Dickinson, in follow-up visits to Laredo, had discovered that two of my sisters, after reporting "some loss of sensation," were diagnosed with a "very mild case of tuberculoid leprosy." I felt responsible and, like Dad, thought that God was punishing my siblings for a sin I had committed. However, I could not figure out what that sin was.

My sisters were told that they would not have to go to Carville. Taking 100 mg of dapsone daily could complete their treatment. Since they were to remain in Laredo, they were strongly encouraged to keep their diagnosis "confidential" in order to prevent mass hysteria. I mailed them more information on the disease—anything I could find. I sent letters, made telephone calls, and I apologized. I wanted to stop the bacillus from growing, to prevent them from the physical and emotional pain I had endured.

Luckily, their infection was localized, and they never experienced physical problems. Later, four other siblings were also diagnosed with "mild cases" as well and prescribed dapsone. All four were involved, like me, in doing work in the fields around Laredo. The "soil, melon, and onion belief" resurfaced.

The diagnosis came after careful monitoring of their bodies, in particular their hands, arms, feet, and legs. The areas where insensitivity was centered included the calf, knee, upper arm, and elbow. Most were diagnosed while in their teens, but a direct cause of how they got the disease could not be determined. My siblings witnessed how extended family and friends came to my support, so they did not fear rejection. However, sensing the health department's concern related to unfounded rumors about an "epidemic of leprosy," they chose to keep their diagnosis within the family. As each became romantically involved, they told their mates. As each got married, they came to Magdalena and me for advice on education and child rearing. Each time, we both recommended that they visit Carville for a minimum of three days so that they could receive a thorough checkup from some of the best leprosy specialists in the world. They all returned home with a much better understanding of the disease and of a unique place that had become my second home.

Mom made a disturbing discovery while taking all of my siblings to the public health clinic for "required" follow-up examinations. She found out that the elderly gentleman who had criticized Dad for placing a notice in the local paper listing my Carville address was also the man who would pay her a nickel a day when she was a little girl to run errands for his wife. Mom, always the social butterfly, met the man's sister-in-law, who was at the clinic for a doctor's appointment. Mom recognized her as one of my many teachers. While engaged in conversation, the woman reluctantly told Mom that she too had been a resident at Carville as a young girl. Before she could relate any of her experiences, her name was called and they never crossed paths again. As Mom was sharing this incident with me in one of her numerous letters written in July of 1968, she could not help asking, "Si yo te pase la enfermedad con mis trabajitos de niña o si la maestra te infectó?" ("Wonder if I was responsible for your illness because of my job as a child running small errands or if maybe the teacher infected you?"). Mom continued to search for an answer on how I contracted HD until her dying days.

By the middle of April 1968 I had gained enough strength to walk to the canteen, rather than use a wheelchair. Additionally, the occupational therapy and physical therapy departments issued me handmade shoes designed to displace pressure from the slow-healing sores on the bottoms of my feet.

The occupational and physical therapy departments had staffs that were miracle workers. I had more contact with these two departments than any other during my stay at Carville. The day-to-day staff was composed of personnel from the public health service system and residents hired as aides. They also had a large number of students coming in to complete their internships—all very eager to learn and with excellent people skills. Their hands did the work in the daily wrapping of a burned or infected foot, but it was their soft, patient, and caring voices and attentive ears that helped people recover in record time. It was this staff who helped me not only to learn *how* to walk again but also gave me the encouragement to *want* to walk again.

When I was once again able to walk, I divided my time among four areas of the hospital: the library, the ballroom which housed the pool tables, the training branch which housed the medical library and office for the tour guides, and the school. The latter two helped me to learn the technical side of the disease, as well as the history of Carville. Jack W., a white-haired gentleman who lived with his wife in one of the cottages, was the official tour guide. He knew a great deal about the disease and the hospital, and answered such a multitude of unusual and routine questions, that I would accompany him on tours just to hear his responses. He would describe the disease from biblical to contemporary times with so much passion that visitors would say they were happy to know the difference between myth and reality. Along with the walking tour of the hospital, Jack would show a fifteen-minute film and distribute literature, including a copy of *The Star*. Jack strongly emphasized to me that it would be "unethical" to solicit tips from visitors who religiously arrived for the 10 a.m., 1 p.m., and 2 p.m. tours. However, it would be "rude to decline" an unsolicited tip such as a one-dollar bill exchanged during a thank-you handshake.

Jack taught me the finer points of being a guide: smile; welcome with a handshake; if it's a small group, ask first names and hometown; set ground rules (no photos); be receptive to questions; emphasize negative connotation of the "l" word ; and start out the tour by stating that you are a resident. The last point was very critical, because it would lessen the probability of painful questions such as "where are the lepers?"

Residents knew that Jack was the tour guide, so most would ignore the group by speeding up on their bicycles. However, three people liked to startle the visitors with a hard stare or a Halloween-style "boo!" These men, Blanco, Soto, and Michael, would make Jack roll his eyes. Their antics would usually increase the amount of the tip—"a good scare," as Jack liked to call these encounters, and he would split the tip with the offenders.

Going to the hospital's school was a joy because Gaston England, the principal, was a very low-key and pleasant man. He had a receding hairline and large muscular arms. He reminded me of my high school football coach in stature and of my grandfather in demeanor, firm but fair.

The school was also home to probably the prettiest and most vocal of the hospital's staff, Joan Hastings. She had a very energetic personality that rivaled the all-business-type demeanor of her husband, Dr. Robert Hastings. Her laughter was contagious and it permeated the one-room school, causing even those experiencing the worst of reactions to at least smile.

In my opinion, the principal, respectfully called Mr. England, and his one-teacher staff, called Joan by everyone, made a good match. Mr. England represented the fatherly authority figure that all schools need, and Joan represented the "new math" of how teachers could teach and also be friends. Mr. England had been the first teacher at Carville and was able to attain certification for the school via the Louisiana Department of Education (LDE), which validated the first diploma ever awarded, to Ray Elwood. In an effort to not further stigmatize the young students, Mr. England persuaded the LDE to list St. Gabriel on the high school diploma instead of Carville. Ironically, my first job after graduation from college was with the Louisiana Department of Education, and Ray married the teacher who replaced Joan.

April 19, 1968, was an exciting day for me, as I was informed by my doctor, John Hull, that I was being discharged from the infirmary and had been assigned room #104 in House 23. An extra surprise was that I had been approved for employment at the school to teach English to Spanish-speaking residents and was offered the opportunity to serve as the weekend tour guide to relieve Jack.

The assignment to House 23 was actually listed in my chart as "discharged to [the 'I'] colony." This, to my surprise, was what the physician routinely listed when a resident was released from the infirmary. Until I discovered this fact in 1998, I and others referred to the area outside the infirmary as simply "the hospital" or "the back" or "pecan grove" (cemetery) but never as "the colony." Using a term such as "the colony," often associated with the offensive "I" word, resurrected the negative myths we despised. This was being done by the very people we believed were educating the public, the physicians. This surprising discovery made me believe that many of those in a position to make referrals in 1968 for psychological services saw us in a stereotypical manner and maybe not in need of such a valuable service.

House #23 was known for its quiet atmosphere. Each of the ten male residents had a job, so they would disappear into their rooms by 9:00 p.m. Three had girlfriends, whom they would visit in their rooms for most of the weekend. Two drank alone and did not infringe on anyone else's privacy.

The men included Sam M. (Mexican American), Blanco S. (Mexican American), Lucio (Mexican), Juanito (Mexican American), Soto (Puerto Rican), Arturo U., or "Junior" (Mexican American), Juan S. (Mexican), Francisco "Pancho" (Mexican American), Juan J. (Mexican), and me. These men would monitor my physical health, tell me when the SSO had conducted a "surprise inspection" of my room, teach me how to keep my room clean, scold me when I drank, and threaten to beat me if I did not do my homework. They were a tough bunch, but they were major contributors to my successes.

One of the first things that the Super 23s, as they liked to call themselves, did was to invite me to visit the Ponderosa. This was an invitation of sorts to the sanctuary of House 23. Blanco, a slim, balding man with a walk that reminded me of a marionette, invited me to join the Super 23s after supper on the first weekend of my arrival in room #104. I felt so honored that I forgot to ask questions, and he did not volunteer any information other than to say, "I'll see you by the canteen at 5:30 p.m." So, promptly at 5:30 p.m., I arrived, and he was waiting on his faded red bicycle. He joked that I needed to get "some wheels" and slowly pedaled to the front of the recreation building. I obediently followed and wondered where he was taking me.

He initiated some small talk about my room, medication, family, and work—things he already knew about me. Blanco directed me toward the road and for the first time I saw "the hole" up close. I had read about this hole and heard many talk about it, but I never dreamed that I would actually use it.

A ten-foot cyclone fence with barbed wire on top surrounded the hospital. The bottom of the fence, though, was not buried in the ground. The residents had dug approximately two feet into the ground and had cut part of the wiring to allow anyone squatting low enough to exit the hospital grounds. Many residents have described their own experiences with the hole: how they ran away, ran off to get married, went to LSU games, or went drinking.

Blanco made sure that we approached the hole while there was no traffic on the road. To my right, I could see the road curve to the right, obstructing the view of the guard stationed at the main entrance to the hospital. To the left the road led to Baton Rouge, but the only building I could see in the distance was a one-room house with a roof made of tin and converted to a bar called the Red Rooster. Directly in front of me was a thirty-foot levee protecting the hospital from potential flooding from the Mississippi River on the other side.

As we arrived on the top of the levee, I was stunned by the magnificent view, a muddy Mississippi River rushing toward the Gulf of Mexico. As a six-year-old in 1954, I had seen the destructive force of the Rio Grande flooding two countries. But the Mississippi was a mile wide, and I could barely see the other bank.

I slowly stumbled down the levee and encountered another surprise. I found myself staring at a one-room hut made of driftwood and discarded lumber, painted in rainbow colors, with a big framed sign saying THE PONDEROSA on the top, reminiscent of the popular TV show *Bonanza*. Inside were all the comforts one needed for a good party or simple time for reading a book. Blanco had several .22 caliber rifles and a hound for hunting squirrels and raccoons. There was also a small garden where Sam and Junior grew flowers and vegetables. Buried within the garden was an odd looking "weed." It turned out to be marijuana.

Laughter abounded as I received a lecture from Blanco, who said that the Super 23s had discovered a "cure" for leprosy. He emphasized that it was not the smoking, but the smoke that was generated from the burning marijuana that killed the HD bacilli. They all emphasized its medicinal value, and guaranteed that I would feel better after trying it. They were all convinced of marijuana's magical powers, as were countless others during the late sixties who experimented with this weed.

I do not recall how many puffs I endured, but I vividly remember that we were drinking beer around a huge bonfire when a police car appeared along the top of the levee. I stood up and nervously looked for a place to hide. No one else moved. They simply waved toward the driver and started to laugh hysterically at my behavior. They all knew the sheriff's deputy who had come by for a "few good jokes," completely ignoring the odd odor.

I became sober very quickly, and I was cautious with my excesses thereafter. The trips to the Ponderosa were very uplifting for my spirits and spirituality, grown men sharing intimate life experiences, and crying without being judged or identified as being weaklings. The Super 23s eventually disbanded because the state police started to patrol the levee by the hospital and "strongly encouraged" the group to "stop growing exotic vegetables." The members also grew older and more sedentary.

During the hot summer months of 1968, many residents wore sweaters and long sleeves. I learned that this behavior was a sign of a reaction, an inflammation of the nerves in elbows, hands, or feet, causing severe pain. It could also include high fevers, open sores, and, predictably, severe depression. Most in this condition were inconsolable and would retreat from others physically or emotionally. My reactions were severe and would normally last two weeks. The reaction would weaken me so much that the result would be readmission to the infirmary, a total of seventeen times in an eight-year period.

The reactions could develop for a variety of reasons, including side effects of steroids, physical or emotional stress, the reaction to the reintroduction of new medications, and unexplained, sudden escalation in bacilli growth. For me, it was like being on a roller coaster with high peaks and low valleys, exacerbated by environmental and mental stresses, e.g., family in Laredo, conflicting philosophies in social treatment of others, and the demands of class work while I was attending Laredo Junior College. Reactions have the potential to be very destructive, making persons experiencing this phenomenon reach a state of cachexia, or general ill health. On rare occasions, reactions had contributed to the death of those affected by this bacillus, e.g., severe pain, open blisters, and secondary infections.

Due to limited success with dapsone during the early stages of my treatment, the medical staff approached me about starting on an experimental drug called thalidomide. I had some familiarity with the name, as did most people of my generation. I was told in technical terms that the drug could cause embryopathy syndrome, or, in lay terms, deformities in the fetus if taken by women in the early stages of pregnancy. At the time I took the medicine and up through current times, women of child-bearing age are denied thalidomide. This drug had caused severe deformities in babies throughout Canada, Germany, and England in the 1960s. It had been administered as a sedative for pregnant women, with horrifying results, and was banned after worldwide publicity regarding its destructive power.

In 1965, a medical team in Hadassah University Hospital in Jerusalem, Israel, led by Dr. Jacob Sheskin, started to experiment with thalidomide as "palliative treatment" (leading to the temporary lessening of pain and insomnia). To their surprise, the drug was found to be effective in lessening the symptoms of HD reaction.

I agreed to take the medication, 400 mg x QID (one pill, four times a day). The drug, a blue capsule, kept me in a daze most of the time. My physician, Dr. John Hull, gave me stimulants to help me stay awake. I took thalidomide until November 26, 1974, each time having to go to the infirmary to be observed by a nurse or to sign documents stating that I would honor the schedule of administration of the medication if I left the station for more than eight hours. On one occasion, when I was scheduled to begin final exams, the medical team decided to place me on placebos. The lack of this unique medicine resulted in a severe reaction and required Vernon Bahlinger, director of social services, to intervene with my professors at LSU requesting an "I" (incomplete) in my grades and rescheduling of exams at a later date. I had already realized the miracle properties of thalidomide and expressed my dissatisfaction to Dr. Hull about the placebo. He simply shrugged his shoulders and said, "Sorry."

In the summer of 1969, *The Star* published a story emphasizing thalidomide's unique qualities in controlling the dreaded reactions and possible prevention of deformities. This story generated much interest from the press and advocacy groups. Among the latter, the March of Dimes and the Thalidomide Victims' Association of Canada placed great pressure on the Federal Drug Administration (FDA) to ban its use. It took many years of research and hearings in Washington, D.C., before these two groups reluctantly agreed to endorse its use, provided that stringent safeguards were initiated.

In July of 1998, the FDA formally approved its use in the treatment of leprosy reactions. Opponents to such action were probably convinced to reverse their stance once they heard from researchers that thalidomide was proving to also be effective in the treatment of certain AIDS-related conditions, some forms of cancer, glaucoma, lupus, Crohn's disease, multiple sclerosis, arthritis, and Alzheimer's disease. It took over forty years for thalidomide to go from being a feared monster to being a trusted friend, a battle that those of us affected by leprosy have not yet won. The FDA approval was equivalent to the renewal of a license for the media to remind the world of our "sinful existence" with headlines such as: "Thalidomide Can Now Cure Unclean Lepers."

One of the places I enjoyed visiting was the hospital's three-hundred-seat auditorium/theater, a popular place on Tuesday, Thursday, and Saturday evenings. These were movie nights. The chair of the Recreation Committee of the Patients' Federation would coordinate the selection of the movies, none of them blockbusters. Once a month, the Mexican Club could choose a Spanish movie. I had the honor and misfortune of helping to select these movies when I served in both organizations at the same time. Rarely was I able to please the audience, but on some occasions I was credited with bringing laughter or a happy moment to staff, residents, and visitors from Carville and St. Gabriel who sneaked in through the hole to come see a quality film.

The theater was a place where controversial decisions would be debated and voted on, such as when federation elections were forthcoming. The excitement would reach such a high pitch that even those in the infirmary would ask for wheelchairs to enable them to attend the meetings.

As my health improved, I stayed busy by working at the school and conducting tours on weekends. However, the thalidomide dramatically affected my sleeping habits. It was a challenge to take four thalidomide capsules daily and stay awake and alert. Dr. Hull told me that I would adjust over time, but this never happened. Additionally, thalidomide did not totally prevent the dreaded reactions. I was to report to work at the school by 8:30 a.m. and I was usually late. Even with an alarm clock, I struggled to wake up. Frequently I would miss breakfast, but I did not miss my morning blue capsule.

Joan Hastings gave me some basic tips on how to develop a lesson plan, even though the class was supposed to focus on daily life experiences. I was diligent in complying with what I understood would be my job—teaching English. However, all of the students were much older than I and usually eloquent speakers in their own language, so they oftentimes taught me how to speak proper Spanish, *Español propio*, even though they could not read.

So, I sought and received permission from Mr. England for us to take walks around the hospital grounds and learn from what we observed around us: door, sliding door, hallway, stairs, screens, concrete, paint, light bulbs, bicycles, birds, sun, grass, garden, dinner bell. *La campana*, the bell, would make all of us lose interest in learning and focus on moving towards the cafeteria. Similar to Pavlov's dogs, we were conditioned to swiftly respond to the clanging of the bell.[6]

I formed lasting relationships with the twenty different students who attended classes on a regular basis. My teaching career ended four months later when I was approved to work at the canteen.

The work as a tour guide was extremely rewarding. I met people from all over the world, some who had come to Carville to complete a pilgrimage of sorts. They had either read Betty Martin's book, *Miracle at Carville*, as a child, or had been inspired by a visit to a "leprosy village" in some faraway land. All visitors were very attentive and observant of the surroundings. Some showed fear mainly because of ignorance. All, however, were receptive to shaking my hand after the tour, with some even leaving a small tip. I enjoyed this job the most while I was at Carville.

People who surprised me with their generosity included a couple from Alexandria, Louisiana, and a nurse from Memphis, Tennessee. The couple from Alexandria purchased a bicycle for me and left it at the front gate with a note stating, "Thanks for the tour, hope this two wheeler helps your feet to heal." Their gift helped me recover at a faster pace during those many times when I had "reactions," and sores on my feet caused discomfort in walking. I emulated the couple's good deed by giving the well-traveled bike to another resident when I left Carville.

Shirley Hart from Memphis was another individual who invited me to visit the hospital where she worked. She said she was on vacation and stopped at Carville in an effort to see what she had read about in *Miracle at Carville* as a child. I always abided by the rule of confidentiality, but this lady was so energetic and persistent in genuinely wanting to know more about the disease that I broke the rule. I took her to the ladies' floor in the infirmary and timidly introduced her to Betty Martin. Betty was so gracious that she invited Shirley to visit later. Shirley spent an hour with Betty after I had concluded the tour.

Shirley unexpectedly gave me a strong handshake and a generous tip, and I left her with Betty, thinking I would never see her again. Within a week, I received a handwritten thank-you note and an invitation, all expenses paid, to visit Memphis and make a presentation at the hospital where she worked. Her administrators had cleared the way for me to speak.

In 1968, being twenty was a hindrance because the hospital was required to receive written authorization from my parents for me to travel to Memphis, and Carville's medical team had to "weigh the risk" of my traveling while on a "strict and experimental" regimen of thalidomide.

Once these obstacles were cleared, I struggled with missing Magdalena's graduation from Laredo Junior College. The doctors and social worker actually decided for me, i.e., I was "not emotionally ready" to travel to Laredo, which would also be a physical strain, as getting there would take over twenty-four hours by car. The round trip to Memphis would last no longer than three days and I would travel by plane. I did not accept the invitation until Magdalena wrote, "Go for it, you may never travel to Memphis again."

The plane ride to Memphis was my initiation with flying. The flight was extremely scary, because it was at night and the Delta propeller plane had to make an emergency landing at some small airport due to maintenance problems. We were escorted off the plane and waited approximately four hours while a part and a mechanic were flown in from Atlanta. My pain must have been obvious because several passengers asked me if I was okay, and the pilot even offered an alternate way to travel, by bus at Delta's expense. I declined and took out my rosary when we reboarded. The plane landed in Memphis after midnight, and Mrs. Hart, alerted by the airline of the lengthy delay, was patiently waiting. We traveled to her home, where I excused myself and went straight to bed.

The next day was a full one; I met many nurses and made a presentation to a small group. I was unprepared and struggled with the presentation. The Q & A session saved me. The questions came rapid-fire, and just as quickly I was able to respond. I was even able to answer some of the more technical questions about diagnosis, treatment, and reconstructive surgery. I had been present at the training sessions when Dr. Paul Brand, internationally recognized surgeon specializing in hands and feet, had explained to visitors how digits "lost to infections and amputations" could be "reborn." This was done by surgically making incisions between the knuckles and forming a facsimile of a hand. I simply learned to quote from the best. The hospital staff was in awe, and I wondered how long it would be before they realized that I was simply repeating what Dr. Brand usually said. Luckily, lunchtime arrived, and I was escorted to the cafeteria.

Mrs. Hart had indicated that she had friends who "might arrange for a meeting with Elvis." She had given me the idea that Elvis might serve as a sponsor for fund-raisers that would assist individuals from institutions in the transition to community living. The meeting never occurred, and the search for a spokesperson has now turned to tapping into the wealth of knowledge found among those of us affected by leprosy. The closest we came to finding a celebrity was Princess Diana.

The day in Memphis ended too quickly, and in the blink of an eye I landed in Baton Rouge and was driven back to Carville.

Upon my return from Memphis, I went to my mailbox and found a letter from Magdalena. Her opening sentence made me sad: "Never have I felt lonelier than now." We used to spend a great deal of time together, and regularly shared our successes and perceived failures, and now we were apart. She had just graduated from LJC but was frightened about the next challenge of continuing college. She was going to visit family in Monterrey, Mexico, before starting a summer job, and I was traveling to Tennessee. Our friends were either getting married or strengthening their relationships, and we were apart. She wondered if she had the "blind faith" and patience needed, according to one of her aunts, to see me cured of leprosy.

I immediately ran to make a three-minute call from the telephone in the recreation hall. Luckily I connected with Magdalena and only focused on the word *fe* (faith) and on how we had to support each other during times of laughter and unexpected depression. We both cried. The operator, hearing our sobs, asked if we were okay, but realizing she was interrupting a love connection, said, "Sorry, my mistake, you have thirty more seconds before I *must* disconnect." We continue to be grateful to that wonderful person who extended our call and made it extra special.

Not only did I miss Magdalena's graduation, but I also missed my sister Margarita's high school graduation. I missed my brother Fernando playing third base in Little League. I missed my brother Rodolfo learning how to drive and shoot pool. I missed hearing Dad play the guitar and singing. I missed home.

Magdalena returned from Monterrey ready to work two part-time jobs. She realized that her parents would not be able to pay for her college education at Texas Woman's University, so she had to start saving early. I also started saving, hoping to visit Laredo in July.

Summer was the time for baseball, and this July Dad wanted to make it special for me. Dad, ever the hustler, had won *un dinero* (some money), playing pool and decided that he would use it for the July 9, 1968, All-Star Game at the Astrodome in Houston. He purchased three ten-dollar field box seats—a small fortune at the time. He also arranged with a Houston policeman he once helped with a case in Mexico to allow two of my younger brothers to enter free as "special guests" in the standing room only (SRO) section. Darryl Broussard also had tickets and offered to drive me to Houston. My parents stayed at an inexpensive motel with teepee-shaped rooms. They slept on the bed and my brothers and I on the floor. The rooms were so cheaply constructed that we could hear the traffic drive down Main Street approximately twenty yards from the room. In the morning we laughed, wondering about the embarrassment of being seen at such a cheap motel. We laughed even harder when we saw Dan Cook, sportswriter for the *San Antonio Express*, sneaking out of the parking lot ahead of us and zooming towards the Dome to cover the game.

The quick trip to Houston was very uplifting for all of us. Mom could not stop hugging me and touching my head. Dad tried very hard to remain stoic but would briefly put his arm around my shoulder as we walked. My two brothers, whom I had shared a bed with until my illness, simply wanted to know if there were any girls at Carville; my response was, "Yes, a bunch of nuns." The three of us giggled like little kids.

Several unique things happened at the game, one of which was that Willie Mays surprised me by tossing me an autographed practice ball as he entered the dugout. He was unanimously chosen the MVP, and the National League won. The ball given to me by Willie Mays mysteriously disappeared during one of the "surprise inspections" of my room, but the memories of feeling special on a hot July day helped me imagine being rid of the HD bacillus.

# First Visit to Laredo

Upon my return to Carville, I found several appointment slips under my door. This was not out of the ordinary, but what appeared odd was the notice to see Dr. Hull at 8:00 a.m. the next day. I sensed something wrong, as I had seen him for a scheduled appointment four days earlier, and he usually made rounds during the mornings. My hope was that I was being granted a pass to visit my family in Laredo. I asked Juan S., my neighbor in room #102, to please wake me up early the next day.

Promptly at 8:00 a.m. on July 10 I knocked on Dr. Hull's door. He had two surprises for me. One was that I had been granted a medical pass to visit my family in Laredo, and the second was that the Texas Department of Health had authorized free transport. My emotions raced to catch up with my thought processes: my anxiety level and blood pressure escalated. When would I go? How would I tell my parents and Magdalena? How long would the trip take? How should I act? Would Magdalena's mother feel I was disgracing her home if I visited, or would she embrace me? What precautions should I take to prevent anyone else from possibly getting the disease? Would I be able to take thalidomide with me?

Dr. Hull obviously sensed my distress as he belched loudly to get my attention, and laughed even louder when I stared at him in disbelief. "Damn," he said, "you all react the same way on your first pass home." "Is there any other way to act?" I asked, wondering if it was inappropriate to feel so excited.

Another surprise came via a telephone call that Dr. Hull received from the lab. Preliminary reports indicated that my bacilli count was "stable," and I might be discharged by December 1968. This was too much for me and I started to hyperventilate. Dr. Hull instructed me to take quick short exhaling puffs and then one long deep breath. Once I regained my composure, he promised not to surprise me with so many bits of good news.

The pass was for two weeks, starting on July 25, with a possible two-week extension if I did not become ill. I would be issued enough thalidomide for one month, but talking about the drug was strictly forbidden as it was still considered "experimental." I was instructed to keep the medication locked in a secure place.

The residents warned me that "R," hired by the Texas Department of Health to transport residents of Texas to their desired destinations, liked to travel by night because "asi no asustamos a nadie" ("we do not frighten anyone")! He had rules that all passengers (five) needed to follow: punctuality—we would depart at 6:00 p.m.; no mention of tips until we were in Baton Rouge; one suitcase per person; and absolutely no passing gas. Considering that I met him only the day before our departure, I could not figure out if he was serious or simply being funny.

The driver was a native of south Texas. The station wagon he drove was bright white with large black print on the door, TEXAS HEALTH DEPARTMENT, and with government license plates. He claimed that assignments for transport were received via telephone. His directives, allegedly, were to arrive at the person's home and wait for hours, sometimes, until "the body"—"*el cuerpo*," as he called his riders—would come out and reluctantly get inside the wagon. Regrettably, many of the residents would often clench their teeth and roll their eyes whenever the name of this short round man clad in khaki uniform was mentioned.

I had already decided that the most I could afford for a tip was two dollars, as I wanted to purchase presents for Magdalena and Mom. The most pressing thing for me was packing only one suitcase for a two-week visit. On my three-day trip to Memphis, I had tightly packed two suitcases. Tony P., a debonair-looking gentleman from Mexico, helped me with the dilemma.

Tony had several jobs, and he was always wearing nicely pressed pants and shirts. He smoked cigarettes with the flair of royalty and had a reputation for being the last man standing when drinking with a group. There were rumors that he had bedded many of the female residents and some staff, but that his true love lived in Acapulco, Mexico. He traveled regularly to Mexico with or without medical passes, but always returned.

He agreed to help me and offered to charge me a fee that was not related to money. He came to my room, asked me to place all I wanted to take on the trip on the bed, and then requested I stand to the side and observe.

He appeared to be thinking out loud, as if it were his trip: plan ahead; try to take only heavily starched pants (can use more than once) folded in half and packed first at the bottom of the suitcase; fill the outer gaps with underwear, socks, and T-shirts; press and button all shirts, neatly fold in the same manner as when purchased at a store; pack all toiletries in used plastic bags and place on very top; and make every effort to take only one pair of shoes. Presto, my clothing was neatly packed in the required one suitcase. Tony, broadly smiling, requested his payment—all of the Darvon I could spare. Tony was addicted to painkillers. "I am doing you a favor," he said, "by getting these killers off your hands." Years later, rumors circulated that Tony had died of an accidental drug overdose.

I kept my neatly packed suitcase ready for the long-awaited trip for one week before we actually departed *para el valle*, to the valley, as south Texas is referred to by many Texans. Magdalena kept writing, almost on a daily basis, and was having to revert to walking to the now bankrupt five-and-dime store called Kress during her breaks from work to write on their thin napkins. "Todavía me digo que son mentiras que vienes por dos semanas" ("I still cannot believe that you are coming to visit for two weeks").

Mom, always praying for my recovery, asked Dad for some type of monument or shrine to be built in front of their home. She wanted the shrine built before my first visit. Dad, who was one of the first persons in the U.S. to be licensed as a private investigator in two nations (in the state of Texas and in Tamaulipas, Mexico) followed up on Mom's request. He accepted a case in Nuevo Laredo, Mexico.[1] Then he bartered for the payment—no cash, just a shrine of the Virgin de San Juan. Mom had Christmas lights adorn the two-foot shrine set on top of a one-foot-high flowerbed and protected with clear glass. She would walk out to the shrine, praying almost daily for my recovery, and later for *otros milagros* (other miracles). My oldest sister, Yolanda, kept this shrine after my parents passed away.

As the days got closer to my departure on July 25, I received more letters from Mom and Magdalena, both asking that I consider spending more time in Laredo. Magdalena lifted my spirits to a new high with her loving and caring words—"lo único que me falta a mi para alegrarme eres tú" ("the only thing missing in my life to make me happy is you"). She added, "I'm not really living, I pretend to—I feel empty without you." She made me feel so special.

When July 25 finally arrived, I got up and dressed for the trip. The day dragged on for an eternity. Promptly at 5:30 p.m., Mr. R., the station wagon driver, pulled up to the front of the infirmary, and four of us responded to his orders: "Vayan todos al baño porque no voy a parar" ("Go to the bathroom now as there will not be any stops later"). By the time we returned and boarded the station wagon, it was 5:50 p.m. He slowly drove to the gate, signed consents for our passes, joked with the guard about how much he should charge us for the "limo ride," and, precisely at 6:00 p.m., he drove away from the gates of Carville.

None of us had realized that a pillow would have made our trip a bit more comfortable, so we tried, unsuccessfully, to get some sleep. Mr. R. spoke nonstop, possibly to stay awake. He drove first to Brownsville, the southernmost tip of Texas, and dropped off a male rider. A handshake and, we all assumed, a tip was exchanged. He then drove to Corpus Christi where one of the two women was dropped off, and then proceeded to Alice, where he dropped off the second woman at the Greyhound bus station. Mr. R. explained that the lady's husband lived in Alice, but the husband refused to have anything to do with her since she was diagnosed with HD, so she was taking a bus to Monterrey, Mexico, to visit her mother. The last stop, at approximately 1:30 p.m. on Friday, July 26, 1968, was at 2509 Locust in Laredo, Texas—my parents' home.

As Mr. R. drove along Locust he encountered some kids, who all seemed to be eight to ten years old, dashing across the street in front of the station wagon. He honked his horn and, as they stared back, I realized that they were all related to me, four brothers and three nephews—obviously all on the verge of getting into trouble. The oldest in the group, Fernando, or Ferny, turned as white as the station wagon I was riding in when he recognized me. He frantically started running behind the station wagon, and the others quickly followed. Ferny reached me as I was coming out of the vehicle, embraced me around my waist, started to shake, and cried. I also cried in a way I don't ever recall crying, hugged him tightly, and then did the same with the other kids.

One of the nephews ran inside to announce my arrival, and before long I was smothered with hugs and kisses. No words were said until Mr. R., who may never have seen such a show of affection, said, "Ya me voy" ("I am now leaving"). My parents invited him to come inside and eat and said "*gracias*" so many times that we started to joke that Mr. R. should change his name to Gracias.

He stayed for over an hour, explaining to everyone, while he ate freshly made tortillas, how he performed an important but "secret job" for the state. He offered to work hard to get authorization to transport me back to Carville after two weeks.

My parents patiently listened, not realizing that I already had the authorization in writing, and bid him farewells with *abrazos* (hugs) and a ten-dollar tip, saying, "Gracias por todo" ("Thanks for everything"). Mr. R. left, broadly smiling, waving goodbye.

Magdalena had a boss at her second job who refused to give her the afternoon off, so she was unable to come over upon my arrival. We did not see each other until approximately 7:00 p.m.

All of my siblings, neighbors, friends, and distant relatives paraded through the house from the moment I arrived. Some would silently stare in disbelief that I was actually alive after such a "dreaded disease" was found in my body. Others kept touching me, looking at my hands and feet as if trying to see where a lost limb might have been reattached, while some simply wept, continuously making the sign of the cross. Others, primarily my parents and siblings, would hug me long and hard—*abrazos del corazón* (loving hugs).

Once Mr. R. departed, Mom ordered everyone to gather around the newly built shrine of the Virgin de San Juan and kneel to give thanks for my return to Laredo. Just as Mom started leading the group in prayer, two carloads of their friends from the prayer group arrived and joined the celebration. Two of Dad's friends from the days when he was on the police force arrived in their patrol cars and joined the circle. To passersby, it must have looked like a circus.

As the praying continued, one of my parents' friends made a comment that still haunts me today: "Dios lo ha seleccionado para sufrir y despúes hacerlo santo" ("God has chosen him to suffer in order to make him a saint"). His comment put a gleam in my parents' eyes but made me feel uncomfortable. The sense of being divine disappeared soon after I excused myself to go to the bathroom.

Sainthood is a unique privilege bestowed upon those who can unselfishly perform great deeds for others. Sainthood is bestowed upon those who suffer great emotional or physical pain in their lives, and millions before me had felt pain that was a hundredfold greater than any I had ever experienced. Sainthood was not for me, but Mr. Vargas's comments forced me to again reevaluate my life, to openly advocate on behalf of those who were diagnosed before me, who were denied opportunities to live lives devoid of fear, and those who came after me, who continue to be denied appropriate psychosocial services to address their own fears of "being discovered."

Mom again took charge after the praying and bluntly told everyone that we had an appointment to visit Guadalupe Church to give thanks for my safe return. That was a message to everyone to leave, as the visit to the church was only for family. We got into a number of cars and proceeded to the church.

As we entered Guadalupe Church, the only church I had known as a parishioner, a flashback of good and not so good times passed through my mind. The church has an elongated dome with huge white columns leading toward the altar. The altar has an ornate frame with the intricate and saintly three-dimensional figure of the Virgin of Guadalupe, encased in a background of blue sky, puffy white clouds, and flying angels.

Nothing could diminish the serenity and comfort I felt walking inside this beautiful church. The whole family walked to the front. The priest, maintenance man, and mother superior, all with reputations for rudeness, were standing at the altar, possibly discussing some upcoming event. They made eye contact with my mom, who was leading the procession. Her silent message, understood by the three at the altar, was "Do not mess with me today." They gently made their palms meet, slowly bowed, and quickly vacated the church.

Even the little kids understood that Mom was in total control, and she would not tolerate any silly behavior from them, so they went to a pew and patiently observed the praying and the long stares up at the virgin. I believe that we all sobbed and laughed at this priceless moment, devoid of judgements and so full of love. Before leaving the church, we took turns lighting candles as an offering for our reunion.

I requested the keys to the car so I could go visit Magdalena. When I arrived at her home, she was waiting and we hugged each other for a long time. She looked beautiful, sweet, and innocent. She was affectionate, tender, and loving. She was silent, like me, as we continued our embrace. Then, with her mom standing by the porch, allowing us a special moment to rekindle our love, she kissed me gently and long, something she would not have done in front of her mom before my diagnosis. Her mother then moved towards me with tears in her eyes and hugged me, saying, "*Gracias a Diós*" ("Thanks to God [that you are well]").

Magdalena and I spent the next three hours talking about our good fortune and doing some serious thinking about our futures. We renewed our commitment to each other and promised to continue sharing our thoughts via correspondence.

Neither of us wanted the evening to end, but we both knew her mother still expected us to respect her "late curfew" of 10:30 p.m., so we trekked home. Her siblings were waiting for us, and they, too, welcomed me back to Laredo.

I returned home at approximately 11:00 p.m. My parents and siblings were waiting, anxiously wanting to know more about Carville in general and my treatment in particular. Everyone cried again when I shared the good news about possibly being discharged in December. Plans were immediately discussed on how we could celebrate by going to a scheduled dance at the civic center with Sunny and the Sunliners, the most popular singing group in south Texas at the time. Following the dance, we could all gather at the Ramirez home with family and friends for some menudo—a soup made of tripe, hominy, and plenty of spices, topped with diced onions, cilantro, and serrano peppers. We laughed and cried some more, until someone mentioned that it was almost 2 a.m. Suddenly, everyone felt very tired and sleepy.

The next day, I woke up to the nostalgic smell of diced onions and serrano peppers being sautéed and mixed with Mexican sausage, or chorizo. The wonderful smell of fresh flour tortillas immediately made me regress to happy summer mornings when stresses were minimal and everyone was in good health. As I walked toward the kitchen I overheard Mom and Dad talking about finances, an ongoing challenge for a family with eleven kids living at home. The discussion ended as soon as I entered our small kitchen. I, of course, acted as if I had not heard their words, and instead I asked for some tape. My parents gave me a puzzled look and both asked almost simultaneously, "¿Para qué?" ("For what?").

In spite of all the information I had learned about HD, I still felt like my family was being exposed to a dangerous bacillus. Therefore, prior to my trip, I had decided that no one else in the Ramirez family would risk having to repeat my painful experiences. An appropriate plan, I thought, would be to mark my drinking glass, plate, and utensils.

When I explained my plan to Mom, she threatened to break the plate over my head just as she had done when I was fifteen years old, when I had stupidly criticized her cooking. She proceeded to dramatically pick up one of the plates and demonstrated what she would do if she ever found anything marked by me. She smashed the plate on the floor. The noise startled even the mice hiding behind the gas stove. My siblings rushed to the kitchen, only to be admonished by Dad to go back to bed. Mom cried and embraced me, saying, "Por favor no me ofendas" ("Please do not offend me").

Magdalena had told me that some friends were getting together on Saturday for a little summer party and said she wanted to take me for some dancing. I reluctantly agreed, not realizing that it was a surprise for me and that many friends and family members would be present.

The long drive from Carville and the excitement of being reunited with family had left me exhausted. I attempted to rest on Saturday, but a long procession of well wishers kept me on my toes, responding to observations and questions: "You look so well." "We are all praying for you." "How long will you stay?" "What is your treatment?" "Where is the hospital located?" "Do you have any friends?"

By the time I picked up Magdalena for the summer party at a small ranch on the outskirts of Laredo, I felt like a zombie. My body was sending me messages that the physical and emotional stress of the visit was starting to affect my health. I had a slight fever, my feet were swollen, and my hands and arms started to show signs of red nodules that were described as *caliente*, or hot, by Mom.

I did not share my discomfort with Magdalena, but she obviously knew that the HD bacillus was starting to affect my personality, and mentioned that I looked "withdrawn." As we entered the party area, a large covered dance floor with bright lights and a loud record player and a barbecue pit at the far end, Magdalena whispered, "This is for you, enjoy but please take it easy." I felt shoved into the limelight and Magdalena moved to the side, smiling but radiating a telltale sign that she did not approve of our physical separation. The guys I had gone to school with came over with broad smiles and bear hugs, saying, "Good to see you again, *vato*" (guy). The girls stared in awe as if they expected to see me in a wheelchair, gently hugged me, and said, "You look so good." I kept glancing towards Magdalena, but kept being pushed more and more to the center of the dance floor, until one of the party goers yelled out, "Vamos a bailar" ("Let's dance"). I quickly moved toward Magdalena and reached out for her hand. She moved toward me and we danced. The rest of the evening is a blur as the physical discomfort eventually displaced the joy of being with my friends.

Magdalena and I left before the party ended. By the time we arrived at her home my fever had escalated and the nodules were bigger. I decided two things: first, I was not ready to participate in such fast-paced activities filled with high emotion; and second, I needed to return to Carville for further treatment. I shared these thoughts with Magdalena and she cried, nodding in understanding. I was showered with emotional and physical contact, but I felt so alone, realizing that I would really never be able to return to the days of the summer of '67. This was a different summer in '68.

For the next two days I stayed at home, attempting to rest, but continued to receive visitors who were "just in the neighborhood." Magdalena did not work on Sunday, but she would usually commit this day to helping her mom clean the house and to making clothing for the upcoming school year. We did spend a few hours together Sunday evening, but we simply were in limbo, unable to plan anything for the future because of the uncertainty of my own future at Carville. We said good night realizing that I could be on the way back to Carville by Monday.

On Monday, Mom called Carville and described my symptoms to one of the nuns who also was a nurse. After a consult with Dr. Hull, I was strongly encouraged to return quickly as I was undergoing one of the dreaded reactions. Mr. R. would not be available for a return trip for at least ten days and a bus ride would be too long. Diane unselfishly gave my parents her whole paycheck in order to purchase a plane ticket for me. It was scheduled to depart Laredo at 5:30 a.m. on Tuesday, so there was little time available for farewells. I was not able to reach Magdalena until 7:00 p.m. on Monday, so she asked a friend for a ride to my parents' home and came at 8:00 p.m. to say *adiós*. We had limited privacy and little time to talk, so she affectionately embraced me and said, "You'll have a letter from me by Friday." We were both saddened by the turn of events and silently wondered when we would see each other again.

My youngest sibling, Rosalinda, only eight at the time, recalls that our early morning trip to the airport was the closest she had ever been to an airplane. She felt that as my plane was swallowed up by the clouds, I had again died and been sent to heaven.

By Tuesday afternoon I was in the infirmary at Carville, where I stayed for two weeks. As Magdalena had promised, I had a letter by Friday. Magdalena had gone home Monday evening and written a beautiful letter, stating that she was jealous of all the attention I received and the limited time to enjoy our company together. She felt confused and betrayed by this odd disease; she had seen me on what appeared to be my deathbed six months earlier, then I was miraculously walking without a sign of the illness, and then the bacillus robbed us of precious time . . . again. "When will it end?" she asked. I did not have an answer, except to respond in my letter that it appeared that a discharge date of December was only a dream.

The two-week stay in the infirmary gave me the opportunity to continue my readings about HD, especially about the new drug called B-663, also known as clofazimine. This was a medication that would turn the complexion a variety of dark colors: blotches of purple, irregular markings of brown and black, and very black. This unique medication was eventually used with other drugs to attack and kill the HD bacillus, the combination becoming commonly known as MDT (multiple drug therapy) in 1981. The possibility of a cure intrigued me, but I also saw how others who were on the medication refused to be seen outside the hospital grounds.

Letters continued to come from my family. They would describe in great detail their accomplishments in school and sports, the wonders of dating and the fears of moving out of town to attend school. With regard to the latter, my sister Margarita started business college in San Antonio, and Magdalena enrolled at Texas Woman's University in Denton, Texas. At the same time that Magdalena received a long list of dos and don'ts as a resident at one of the many dorms on campus, mostly don'ts, I received a one-sentence letter from Laredo Junior College: "Your transcript has been mailed to Mr. Mike Garcia of the Texas Vocational Commission." This short letter validated my suspicions that discharge would not occur in 1968.

During September I experienced another serious reaction, and again I was admitted to the infirmary. Dr. Hull and Dr. Bauschard came to visit as a team and said that the reaction would probably continue, eventually resulting in irreversible damage to my hands, feet, and legs. They showed me pictures of persons with the damage they described. They said the only way to prevent further damage was to take B-663, along with thalidomide and dapsone. I asked for time to think about it. Their response was, "How about tomorrow morning?"

I scurried to consult with my parents and Magdalena, explaining the visible side effects, as well as severe constipation. Their response was predictable—do what will cure you. Well, my response the next day was "yes."

Within weeks of starting on B-663 my skin started to change. Ironically, my complexion was already a dark tan and many of my friends would call me "*negro*," a term of endearment in Laredo. However, the change with B-663 was much more dramatic than I had anticipated. I would often receive stares from residents and staff, as well as strangers I encountered outside the hospital grounds. The stares made me uncomfortable and angry, since I already had an annoying label.

I felt anger as people also called me "nigger" and "boy." The longer I took B-663, the darker I became. As I started to venture out to the communities of La Place, Gonzales, White Castle, Geismer, Prairieville, and Baton Rouge, the more I felt the stares and the more I was blatantly denied service at convenience stores. More sheriffs' deputies and state police stopped me because I looked "suspicious." I was never arrested, but most of the time when I was stopped, the police would make sure that I saw they were holding their guns outside their holsters. It's possible that the reason I was never arrested was because the police found it difficult to believe that any black man would speak with such a heavy accent, or have a name like José Ramirez.

October 1968 started out with another two-week visit to the infirmary, because the reaction had returned. Each time it was more powerful, incapacitating me and leaving me very weak and despondent. Mom and Magdalena would consistently ask in their letters for more details of my treatment progress or relapses. Well, Dr. Hull and Dr. Brauschard would get an earful from me because I remembered a promise that if I took the B-663 all reactions would disappear. Both denied ever making such a promise.

While still in the infirmary, I received an unexpected call from Mom. She wanted me to know that funding from the Texas Vocational Commission had been approved for me to attend Louisiana State University in January. Wow, what scary news. The thought of attending such a huge university overwhelmed me. I called Magdalena and gave her the good news as she was preparing for an exam. As is her nature, she did not say anything about her challenges in school and living in a dorm. Instead, she focused solely on my acceptance for funding to attend LSU, describing this as an "early Christmas gift."

Within an hour of receiving the news from Mom, Vernon Bahlinger, the hospital's social worker, came to visit. He congratulated me on the funding and then surprised me with the news that my Social Security Disability Insurance (SSDI) payments would start in November, retroactive to September.

Things were going so well that I had to pinch myself. Just then Darryl Broussard walked into my room, saw me pinching my arm, and sarcastically said, "Son, once you lose the feeling you never get it back," referring to the loss of sensation with HD. He added to the good news by saying I had been accepted for membership in the Lions Club and ordered me to "get well for your initiation." The hospital at Carville and the Kalaupapa HD Settlement on the island of Molokai, Hawaii, had very loyal members of this international organization. I was eventually appointed secretary, because I had a typewriter for recording the required minutes.[2]

Mr. Bahlinger and Bob Miller of the hospital's rehabilitation department initiated the process for me to be accepted into LSU. My grades were good enough and all of my credits were transferable. However, I was required to successfully complete a three-hour exam in order to be "certified proficient in English." This was a requirement for all new students because, to my surprise, people were graduating from high school or junior college without having the ability to read or write. In December, I received my formal letter of acceptance.

What I did not know until thirty years later was that the medical staff had strongly advocated on my behalf to encourage LSU officials to change their policy about accepting "in-patients" from Carville. The LSU policy was that no person with "bacteriological positive HD" would be accepted as a student or employee. The fight to change school policy was led by the hospital's director, Dr. John Trautman. To my surprise this battle was also strongly supported by the chief surgeon and the SSO. Dr. Trautman had to meet with the president of LSU to get the policy reversed. Dr. Trautman's victory was not just on my behalf but on behalf of all persons with HD.[3]

The news of receiving funding from TVRC, approval for SSDI, acceptance to LSU, and an invitation to join the Lions Club was very timely. This greatly lessened the disappointment of being notified by Dr. Hull that "in consultation with the Medical Director, Social Services Department and Rehabilitation Department, [I] would not be issued a medical pass for either Thanksgiving or Christmas." No one, including me, believed that my body would be able to handle another visit to Laredo, especially after the resurgence of the HD bacillus in July. I reluctantly accepted their recommendation and directed my energies to helping the Lions and Mexican clubs host bingos during Thanksgiving. For Christmas, I assisted the school staff and others in planning a Christmas show on December 24.

By age ten, José had made his first communion. Ramirez family photo, 1958.

Magdalena and José in 1966 at one of two high
school proms. Numbness had spread to parts of
his legs and hands.

José, age fifteen, with his family. He noticed numbness in his forearms at
this time. From left, standing: Javier (nephew), Idalia, Rudy, Mague, Diana,
José, Raquel, Javier, Yolanda, Sandra (niece); sitting: Ramiro, Rene, Father,
Gerardo, Mom, Rosalinda, Fernando, Daniel (nephew), David (nephew).
Family photo taken at Guadalupe Housing Project, 1963.

Magdalena and José on last trip to annual fair in Nuevo Laredo, Mexico, 1967. Bouts of severe pain and difficult-to-heal sores had started. Photo by street vendor.

One-inch article in the *Laredo Times* resulted in hundreds of letters of support. Article paid for by José's father, 1968.

Aerial photo of the 350-acre U.S. Public Health Service Hospital in Carville, Louisiana. A road along the Mississippi River was the only way to the hospital. Photo by Gleason Photography.

Entrance to the hospital taken in 1968, two months after José's admission. Ramirez family photo.

José's mom making tacos for Sister Joanna during first visit after admission. Ramirez family photo.

Dad and Mom enjoying a paddle boat ride at the hospital's lake. Ramirez family photo.

José, representing the Patients' Federation, awards the trophy to the winners of the annual Carville tournament. *Star* photo, 1970.

José and Jim Haley (left) walking in front of the Tower, best known of all buildings at LSU. *Star* photo, 1971.

Proud day following graduation exercises at LSU in May 1971. Ramirez family photo.

Wedding photo of José and Magdalena, high school sweethearts. Experimental medication B-663 changed the color of his complexion. After they got married, José continued residing at Carville and Magdalena lived in a small apartment near LSU. Ramirez family photo, December 24, 1972.

Diana, "the cheerleader," with husband, Roberto, congratulating Magdalena and José at the wedding reception. Ortiz family photo.

José with J. R. and Erika. Ramirez family photo, 1986.

José, Darryl Broussard (real name Wasey Daigle), and James Carville at the centennial celebration. *Star* photo, 1994.

Mary Ruth and Darryl Broussard, surrogate parents to José. *Star* photo, 1994.

José with Betty Martin, author of *Miracle at Carville*, at the centennial celebration. *Star* photo, 1994.

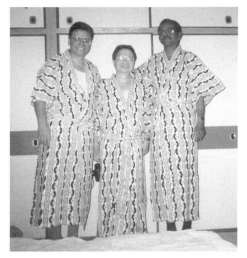

José, Dr. Due from Vietnam, and Dr. Gopal on visit to Hansen's disease sanatoria in Japan. Ramirez family photo, 1996.

José with Dr. Gopal from India in Washington, D.C., at ILEP (antileprosy organization) meeting. Ramirez family photo, 1996.

José at the top of the cliff where Fontilles was built in Spain. Stone walls look like the Great Wall of China. Notice the opening to allow guards to shoot escapees from leprosarium. Ramirez family photo, 1997.

José and Bernard Punikai'a, hero of Molokai, and possibly better known than Father Damien in some parts of Hawaii. Photo by Pamela Parlapiano, 1997.

José and Dr. Türkan Saylan at World Leprosy Day, January 31, 2000, in Istanbul, Turkey. José received the Etem Utku Medal for "Outstanding Work in the Field of Leprosy." Photo by Magdalena S. Ramirez.

Simeon Peterson, a.k.a. "Dr. Pete," at the International Day of Dignity and Respect on March 11, 1999. Photo by Pamela Parlapiano.

Family photo taken in 2003, two years after the loss of their home to Tropical Storm Allison and Magdalena's recovery from cancer. Ramirez family photo.

The theater, with heavy blue curtains, had been the site of many holiday activities. In December, I was the master of ceremonies for the Christmas play, choreographed by Julia Rivera. At the end of the play, I was standing beside the curtain, and Lala Williams, a muscular Samoan, was attempting to remove some props from the center of the stage. Suddenly, the curtain came crashing down on both of us, creating a cloud of dust throughout the auditorium and nonstop laughter. For years thereafter, December would bring a smile, if not uncontrollable laughter, to those of us who witnessed this unique display of vaudeville.

# Manhood and Beyond

The year 1969 started rather gloomily for me. I was away from family during a time when I felt manhood was just around the corner, as I was turning twenty-one in February. The gray time of the New Year turned very bright during the first week in January when Dr. Hull and Mr. Bahlinger surprised me with a two-week medical pass to visit Laredo. Mr. Bahlinger had even prearranged with the Mexican Club to pay for a round-trip bus ticket. He had also called my parents, which gave me little time to contemplate making a decision about the trip. So, within twenty-four hours of being informed of the pass, I was on the bus to Laredo.

The ride to Laredo didn't seem as long as the ride in the Texas Department of Health station wagon. It was also a lot more comfortable riding in a Greyhound Express to Houston and then transferring to another express bus to Laredo.

Much of the ride home occurred at night, so when I arrived in Laredo at approximately 9 a.m. on January 8, I felt rested. My siblings, my parents, and Magdalena told me that the border patrol had uniformed officers with dogs at the station. "They stared at us a lot," said Magdalena.

Nevertheless, the Ramirez clan gathered around for *muchos besos y abrazos*, many hugs and kisses. We drove home in several cars and arrived to see a number of friends and neighbors waiting to greet me. Most noticed how dark my skin had become but did not ask for details, even though their eyes conveyed many questions.

Dad had woken up at 5 a.m. to make some *carne asada*, pieces of flank thinly sliced and marinated overnight in fresh juice from a key lime. He cooked the meat by placing it on a grill heated by fire from mesquite wood.

Dad had been taught at a very early age that, even though as a man he was not expected to toil in the kitchen, he was required to know how to make tasty, succulent *carne asada*. Any male in Laredo wishing to be called manly must first learn how to make good *carne asada*, complemented with a spicy sauce made of tomatoes, onion, chile serrano, cilantro, and fresh lime juice. Dad learned his lesson well and he passed this skill on to all of his sons.

The term *"carne asada"* is rarely used now. Instead many people prefer the word "fajitas." According to Professor Homero Recio of Texas A&M, the term "fajita" did not appear in print until 1975.[1] However, butchers in the Rio Grande Valley used the word, a derivative of *faja*, or belt, in the 1940s. Fajita refers to the diaphragm muscle of a steer, which looks like a belt.

One of the people present at the fajita feast was Amparo Meza, the same lady who had sponsored our trip to Monterrey in 1967 to see the *curandero* who unofficially diagnosed my illness. She had made a promise to the Virgin of Guadalupe that she would take me to Monterrey on a pilgrimage if I regained my health. So on January 10 we took another trip to Monterrey.

We went by bus, first class, which meant a bus that had a bathroom and that also prohibited passengers from taking live animals along. The trip went smoothly, but I kept thinking about our last trip to this beautiful city embraced by the Sierra Madre mountain range. Magdalena accompanied us on the trip. We spoke little, and for the whole day it seemed as if we were inside a sanctuary, with much silence and occasional whispering, as if praying.

Mrs. Meza insisted on taking us to a church she knew about. We entered on our knees and "walked" all the way up to the altar. We prayed individually, received the holy sign of the cross from one of the priests, and lit candles as a token of our appreciation for improving health. Both Mrs. Meza and Mom stuffed the donation box with pesos.

Leaving the dimly lit church and walking into the bright sunshine made all of us feel cleansed of all sins, as the light from the heavens seemed to be saying, "Your life can start fresh again." The four of us formed a circle of embraces. We bought some tacos from a street vendor, boarded the same bus for the return trip, and quickly fell asleep.

The remainder of my time in Laredo was spent visiting many relatives and friends and, of course, strengthening my relationship with Magdalena. My daily routine was focused on plenty of rest, no late-night parties, and on constant monitoring of my legs. The medication kept the HD bacillus in check, but I still had sores, which stubbornly refused to heal. Thus, I had to soak my legs in warm water three times a day, apply petroleum jelly and powdered medicine, cover them with sterile gauze, and protect them with support hose that went up to my knees. Additionally, I looked for hot spots on my body, especially on my arms, and every four hours I checked for fevers with a thermometer. Dr. Hull and the nurses, especially Sister Joanna, had trained me well to keep myself from becoming ill with a reaction. Another weapon I used during my pass was prednisone, premeasured in a syringe.

Sister Joanna, who was a robust lady with horn-rimmed glasses and a baby face, was only seven years older than I. She had a master's degree in nursing, and had volunteered to teach me about self-injections. First, she carefully noted the dangers of using incorrect dosages of prednisone. Then she had me practice injecting the medicine into an orange. Finally, I practiced on my own thigh. She kept saying it was "no big deal" and emphasized the alternatives to not learning about self-injections, i.e., I could get a severe reaction, which would cut my trip short.

Magdalena had to return to school at Texas Woman's University in Denton before my pass expired. So my brother Rudy and I drove her in a borrowed car. As with our initial ride to Carville, we had a minor car problem, a flat tire. Magdalena directed the changing of the tire as she slowly, and jokingly, repeated her presentation titled "How to Change a Flat Tire," made in speech class at Laredo Junior College in 1966.

Soon after I returned to Carville, one of my first friends at the hospital, Jimmy, died of a heart attack. Jimmy wanted to be buried in his beloved New Orleans with a package of Kool cigarettes in his pocket. He was the first of my many Carville brothers and sisters who died at the hospital, most of whom were buried in the now-historical cemetery located at the rear of the hospital grounds.

Jimmy was fifty-five when he died. The average age of the residents at the time was fifty-five. Jimmy's death gave rise to renewed concerns about maintaining good health, but little was done at the time to change the eating and drinking habits of the residents. Something, however, was done differently which positively affected their life spans. By 1999, the average age of the residents at Carville was eighty-five, which was comparable to other leprosy hospitals throughout the world.

The closer the starting date of the spring semester at LSU got, the more concerned I became with finding a way to get to school, which was twenty miles from the hospital. I had managed to save $160 from my jobs and money from parents, so my selection was limited. Advice from Dad was "compra algo que este limpio, te ahorre gasolina y que tenga buenas llantas" ("buy a vehicle that is clean, not a gas-guzzler, and has good tires").

Two other residents and I drove in a borrowed car to the small town of Gonzales. The town's name just didn't connect with most Louisiana names such as Landry, Landrieux, Boudreaux, and Broussard, but Louisiana was under Spanish rule for a long time, so Spanish influence in architecture and names of towns is obvious throughout the southern part of the state. The Catholic faith is also evident in the state, so I prayed for getting a salesman who was a good Catholic and had a Spanish surname. I believed that these traits would help me find an honest deal in a used car.

My purchase, for $150, was a white '63 Plymouth Valiant station wagon. "The car is very economical," the salesman by the name of Perez told me. He urged me to focus on how white and clean it looked and to disregard the rust on the lower part of the frame. "This is a steal," he said, gently kicking the retread tires that looked new. "Everyone will be jealous." I meekly signed on the dotted line. Within six weeks, I had three flats, two burned-out headlights, and a dead battery, but I was the owner of a "new" car and learned the importance of regular maintenance.

Even though I was elated about the vehicle, an absolute necessity, I was pained by the financial struggles my parents were experiencing due to Dad's unemployment status. I also felt a tinge of anger and jealousy from some residents who had not been offered the same opportunities as I. So I said little about the Valiant and parked it next to the cemetery, away from the view of other residents.

I knew about the financial strain at home because Mom, without realizing it, would let me know. Each of her letters started with a salutation that was more like a prayer. She thanked God for my continued health and described the day or night in terms of weather. Occasionally, she would also ask for a prayer for Dad to find a job. In any case, she always accentuated her love for me and everyone in the Ramirez family.

Dad also relayed distress messages whenever he discussed Mom in his letters. Normally, he would provide infinite detail about the sports activities my brothers were involved in. But if he mentioned my mother in a saintly way, he was conveying a message of financial burden.

The date to register at LSU finally arrived. I drove to school early and found myself engulfed in a sea of white faces. I simply followed the signs that led me through the confusing registration process. Then I found the fraternity tables. As I approached one of the tables, a student jumped up from his seat and firmly pointed away from his turf, saying, "Your kind is over there." He was pointing to a group of students from India. I looked at him with disdain and anger, calmly voiced a few curse words in Spanish, smiled, and, feeling much better, walked away.

I was overzealous in my goal of catching up to my friends who had graduated from high school in 1966, so I signed up for sixteen hours. This was a huge mistake, because even though I did complete the hours, I struggled to keep up with the demands of one lab and five classes.

The daily school routine that I followed was maintained for the duration of my enrollment at LSU. I would have fellow residents wake me up at 6 a.m., get to the hospital cafeteria for oatmeal and a box lunch prepared by staff, and be on campus by 8:30 a.m. I stayed at the university until approximately 6 p.m., regardless of the number of classes I had. Most of the time I would be in the library. Thalidomide is a powerful sedative, and I did everything I could to stay awake while driving or studying—pinching myself, yawning, screaming, stomping my feet, moving my head to stimulate the neck muscles, and turning up the volume of the car radio. Most of the time, thalidomide won, and I would fall asleep with my forehead resting on top of my textbook. While driving, I simply stopped on the side of the road and napped until I was alert enough to continue on my trip. The distance between the hospital and the gates of LSU is exactly twenty miles, and 90 percent of the drive is in a straight line, so it's a wonder I never crashed while taking thalidomide.

Mom continued to keep me informed about all the Laredo *chisme*, gossip. One of the events, which seemed to be repeated with much regularity, was a wedding. One big wedding that my parents and Magdalena attended was that of our high school friends Yolanda Luna and Quintin Vargas. Quintin's father had been the person who got my parents involved with the *cursillistas* and coordinated the marathon prayers for my health.

Magdalena had traveled with her high school girlfriends and college roommates, Hilda Cabrera and Laura Duran, to the wedding. Mom reported that friends had asked about my status and each offered a prayer on my behalf. Mom said, "Amigos que no te han dejado son amigos de verdad" ("Friends who have not abandoned you are true friends").

My relationship with Magdalena continued to face challenges. Our mood swings escalated and de-escalated, similar to the country's ongoing debates about the Vietnam War. We were constantly in battle with our own demons of adjustment, depression, loneliness, fears of failure, and the ever-present adult responsibilities of making decisions about life.

Adulthood for me became even more obvious as I turned twenty-one years old. Magdalena, attempting to bring a feeling of home to Carville, mailed me a package of homemade flour tortillas. Homemade tortillas do not contain the special preservatives used by commercial distributors to keep them soft. Therefore, Magdalena's special tortillas were hard as rocks and could be easily thrown like Frisbees over the spacious golf course at Carville.

When I shared my good fortune with the other residents about receiving the tortillas from Magdalena, they laughed. However, Tonia, who was employed as the cook in the small kitchen of the canteen, volunteered to make the tortillas edible again. Tonia, who had been diagnosed as a teenager, had lived at Carville for almost thirty years. She was one of the many women who met some of my needs, first by ironing my shirts for twenty-five cents each and later starching my khaki pants for fifty cents. She specialized in making fresh flour tortilla tacos, usually with ground meat and potatoes. This menu item was so popular that she would usually run out of tortillas by 6:30 p.m. Considering that I would regularly not get back to the hospital until after the patients' cafeteria had stopped serving, Tonia would save me two tacos. She would add lettuce and tomato and freshly made salsa, making the tacos look huge. The other residents, usually men, would predictably yell and complain not only about the size of the fifty-cent tacos, but also that she had already announced before I arrived that the kitchen was closed. Her firm and motherly response to the complainers was always "Callense, él es mi hijo" ("Shut up, he is my son").

She softened my birthday tortillas by slowly heating them over a low flame on the gas range. She further surprised me with a plate full of *picadillo* (ground meat made with many spices and diced potatoes and bell peppers), fresh pinto beans, and *fideo*, vermicelli with many spices and tomato sauce. Tonia knew about my twenty-first birthday because she had read an announcement in the *Q.M.* (*Question Mark*), which was a weekly publication that was developed, printed, and distributed by the teachers who worked at the school.

My family sent me birthday cards with one-dollar bills inside. Mom indicated in her letter that February was simply not the same without me. Family involvement in the annual Washington's birthday parade had become a tradition. Magdalena and my sisters had been participants in the parades, marching with their school's pep squad, and I used to sell raw peanuts in small bags as a way of making spending money. Thus, in 1969, with no one in the family participating in the parade, the celebration was *como un nido abandonado*, like an abandoned nest.

Towards the end of February, I was invited by a number of residents to visit the Red Rooster. The Rooster was a one-room bar approximately one mile from the hospital. A family who had two brothers living at Carville as residents operated it. The family was black, of Cuban ancestry, and thus they spoke Spanish. The bar was frequented by the whole community, but it had a reputation for "boys being boys," and attracted young women interested in dancing. It was not uncommon to have a game of dice going on in the parking lot.

The invitation to go to the Rooster, not my first visit to this establishment, was actually for me simply to provide transportation. Since I had a school pass, I could leave the facility without requesting other forms of written permission.

The plan was to leave the hospital and pick up five of the residents by the hole at 8 p.m., after the canteen closed. I picked up the group, which included Johnny M., who had helped me choose the station wagon.

We were at the Rooster for approximately two hours, drinking beer, eating snacks, listening to music, and telling jokes. The party, at least for me, came to an abrupt end when our conversation veered to examples of perks enjoyed by many staff, e.g., great pay, easy jobs, etc. Then, the discussion turned to resident perks, e.g., large apartments, easy jobs, etc. Johnny, by then the most drunk in the group and slurring his words, accused me of getting school perks, adding, "Yo nunca pude ir a la escuela" ("I was never able to attend school"). My wonderful, articulate comeback was nothing more than a mix of four-letter words, and he responded with a punch, more like a slap, to my face. Being over twenty years younger and about five inches taller, I dropped him to the floor before others intervened.

Both of us ended up with black eyes. Neither of us talked about our fight, but others had plenty of versions about what occurred. Johnny and I privately apologized to each other, but I learned a valuable lesson—never overlook the experiences of others.

Johnny and most of the other residents had many painful experiences, including losing families and opportunities, after being diagnosed with HD. My own experiences, though painful, paled when compared to theirs. I made a commitment to repay my Carville family by educating the world about their losses.

Six weeks after starting school, I had my first experience with a dead battery in the stadium parking lot. With the exception of the huge Tiger Stadium parking lot, parking space was at a premium at LSU.

By March, I already knew most of the starting lineup for Coach Charlie McClendon's Fighting Tigers. One of the players was a linebacker from Gonzalez, a walk-on without a scholarship, who was only slightly bigger than me. To my surprise, he was friendly and had some knowledge of cars. I had assumed that the football team would consider it belittling for them to look at, much less speak to, the students who were not on the school's athletic teams.

He must have seen my look of panic as I attempted to tinker with the wires after being unable to start the car. He calmly walked over and said, "Do you need some help?" He asked me to try to start the station wagon and then quickly diagnosed the problem. He was able to jump-start the car and instructed me not to stop anywhere; otherwise I would need someone to help me with the jumper cables. My appearance, accent, or place of residence never affected his willingness to help. Is it possible, I wondered, that the fear of rejection was all in my mind? This young man, though he didn't know my name, was the first peer at LSU to make me feel at home. The LSU fans, fanatics about football, learned to admire his reckless drive to make a tackle.

As I left the parking lot and passed the school's golf course, the station wagon simply died on me, and I coasted to the shoulder of Highway 30. Luckily for me, two fellow students stopped to help. They did not have jumper cables, but they offered to give me a ride in their two-door '57 Chevy to wherever I was going.

In spite of my good fortune in receiving assistance from fellow students, I was still on guard about possible rejection and chose not to mention Carville. As we proceeded down the road, they became more inquisitive and I less talkative. Finally, the grounds of the hospital came into view and both stopped asking questions, sharing panicked glances. My hands started to sweat and my heart ached for not telling them about my "home," but it was too late. I finally said, as we approached the guarded gate, the only entrance/exit at Carville, "Here is my home."

Mike, who was driving, slammed on the brakes so hard that the car skidded on the loose gravel and got the attention of the security guard. Larry quickly jumped out, held the door open, and, with his mouth wide open, frantically motioned for me to exit the car. I was frightened at their behavior and got out. Before I could say thank you, Mike and Larry sped away. The security guard patted me on the back, smiled, and said, "Betcha they didn't know you lived here!" He added, "I see it all the time," and we both laughed. Then we laughed even harder as Mike and Larry zoomed by the Carville gates again, and disappeared over the horizon. Neither of them knew that the road past the Carville gates was a dead end, so they were forced to breathe Carville air for a second time as they drove to Gonzales.

That same evening Darryl Broussard drove me to Gonzales to buy a battery, coincidentally from the same man who had guided us to Carville over a year earlier. He had a contagious laugh, and we all joined in as we reminisced about the ride to Carville and then about my most recent experience with Mike and Larry. He offered to drive me to Baton Rouge and replace the battery. We exchanged handshakes and a five-dollar tip.

A week later, I once again saw Larry. He was using the urinal in the men's room. I stood next to him. Our eyes met, he turned pale, and his flow was redirected to his right leg, wetting his trousers. He turned and rushed out of the men's room, his penis still exposed. I can only imagine his embarrassment when he realized the consequences of his rapid exit. I never saw Larry or Mike again, but their names kept coming up whenever the other residents and I compared stories about ridiculous incidents related to ignorance about HD.

Dad's response to the incident with Mike and Larry was "Marzo loco y abril otro poco" ("March is a crazy month and April a little more"). This old Spanish saying was in reference to the unpredictable weather in March and its influence on behavior.

Magdalena compared my struggles to her own—dealing with racism and discrimination on a daily basis. She sought support from other Mexican American students who belonged to La Raza Unida (United Race). La Raza was conceived in the small town of Crystal City, Texas.

Besides giving birth to La Raza Unida, Crystal City had an added special significance for Magdalena and me, as it was the place where our relationship was anchored in December of 1964. The welding of this anchor started in October of 1963, when we went on our first official date to a dance sponsored by members of Martin High School's ROTC. We enjoyed each other's company so much that in January of 1964, I decided to give her my high school football sweater as a prelude to "going steady."

The following school year, after my return from doing migrant work with Mom and four siblings in the sugar beet fields of Montana and cucumber fields in Wisconsin, I was forced to continue my education at the new high school, J.W. Nixon High School, located in an area closer to our home.

Magdalena and I had corresponded during my brief "vacation," which was an eyeopening experience since we and five other families traveled in the back of a ten-wheel truck. We were stopped by three different state police to "check the Mexican load." We were stared at whenever we stopped to buy fuel and eat. We were refused services at various grocery stores in Helena, Montana. Behind our backs, but in a manner loud enough for us to hear, we were referred to as "greasers" and "spics."

Our return to Laredo, after "visiting" some northern states, came a few days before the start of two-a-day football practices, so I had limited time with Magdalena. Once classes began, we would see each other on the weekends. This continued through December. The week before the long Christmas holidays, Magdalena returned my sweater via my sister Diana, who, as a senior, had the choice of graduating from Martin or Nixon High School.

Diana left the sweater on my bed. Upon seeing it, I quickly went to Diana, knowing that she would be the "messenger" since both she and Magdalena attended Martin High School. Diana heard me rushing towards her, and anticipated my demand for a detailed explanation. Her comment, before I could utter a word, was that "she did not tell me why, but if you want her back, you must do it face to face."

I was in a panic and pleaded for guidance. Diana simply shrugged. I attempted to call Magdalena, but she refused to accept my calls. I went to her house, but her family told me she was out.

The Christmas school break finally arrived and still no contact with Magdalena. I made one more visit and begged her sister, Marta, to tell me where she was. "Okay," she said, "I'll tell you against my better judgment. She went to Crystal City with Marta Villa [her best friend]". Coming to the realization that Magdalena was special and I did not wish to lose her, I asked Dad for permission to use our car to take the ninety-mile drive to Crystal City. Dad had seen me drive part of the way from Wisconsin after buying a '57 Plymouth with money earned from migrant work, so I figured he knew I could handle highway driving.

Surprisingly, he said, "Está bien, pero tú buscas el dinero para la gasolina" ("Okay, but you find the money for the gasoline"). Showing too much excitement would have been disrespectful regarding Dad's important decision; plus it would have been a sign of my own immaturity. So I waited until I left his sanctuary, the bedroom, to celebrate by dancing a Mexican polka with an imaginary partner.

Magdalena has described my unexpected visit to Crystal City as "*como un ataque de corazón*," a real shocker, like a heart attack. It was our first time to honestly discuss open communication, perceptions, and trust. It was the beginning of a wonderful and long-lasting relationship. So Crystal City became a link to our heritage and our love.

Back home, three of my sisters were experiencing unique changes in their lives, and each wrote me describing their struggles. Margarita (Mague), who left Laredo to attend Durham Business College in San Antonio, was faced with the ongoing fear of being away from the familiar surroundings of home. Additionally, she too was exposed for the first time to the practice of labeling.

Another sister, Idalia, age sixteen, wrote about being forced to face the "expectations of being a girl in our family." With the older sisters married, working, or in college, she was expected to take on the "role of maid" as she described her chores—help to make tortillas, prepare supper, and wash dishes. Unfortunately, we as brothers lacked the parental teaching to express any compassion about her complaints.

Rosalinda, the youngest sister, had started to get her orientation to becoming a woman in Laredo by helping Idalia wash dishes. She wrote her first letter to me, wishing me a happy Easter, expressing "sadness" about my illness, and stating how happy she was to be learning "how to cook for the boys [brothers]". Luckily, my brothers and I eventually learned to assist our soul mates with household chores and not to simply *dejar a la mujer que lo haga*, let the woman do the chores.

Magdalena had expressed a desire to "get away from everything at TWU" during her spring break, but not go to Laredo. I immediately extended an invitation to visit me in Carville, as I could not leave. Magdalena accepted.

The lack of financial resources was a big barrier to both of us, so we learned to become very frugal with our spending and liberal with our savings. This practice made it possible to tap into my "savings" (piggy bank of quarters). I purchased a $25 Trans-Texas Airways ticket from Dallas Love Field and a $12.50 Greyhound bus ticket for her return trip. We used this system of saving to visit each other on future trips.

I received mixed reactions from residents and staff about Magdalena's visit. Mr. Bahlinger, chief of the social work department, remembered Magdalena from her initial visit to Carville. He wrote in my chart that he considered her visit "very therapeutic for [my] mental health." He convinced other staff "not to object to [her] visit" (as opposed to supporting the visit). This action, he later told me, opened up the opportunity for him to offer Magdalena a free room in House 25 and meal tickets.

Magdalena arrived in Baton Rouge on the afternoon of April 1, 1969, and left Sunday, April 6, 1969. Everyone at the hospital learned to love my girlfriend. We had a wonderful time together. We attempted to play golf (mostly rode the golf cart), rode the paddle boat on Lake Johansen, played pool, crossed the Mississippi River on the ferry, flew kites Magdalena had brought on the trip, visited the LSU campus, ate hospital food, and studied together. We expressed our continued love for each other and relished the time spent together.

Even though I would never exchange Magdalena's visit for anything else, I still missed being in Laredo for Easter. My parents had initiated a tradition that is still talked about by my siblings and extended family. The Easter festivities were held at the Casa Blanca Lake in Laredo or on a small ranch owned by my sister Raquel and her husband, Julian. There was always plenty of food, drink, dancing, silly games such as sack races, and, of course, many dozens of *cascarónes*.

*Cascarónes* are eggshells emptied of their contents through an opening on the top the size of a quarter. The eggshell was then rinsed and put away in a carton. Approximately one week before Easter, Mom would form an assembly line with all the smaller kids to make the *cascarónes*. We would boil water to melt coloring tablets, and then dip the empty eggshell into the dye. The dyed eggshells were placed upside down on paper and left for ten minutes to drip dry. They were then filled with multicolored confetti, and occasionally one was filled with flour. For added attraction, the eggs were decorated with wax pencils. Finally, the top was sealed with school glue and thin wrapping paper. The paper was cut in a circular design to give the appearance of an unbroken egg.

On Easter Sunday, Mom and Dad and the older siblings would hide the *cascarónes*. Dad would give a loud whistle, and *todos los niños*—all the kids—would dash out to find the most and best-decorated eggs. This was followed by the *cascarónes* being cracked on everyone's head.

Considering the fact that the preparation for this special event took all year and required the involvement of everyone, regardless of age, it is no wonder that all of us in the Ramirez family fondly reflect on these annual activities. This event has become a family reunion.

After Magdalena's visit, I started to save again for the next trip. I applied for a job that I was very familiar with, umpiring slow-pitch softball games. Graduate students in the recreation department coordinated the LSU Intramural League, so I met with some students for an interview. Almost immediately, the students attempted to discourage me from completing the interview, citing how difficult it is to learn all the rules. They had looks of disbelief when I mentioned my experience in umpiring, and they agreed to "test" me at a practice game that same day.

Being the sole umpire at a game is not easy. Knowing the rules is the easy part, but consistently making the calls on a ball passing the strike zone in a looping ninety-degree drop as opposed to a straight line requires much skill. Additionally, positioning oneself for making calls on the base paths requires almost robot-like movements. Making calls at a softball game played by guys my age was not a challenge compared to the games in Laredo with players much older and more experienced than I. I easily passed the test. My good fortune, however, proved to be costly.

During one of the softball games, a player known for his aggressive running hit a ball toward the gap in left field. Almost from the moment he hit the ball, everyone knew that he was going all the way—a home run. Anticipating a close play because the relay throws were being played to perfection, I positioned myself close to home base, behind the catcher, who was planning on blocking the plate and making the out. The runner abruptly stopped approximately five feet from the plate, which confused the catcher, and the ball zipped past him, hitting me hard on the inside part of my left leg, below the knee. I immediately felt a painful sting and saw blood on my leg. Luckily that was the last play of the game, and I hopped to my car.

Upon arriving at Carville, I went straight to the infirmary. The nurses realized that I had a serious injury and received authorization from Dr. Jacobson to admit me. The next day, I had visitors from the P.T. and O.T. departments. The staff lectured me again on how to protect my hands and feet from injury. "This is how deformities start," I was told, "and if you don't take this seriously, you will live to regret it." I knew that Mrs. Helen Woods and John Sturdivan, chiefs of O.T. and P.T., respectively, were correct.

The nurses performed their magic on my leg, dressing it twice daily. The staffs from O.T. and P.T. worked jointly to develop a guard for my leg. The guard was very similar to the shin guards worn by soccer players. This allowed me to continue umpiring even though the injury took months to heal. The most important lesson I learned from this injury was that leprosy affects the skin in a very unique manner—its thickness is reduced almost by half. This and the resulting poor circulation make quick healing difficult.

In May, I started to feel very tired, lethargic, and feverish. It was similar to a reaction, but minus the hypersensitivity to pain. This tired feeling continued until I realized that focusing on this made it very difficult to concentrate on my studies.

I went to see Dr. Hull, who said he could not find anything wrong to explain my "problem." I then went to see Dr. Jacobson for a second opinion, without notifying Dr. Hull first. Dr. Jacobson calmly told me that I had been placed on "special medicine" for two weeks and maybe it was having a side effect. He called the medicine a "placebo" mixed with my other medication. I went straight to the medical library and looked up the definition of placebo. I had been taken off thalidomide to determine if I could manage without it. I had been randomly selected to take the placebo as part of the experimental protocol.

Unfortunately, I was unable to convince Dr. Hull to place me on the real medicine. As a result, I experienced a severe reaction, and sores sprouted next to the softball-related wound. My fever shot up to 103 degrees, my hypersensitivity to pain escalated, my nostrils became blocked, making it difficult to breathe, and the ability to concentrate on my studies disappeared.

I managed to take exams in only two subjects. Mr. Bahlinger intervened on my behalf, and the LSU officials authorized an incomplete in the other three courses. I eventually recovered and completed my exams. Recovery came after the physicians realized that my condition was not going to improve, and authorization was granted for me to renew taking thalidomide.

During the brief time that I was on the placebo, my parents, siblings, and Magdalena strongly urged me to drop my classes. Magdalena argued in her letters that the stress of school and the lack of proper medication would only make my condition worse. I was definitely stubborn about continuing my studies. However, I was more determined to prove to myself that I was not a quitter. I pressed my luck and wound up in the infirmary once again.

A week after being admitted to the infirmary, I felt strong enough to eat solid foods. My fever was no longer consistently above 101 degrees, but my open sores lingered. They were treated twice a day by being soaked in warm water with Alpha Keri. Topical antibiotics were then applied along with Synalar cream and occlusive dressing, and petroleum jelly was put on noninfected areas. My legs were placed under a tentlike cover with a low-wattage lightbulb hung from the center. If I requested a trip to the canteen, my legs would be covered with Ace bandages from my toes to my knees. The other residents never gave me a second look, but I wondered if visitors might ask themselves, "What the heck . . . ?"

That is exactly what happened when Mom and Dad and three siblings showed up for a surprise visit during the last week in May. I recall that they arrived on Friday afternoon, at approximately 3 p.m. They went straight to the infirmary and gasped when they saw me. Mom whispered in a painful tone with hands holding her jaw, *"Madre del alma,"* oh, my God. I too was speechless. Unable to get out of bed, I simply reached out my arms, begging for a hug. And the tears of joy then started for all of us.

Most of the residents and staff knew about the visit, so many were outside my hospital room. They were all smiling and applauding. Some of the residents later told me of their fantasies of having their own families come to visit. Everyone was happy for me, realizing that my parents were a unique couple. They were financially challenged, but rich with hope and love.

The hospital's social worker, Vernon Bahlinger, was aware of the financial strain on families coming to visit Carville, so he would make arrangements to allow them to stay at a house in St. Gabriel rented for "hospital guests." Mom would bring all of the necessary supplies for cooking. One of the meals Mom prepared was a favorite of Sister Joanna's—deepfried corn tortillas molded into a taco and filled with diced potatoes, freshly cooked ground meat, lettuce, tomatoes, onion, and salsa.

Three of my sisters, Raquel, Diana, and Rosalinda, had accompanied Mom and Dad. They started to pamper me by adjusting the bed, my pillows, and the TV set that was locked in place on the wall. They offered to clean my room, do my laundry and make some fresh salsa. They all knew how much I liked freshly made salsa—green serrano peppers finely ground with a *molcajete*, a mortar and pestle made of pumice rock. Diced tomato would then be added and this, too, was ground. A little salt and diced white onion would make the salsa ready to eat with fresh flour tortillas. My parents taught me well to appreciate my ancestry, as Aztecs ate hot peppers rich in vitamin C on a daily basis.

Mom was well known to the residents. They also knew that she never came empty-handed. So, as my friends came to say hello, Mom would give them some chorizo (a spicy pork sausage), canned goods (primarily jalapeños), and *novelas* (written versions of soap operas). Dad would bring his own magic. He enjoyed meeting people, giving them one of his hypnotizing smiles. He had a special way of telling stories, mixing actual incidents with outrageous outcomes. Most people would listen attentively, anticipating a wonderful punch line, and finally end up laughing hysterically. Residents and staff always knew when my family was in town.

Promptly at 4:30 p.m. my supper was delivered to my room and the family retreated to the cafeteria. By the time they returned, we were all in a joyous mood. Mom and Dad kept asking me if I liked their surprise visit but had their eyes focused on the long, tree-lined street which led towards the infirmary. It was as if they were expecting someone else from our large extended family to arrive.

At approximately 6 p.m. I heard a familiar voice in the hallway and my parents walked out of the room. They soon came back, escorting four of my high school friends, Reynaldo Godines, Edmundo Ramirez, Juan Cisneros, and Victor Treviño.

Of all the visitors I had at Carville, these four guys were the last I expected. They were nervously giggling at the fact that they had made it this far without any major problems. Their eyes kept shifting all around; they were possibly expecting to be attacked by the residents, who had heard of their arrival and came to do their share of staring. The four of them finally moved towards my bed, hugged me, and asked, "What the shit is this?" They pointed at my leg tent. Their question simply evoked laughter in everyone. It was a while before we became serious enough to explain the lighted tent.

Juan was unpredictable as usual. None of us ever knew when his comments were serious. Thus, when he loudly asked, "Is it safe to be here?," silence permeated the room until Mom nervously started to laugh, and we all joined in. The fact is that he asked the very question that many first-time visitors undoubtedly silently asked themselves.

Dad sternly responded to Juan's question by saying, "¿Estás loco?" ("Are you crazy?") "No hay peligro en este hospital. Es el mejor lugar en el mundo para curar esta enfermedad" ("There is no danger in this hospital. It's the best place in the world for treating this illness"). Then, after a brief pause, he continued, "El miedo es en perderse en los caminos de Louisiana y caerse en un arroyo lleno de lagartos." ("The fear is in getting lost in Louisiana and having your car fall into a ditch full of alligators"). Everyone laughed.

Victor and Edmundo respectfully agreed with Dad and added that their limited knowledge of the bayous was that they were infested with snakes. "Naw," Dad said, "*solamente un tiburón*," only one shark. Again, everyone laughed.

Reynaldo, who had persuaded the other three to make the trip, kept asking about my treatment and the oddity of using lightbulbs to heal my sores. The foursome gave me another surprise. An hour and a half after their arrival, they were ready to party. They had persuaded their parents to give them spending money for their visit to Carville. Their real mission was to visit the French Quarter in New Orleans.

They promised to stop by on their return to Laredo. However, all they could manage was a card saying that they had arrived safely back home. They had run out of money and energy. Their brief visit was one of the best one and a half hours of my stay at Carville, and it gave me a great emotional boost.

My folks could afford to stay for only three days, so on Sunday afternoon they departed for the twenty-hour ride back to Laredo. Their brief visit was just long enough to help me confirm my faith in the magic of family.

Within a week after their departure, the hospital was abuzz with a minis-candal. A social work student had completed a study at the hospital, with a focus on the "rejection rate" by medical and paramedical professionals of seven different illnesses. The respondents in the survey consistently rated leprosy as the disease they would least like to be associated with. In other words, they would reject the person with leprosy, and social workers had the highest mean rejection rate.

This type of information was not readily accepted at Carville. It portrayed flaws in the way the hospital community wished to be perceived—warm, accepting, understanding, and fearless of the disease. Refusing to discuss the findings of the survey, the staff initiated an effort to extinguish the perception that fear of HD could even remotely be considered to exist at the hospital. The survey revealed conflicting attitudes—it was off to work at Carville, just don't associate with anyone who lives at Carville.

In later years, other surveys showed how ignorance of this disease could result in rejection of persons affected by leprosy and fear of infection. In 1980, a Gallup poll found that most people in the U.S. had the greatest fear of leprosy when compared with nine other diseases.

According to the sociologist Erving Goffman, "Stigma is a situation which results in an individual being disqualified from full social acceptance."[2] Unfortunately, society continues to justify stigmatizing people affected by leprosy due, in large part, to references to "lepers" as described in the Bible, but with limited explanations about contemporary leprosy. I developed my own definition of stigma based on personal experiences: an act of rejection, labeling, or unexplained fear of a person or self.

My definition of stigma takes into account that most persons who are stigmatized experience being feared, labeled, *or* rejected. However, persons affected by leprosy are routinely feared, usually for reasons which cannot be quickly explained. The fear leads to a horrible label, defining us as the illness, and then to rejection. The power of ignorance has proven to be riveted to the formation of attitudes.

One person who impressed my parents because of her willingness to socialize with the family and ignore the stigma usually associated with leprosy was Dr. Dickerson's nurse from the Texas Department of Health. Her job was to coordinate follow-up with residents of Texas diagnosed with HD. Her philosophy was that there was no need to perpetuate the existing fear about HD; thus home visits were always made with the consent of families, and she never arrived in a state vehicle with markings on the doors that announced her affiliation with the health department.

This nurse informed my parents that her practice in medicine was to take a holistic approach in understanding the dynamics of emotional healing. Thus, she not only made home visits, but also attempted to socialize with the families. My parents, being overt social butterflies, gladly embraced her visits, and made fresh flour tortillas for her. They also enjoyed taking her to Nuevo Laredo to visit the marketplace, clubs, restaurants, etc. My parents believed that laughter, music, and food could heal any emotional/financial ailment. The nurse from Austin learned to appreciate their philosophy.

In June of 1969, *The Star* published an article about me that focused on the challenges I faced being a resident at Carville and a full-time student at Louisiana State University. The author of the story chose to use an alias rather than my own name, as a way of protecting my identity. Even though I never consented to such an omission, a condensed version was published in a national tabloid. The headline, "Leper Attends School at LSU," was bigger than the story. Someone at LSU saw the article and pasted it on an outside wall at the student union with the warning: "Beware, this guy may be in your class—shoot him." I destroyed the paper as soon as I saw it, never knowing how many people might have read it.

This incident might have been my inspiration to finally publicly scream out, "Enough with this bullshit!" Since I was on thalidomide once again and my legs were healing nicely, I embarked on another academic journey and enrolled in three classes.

One of the classes was called Social Problems. The professor was a recent recipient of his doctorate degree. He was popular with the students because of his teaching style, which included lectures on his personal experiences and discussions on contemporary issues. During one of his lectures, he considered persons with HD, described as "lepers," to be social problems, adding that these individuals are a curse to society because of their impact on medical costs, not to mention "cost to the clergy for making them bells for their necks" as he put it. "Furthermore," he said, "hundreds of them live just down the road in Carville." His comments elicited laughter from my classmates, but anger from me.

With each stabbing word he said, my heart rate and body temperature increased. I could no longer control my anger, and I screamed, "Persons with leprosy are not 'lepers'!" I struggled to have my words keep up with the anger I felt throughout my body. "These persons are not social problems." With a startled but authoritative look, he asked, "And what makes you such an expert?" "Because," I responded, "I am a leper!" Shocked at my own words, I quickly added, in a softer tone, "Because I have Hansen's disease, more commonly known as leprosy." That was the first and last time I have described myself by the "l" word.

My peripheral vision had detected some rapid movement away from me on both sides of my desk. The movement was that of two very pretty, long-legged blondes sitting next to me. These ladies, nameless to me to this date, looked as if their bodies had jumped away from me so fast that their pale skins had stayed stationary, lost in time. Their eyes and mouths were wide open.

The professor stared at me in disbelief, and I felt a strong desire to make a dash for the door and escape from this awkward moment of silence. "Oh," he finally said, "then maybe you can tell us a little bit about this disease." The bell to dismiss the class saved us all from continued embarrassment.

As the students vacated the classroom, the professor requested that I stay and discuss "our problem." He apologized for his comments and asked me many questions about HD, Carville, and my personal experiences. He acknowledged his ignorance and promised to "do better." He explained that his intent was to educate the students as to how society has the unique power to label a person, thing, idea, illness as a social problem, oftentimes unfairly. He agreed that his delivery was "unacceptable" and requested written information on leprosy. I countered by inviting him to visit Carville. He accepted, and a friendship was born.

For the balance of the semester, the professor utilized Carville and its residents as examples of how we all must attack prejudices and social isolation. He became a strong advocate against injustices. The blonde girls never spoke to me and kept their distance for the remainder of the semester.

The ongoing discussions about HD in the classroom gave me the confidence to participate in other activities resulting in change. So, when approached by several residents about running for one of the vacancies on the Patients' Federation, I agreed to place my name on the ballot. To my surprise, I was elected to the federation.

At my first meeting with the other federation members, I was informed that this organization was the residents' link to the hospital's administration. The federation played an important role in the life of the community. It had oversight of the canteen, provided advice on policy, awarded trophies during the annual golf tournaments, ordered movies, and awarded travel stipends to residents on "pass." Considering my age and short time at the hospital, the other members appointed me to an "easy and stress-free" position.

So, as the chairperson of the Entertainment/Recreation Committee for the Patients' Federation, I proceeded to find a way to initiate group activities. When I discussed my ideas with other residents at the cafeteria, one of my eating partners mentioned the wonderful fun everyone had when the residents participated in the Louisiana River League (fast-pitch softball) and won the league championship in 1951.

I discovered that most of the Carville softball team was still living at the facility. Some of the men, then in their late forties, were still willing to play a few games. So, I started to recruit residents and staff to form a team. Some refused to make a commitment to play or even practice unless I had some games scheduled.

Members of the original team refused to travel elsewhere and agreed to play *only* if the game was played on Carville's field. This attitude was a carryover from the times when they were authorized to play in the league, but not allowed to play as "visitors" away from the hospital. In 1951, the Carville softball team, the Point Clair Indians, composed of young men with chronic fevers and ulcers on the feet, wearing thin baseball gloves that provided little protection to hands void of sensation, and ostracized by society won the Louisiana River League Championship. Collectively, the team was able to symbolically reverse a called third strike. If any story deserves a spot at the Baseball Hall of Fame, it is this one.

The 1951 team was composed of a diverse group of four Mexican Americans, three blacks, one Hawaiian, one Samoan, three Japanese Americans, and four whites. Their competitors were teams of either all black or all white players. The opponents' families and guests attending the games at Carville were required to sit only on the visitors' side of the bleachers; desegregation for visitors was practiced in the stands, but residents were still segregated from visitors.

My plan was to find a team from the community. I realized that I did not have to go far to find a quality team, the champs of the LSU Intramural Softball League. The team, primarily students enrolled in the physical education program, accepted the challenge—I had umpired many of their games. Everything was so simple to me. I recalled that, for those growing up in a housing project, anybody with the urge for a sandlot baseball game could easily find someone eager to play. Playing the game of softball as adults, I found out, is not so easy.

I met with the director of recreation services and shared with him my idea about the game set for a Sunday night, when things were usually quiet. My meeting with him occurred on a day when alcohol made him agreeable to almost anything, so he verbally endorsed the game. Unfortunately, several days before the game, the director received a verbal reprimand for authorizing a resident to coordinate a game "with outsiders." The same man who had enthusiastically supported the game pleaded with me to cancel the event. When I refused, he approached my "surrogate father," Darryl Broussard, and claimed that I was misrepresenting the Patients' Federation. He alleged that he never approved the game.

Darryl and numerous other long-term residents never doubted my side of the story, but they were concerned about the fear of change some administrators had, especially if the change was initiated by a resident. Nevertheless, we played a doubleheader twenty years after the Indians had won the Louisiana River League Championship. The first game was a slaughter, but fun. The second game, which the younger, stronger, faster team from LSU let us win, gave us a split, and was watched by over a hundred residents. We had a victory in more ways than one. The groans from aches and pains could be heard throughout the hospital grounds for over a week.

The morale was so high that the complaints about scheduling the games ceased. The director of recreation services did not speak to me for months, but the issue of allowing "outsiders" to visit the hospital would come up again when I was a senior at LSU.

Summers in Louisiana can be brutal. The high temperatures and humidity made days and nights extremely uncomfortable. The heat gave rise to another idea. During Magdalena's Easter week visit, she observed that the weather was already warm, and there was a swimming pool for staff but none for the residents. She thought that this was discriminatory, and so did I.

Possibly because of the hot days and even worse nights, I was not willing to accept bureaucratic responses to the question "Why not a swimming pool for the residents?" And the responses were numerous: none of the residents can swim; unsanitary with so many residents having open sores; not enough interest; cannot afford lifeguards; and too expensive to build another swimming pool.

These excuses piqued my interest. Where was this pool? How come the residents did not know about this secret pool? Well, I found out that the only person who did not know about the staff pool was me. The staff pool was off limits to residents, just as were the staff dining room, staff golf course, staff parking, and staff pews at the churches. I could not find general support among the residents to fight this ridiculous rule of restricting the swimming pool to staff only.

On one especially hot evening, I found two friends willing to fight this rule. They were my age—Roberto from Corpus Christi and Chuy from Reynosa, Mexico. We were also drinking buddies. So, one evening in July, with much courage from several beers, we rode our bicycles to "the staff side," cautiously looking out for the ever-present guards who patrolled the grounds every evening.

We managed to arrive at the pool. A chain-link fence with a padlock surrounded the pool area. Surprisingly, a stepladder had been left leaning against the fence. We took turns climbing the fence, disrobed, and quietly slipped into the pool. Roberto and I were looking at the gray sky, made visible by moonlight, when we heard splashing. Chuy was struggling to stay afloat. We found the incident both funny and frightening. Chuy did not know how to swim, and he was drowning. He was so fascinated with the pool that he forgot about its depth.

Luckily, I had learned how to swim since my near-drowning incident at age thirteen. We both swam over to him and pushed him to the side of the pool, avoiding his flailing arms and hands. Once he made it to the side, we helped to pull him out of the pool. Both of us kept hitting him on the back as if that would save him. Chuy finally brushed us off and said, "Chingado, ya no me peguen!" ("Damn it, stop hitting me!"). We realized how close he had come to drowning, and the fear could only be lessened with laughter. So we laughed hysterically.

We stayed at the pool for approximately one hour, savoring the forbidden fruit. While Roberto and I leisurely and quietly swam, Chuy restricted his activities to getting his feet wet by the edge of the pool. We returned to the "patient side," went to our respective rooms, and slept soundly, with happy grins on our faces.

The three of us realized that we had jointly broken a major barrier at the hospital—separate but allegedly equal status. Unfortunately, we could not scream out our victory, but it was a victory nevertheless.

Others had also experienced silent victories. Men and women had refused to be segregated by sex. Women rejected the practice of giving away their newborns, and instead escaped through the hole and nurtured their babies. Many continued their faith in religion even though religious leaders labeled them as "sinners" when Leviticus became part of the readings during Sunday service. Many refused to give up their name and culture, retaining their identity via language, customs, values, and dress. Many challenged state laws by successfully having a life in their hometowns. Darryl Broussard deceived the federal government by using a small oven that made sounds and smoke but did not actually sterilize money or outgoing mail. Many did not allow their disabilities, in particular their loss of sight, to prevent them from living a productive and happy life. Stanley Stein used his verbal and written skills to initially chip away at and then later forcefully attack the power of ignorance— a quest to eliminate the odious "l" word.

Roberto, Chuy, and I were very proud of our role models.

Ironically, while we had enjoyed a swimming pool for one hour, others back home were utilizing this refreshing activity without having to hide their pleasure. Magdalena signed up for an elective class in swimming; my younger siblings were rewarded for their occasional good behavior by being allowed to swim at the public pool. Javier, my brother, and Beto, Magdalena's brother, successfully completed a lifeguard class, and had earned money to take a dip in the pool and look at girls. What a difference 750 miles made!

July of 1969 was a particularly harsh time for residents. The social work and rehabilitation staffs were instructed to pressure residents with few or no medical limitations to go home. Employees, cognizant of the fact that the hospital's budget was based on bed capacity, i.e., number of residents, silently objected to this new trend.

Until the moment that the facility was returned to the state of Louisiana in 1999, the employees panicked whenever changes were initiated. All were extremely concerned about losing their extra 25 percent hazardous duty pay. The bureaucrats in Washington would walk a tight rope at budget hearings. They emphasized the decline in leprosy cases, but then strongly defended hazardous duty pay because of the "dangers" of working at Carville.

The dilemma of possible discharge gave rise to much paranoia. The residents were concerned about what they had to return to, considering that the families of many long-time residents had stopped waiting for their return. Magdalena likened this dilemma to a wish from Washington administrators to resurrect people already deemed dead by some families. The residents did not see resurrection as a viable option.

The fear of being pushed out of the facility created a wave of compliance. Conformity was seen everywhere. Only a few realized that rights could no longer be taken away at the whim of some bureaucrat; most of these few were individuals assigned apartments or cottages to live in. In an effort to save jobs, the administration quietly resisted the new movement to evict residents by lessening the pressures for discharge. The belief among everyone was that eventually the discharges would occur, regardless of the lack of community resources.

The heat of July seemed to have an impact on the rotating physicians more than anyone else. The doctors would come and go, which forced the residents to constantly educate new staff about the disease. We felt disrespected by administrators because the lack of continuity in staff affected our own general physical and mental health.

Another major event occurred in July. This event—the moon landing—had worldwide implications. Everyone was excited about this historic moment. The administration, acknowledging its significance, instructed the guards who patrolled the grounds at night *not* to lock the TV rooms that were located in the recreation building. These guards carried an object that resembled a square World War II canteen that had a keyhole designed to receive a pencil-like piece of metal, to record the time they were at designated locations (a clock box). They knew all the residents by name and were usually the first to detect if someone was missing, drunk, or dead. They did not carry guns, but their written reports were like bullets to anyone caught at the wrong place at the wrong time.

The night of July 20, 1969, made all of us equal—guards, doctors, nurses, committee chairs, and residents. Many of us stayed up all night, alternately watching TV and walking outside to stare at the bright moon.

The most revered newscaster at the time was Walter Cronkite. So we listened in amazement as he attempted to describe what the astronauts were seeing. He wondered out loud how the craters might have been created, making most of us laugh. We obviously knew about "craters"; they were all over our bodies, and we did not have to fly to the moon to find them. Staying up so late with little sleep made us say things that normally we would not even think about saying.

We finally called it a night when Cronkite was heard around the world to say, "The astronauts will be in quarantine after their return; no one knows what diseases might be on the moon; leprosy might be one of those diseases." His words pained us so much on an evening when everyone was supposed to be rejoicing. One of the residents recalled a similar incident that occurred during the 1937 Giants vs. Yankees championship game when the radio announcer stated, "The umpire is the 'leper' of the game."

We all got up from our chairs in sync, as if choreographed. Once again, a clueless individual had reminded us of our plight at Carville, that the HD bacillus, whether found on earth or on another planet, was an organism to be feared and we were to be isolated from the general populace. We instructed the guards, who silently expressed their disgust at Cronkite with tightly pressed lips, to turn off the TVs and lock the rooms. We walked to our rooms past large cockroaches scurrying for safety, away from our unforgiving feet.

Magdalena, too, was in awe of the achievements made by the space program. However, as she got closer to her twenty-first birthday, she also faced challenges more applicable to everyday living. "Administrators at Texas Woman's University [TWU]," she wrote, "are also taking giant steps like the astronauts by letting us wear pants."

Sarcastically, she wondered if TWU would ever be on the same page as other universities. "What's next, shorts in the classroom, co-ed dorms?" Obviously, Carville was not the only place where changes were slow in coming.

With the summer months coming to an end, I began to plan for a drive to Denton, Texas, in my station wagon. This plan never materialized, as I had another severe reaction. Magdalena called me and found out that I was in the infirmary. She did not hesitate to send me a letter emphasizing again that I should take better care of myself. Having grown weary of constant reactions, I wrote back stating that she worried too much. Typically for Magdalena, she once again lifted my spirits and motivated me to learn more about HD. "The moment I cease to worry about you is the moment I will cease to care."

As the 1969–1970 school year started, Magdalena began her tenure as president of the Laredo Club. There were so many young ladies from Laredo, most from working families, that having a formal club provided a support system away from home and made it affordable to rent a bus at group rates for return trips home on holidays.

Magdalena encouraged me to participate in a school activity as a means of broadening my friendship base outside of Carville. The publication of an article in the *Daily Reveille*, LSU's school paper, helped me to decide on running for the position of president of the Sociology Club for the 1970–1971 school year.

The school paper described members of a losing football team as "lepers." I was angry with the *Reveille* staff, especially with Carville being only twenty miles from the school. So I wrote them a letter to educate them about the offensive connotation of the "l" word. I developed a flyer on my candidacy, distributed copies throughout campus, and won. I immediately scheduled a tour of Carville, and invited staff from the *Reveille* to accompany the group. They declined the invitation, but I was invited to write an article on the tour. Unfortunately, the two-page piece was never published.

I had learned about protocol at Carville when I coordinated the softball game, so I formally requested permission from the director of the hospital to host the tour. Dr. Trautman did not hesitate to authorize the tour and assigned Vernon Bahlinger to handle the details for me.

My confidence level rose with the opportunity to educate many of my peers about HD. Even though I was not scheduled to be sworn in as president until May of 1970, I decided that November of 1969 was a good time for the tour. Two fellow Sociology Club members, Doug Burns and Donna Bunce, agreed to help me with the arrangements. We were unable to secure a bus to transport the twenty-five students and professors who signed up for the tour, but we managed to form a caravan of six cars.

The tour was well covered by *The Star* and *Q.M.*, the hospital newsletter. One thing that was not printed was that I had inadvertently participated in breaking down a forty-eight-year-old rule, i.e., that only staff and visitors were authorized to eat in the staff dining room, located next to the administration building.

The tour, conducted on a Sunday morning, included a film, panel discussion with me and other residents, and lunch. Mr. Bahlinger left after the presentation, believing that after lunch the students would return to Baton Rouge, opening the road for further education of their peers on HD. And so did I.

The students had arranged to stay for lunch, so I escorted them to the staff dining room. Without hesitation, I started to leave, and Donna Bunce, who was from Towsun, Maryland, asked why I was not joining the group for lunch. Not having a logical response, I decided to get in line with them. As I proceeded down the serving line, one of the dining room staff apologetically told me that they could not serve me. I had to go to the "patient dining room." Suddenly, I had a real reason to join my peers for lunch!

The person who was the messenger for the head cook had been recently promoted from a position in the lab to supervisor and was working that weekend to expedite his orientation to a new job. He spoke softly, attempting to keep my colleagues from hearing his plea. I was unsympathetic to his embarrassment. I asked him what would happen if I did go through the serving line. His response: "I'll probably get into a lot of trouble, maybe even lose my promotion." When I asked him what he thought of my predicament he said, "Aw, come on, José, you can break this rule some other day." His dark skin turned pale as I walked away to join my fellow students.

The serving crew reluctantly filled my plate with selected foods. Their hard stares, telling me that their jobs might be in jeopardy, went unnoticed by the students. They never knew that they had just made history. Ironically, the serving crew was primarily black, themselves victims of unfair rules and discrimination.

The staff dining hall is now the National Hansen's Disease Museum and no one is denied entry.

I do not know if the newly promoted supervisor or serving crew was reprimanded, but by Monday morning everyone knew about the incident. There were mixed messages relayed to me by staff and residents that ranged from facial and hand gestures in support of my actions to complete silence, which registered dissatisfaction with my simple act of defiance.

My mother's response was that only God's judgment counted, not man's, "Asi es que no te preocupes" ("So don't worry"). Magdalena called my action "courageous." For months I called it stupid because of the possible consequences to other residents such as loss of some privileges or their jobs. In the end I was not impressed with the food. It was identical to that served in the patients' dining room.

Not long after the breakthrough at the staff dining room, I was confronted with a terrible setback. Mom wrote a lengthy letter describing in great detail how Javier, a senior at J. W. Nixon High School, was excelling on the football field. She said how proud Dad was, especially when he showed up at Shirley Stadium Friday nights and his peers would whisper, "Él es el papá de Javier" ("He is the father of Javier"). I too felt very proud of my little brother.

As always, Mom started her letter with the most positive of news and gradually progressed to less positive information. Her second paragraph described Dad's efforts to get a job. After many years of security at the Laredo police department, he was now constantly struggling to find even part-time employment. With so many young kids at home, this dilemma placed a great hardship on my parents. I felt responsible because, as the oldest son, I had been brought up to understand my role as substitute breadwinner in the event my dad was ill or unemployed. This expectation caused me so much stress that it affected the severity and length of my reactions. My illness and the distance from home prevented me from fulfilling my cultural role. Many times, my continued enrollment at LSU as opposed to having a job at home affected my grades. I was unsure of how to relay accomplishments to Mom and Dad, such as when I was voted president of the Sociology Club. Of what significance was this to my parents when they were struggling with mortgage, food, and other basic needs?

Predictably, Mom closed her letter with the following note: "Estamos muy orgullosos [de Javier], pero Diós nos manda de todo, así es que pedimos que sigas fuerte y no pierdas la fe" ("We are very proud [of Javier], but God sends us a little bit of everything [successes and grief], so that is why we ask you to stay [emotionally] strong and not lose your faith [in God]").

In sharing my despondency over Mom's letter with Magdalena, I mentioned my feelings of failure and desire to move on to another stress-free life. I had contemplated suicide before, but this time I actually had a plan and it scared me.

Magdalena sensed my desperate plea for help and, once again, found the words to help me through this crisis. Magdalena wrote, "La vida es muy preciosa" ("Life is very precious") "y tenemos que hacer lo mejor para preservarla" ("and we must do all we can to preserve it") "y tu vida es la más preciosa para mí" ("and your life is the most precious for me") "déjame ayùdarte a preservarla" ("let me help you to preserve your life"). Magdalena added humor to her very serious letter, stating that she was earning *"mucho"* volunteer dollars. She hoped to use these dollars to buy a jet so that she could fly at a moment's notice to Carville and "slap me" out of my "silly thoughts."

The volunteer dollars she referred to in her letter were related to the work she did at TWU's bicycle shop. Coeds were allowed to rent bicycles for twenty-five cents per hour. They were required to sign a form and list their home address. To her surprise, while scanning the sign-up list, she noticed a home address given as U.S.P.H.S Hospital, Carville, Louisiana. Neither of us was able to figure out who this coed was, except to speculate that she was the daughter of one of the P.H.S staff.

Magdalena's words were magical. It reversed my "poor me" thinking. Luckily, I listened, because in December of 1969, while recovering from another reaction, Sister Joanna, or Sister Jo as many called her, came to my room with a wheelchair. "Get in," she ordered, "we are going for a ride." Sister Jo's orders were not easy to dismiss, so I meekly got in the chair. She wheeled me to the outside corridor into the bright sunlight and a cool breeze. She laughed heartily as I repeatedly asked, "Where are we going?" We ended up in the dreaded training room, where I once had been humiliated when I was forced to disrobe in a room full of strangers, all gawking at my ill body. This time, it was a room full of familiar faces, all applauding as I entered. I was in shock! It was not my birthday and still too early for Christmas. Sister Jo finally said, "Congratulations." Still, I had no clue.

The special services officer came forward and, in an unusually hesitant tone, started to say, "Several people are being recognized for their work." He then asked another person to proceed with the ceremonies. Several staff were mentioned for "outstanding achievement" and presented with plaques, certificates, and a check. I was honored with a "Superior Performance Award" and given a fifty-dollar check, a small fortune for me.

Sister Jo had nominated me for this special award. Surprisingly, my supervisor, the hard-nosed, no-nonsense epitome of a professional, had supported my award. At times, especially during my down times, I envisioned everyone as the enemy. How wrong I was. How sad that my tears would blur my vision, my thinking, my opportunities to enhance and establish friendships.

Another friend who came through for me was Carol Ann Addington, an occupational therapist from Ohio. Carol Ann, a good friend of Sister Jo, offered to give me a ride to Laredo for the week of Christmas. She had never been to Mexico, and having me as an extra driver was ideal for her. It proved to be mutually beneficial, as I was finally able to spend special time with Magdalena—a real Christmas treat for both of us.

Like everyone else who worked or lived at Carville, the friends who gave me support, advice, a nod of the head, a scream, a beer, a ride on a wheelchair, a job, a pat on the back, a kick in the butt left me a better person.

# The Magic of Dreaming

During my early adolescent years, I would respond to stress by limiting my verbal communication and internalizing the stress, which resulted in dreams that had me falling from an airplane. I would always wake up before I hit the ground. The instant I awoke, I felt the sensation of desperation and terror mixed with cold sweat, pulsating heartbeat, and dark silence.

The stress I felt in January of 1970 came from the realization that my return to Carville meant more time away from family, girlfriend and familiar surroundings. Each return trip to Carville resurrected my self-doubts about being a worthy human being. Each return trip to Carville meant being exiled once again. Each return trip to Carville strengthened the belief of my future mother-in-law that I was never coming out to live a normal life ("Nunca va a salir a vivir una vida normal").

In January of 1970, stress and depression saw me falling from the sky nightly. The dreams continued until my attention was redirected to studying for a full load of classes. The depressing thoughts of January carried over to February. I attempted to bury my depressive moods in the TV lounge, glued to the tube.

Other residents at the hospital monitored my grades and time spent watching TV. When they realized that I was not doing well in either area, they established a network to monitor my whereabouts and pressure me to "go study."

Their efforts certainly contributed to my improved grades and disposition. The positive impact, however, did not occur immediately. It was weeks before their group efforts took effect. I continued to experience roller coaster rides where I faced mounds of ignorance about leprosy that often resulted in an attack on our dignity.

On the morning of February 19, Hugh Downs of the TV show *Today* interviewed Dr. Stanley Browne, a highly respected physician in the field of leprosy. During the few moments that he spoke to Dr. Browne, he said "leper" seven times. In each instance, Downs made grotesque facial expressions and simulated body shivers that automatically occur when one is faced with fear or horror. Friends at LSU and Laredo, who knew of my living at Carville, could only focus on Downs's extreme fear of the disease. He was totally oblivious to Dr. Browne's comments about treatment and about how most of the world's population is immune to the bacillus. Hugh Downs never responded to my request, or *The Star*'s, to educate his audience about HD.

To my horror, country singer Johnny Cash sang a newly composed song. The lyrics said, "Christ cured the lepers and the lame." His face portrayed a message of sin and tragedy. Johnny Cash also did not respond to my letters.

Two days later, the Smothers Brothers had a comic on their show who thought it would be a good idea to imitate a person with HD. He grossly mimicked loss of limbs, stone throwing, and facial disfigurement. The alleged joke was crude and cruel. I did not bother sending the brothers a letter.

February was a time of much anger for me. So many individuals started to have wide access to the public via television, and the public's endless hunger for "jokes" that centered on drugs, alcohol, and depression—and leprosy—resulted in the constant labeling of my family at Carville, and perpetuated my anger.

Jokes, labeling, rejections, isolation all pointed toward trouble for me. The reading of Leviticus ("Aaron the priest shall . . . pronounce the leper unclean") during Mass triggered a wildfire effect on my emotions.[1]

No longer could I simply stand still and internalize my anger. No longer could I watch as my family at Carville tightly closed their eyes in a squinting manner in an unsuccessful effort to block out the constant use of the "l" word. No longer was I willing to accept the principle of "equal but separate" whereby staff and residents would sit at opposite extremes at the hospital's Sacred Heart Catholic Church. The church was built in 1934 with a fifty-one-thousand-dollar gift from the Catholic Church Extension Society and blessed by the archbishop of New Orleans. According to the *Baton Rouge Advocate*, one hundred visitors attended the ceremonies, as well as "75 of the leper patients . . . [who] . . . stood behind a barrier separating them from the visitors."

The church has a unique "T" design. From the outside, with its reddish-looking brick and the pastor's small cottage and garden to its side, the church looks like a box. Walking inside and seeing the stained glass windows which depict biblical scenes gives the visitor an entirely different perspective. Anyone flying over the church can see the design of a cross.

The four-hundred-seat church faced the large power plant. Visitors from the outside and residents who drove to the church would park on the small lot blanketed with white seashells. The entrance would allow the visitor to God's home to view the elevated altar, the huge cross made of cedar, the high ceiling, stained-glass windows, and two rows of pews flanking the middle aisle leading toward the altar.

The church extended to the left with more pews and an automatic sliding door that led to the covered walkways. The architect had creatively blended in the needs of people in self-propelled wheelchairs and bicycles. The Protestant chapel, thirty feet from the Catholic church, was also connected in the same manner. I loved this ingenuity. It was done decades before the first President Bush signed the Americans with Disabilities Act in 1990.

To the right of the altar, more pews were arranged in a similar manner. The door to this side of the church was used exclusively by staff and the Sisters of Charity. They had a very good view of a life-size canvas of the Virgin of Guadalupe painted by one of the talented residents, John Karver. Persons of Mexican ancestry outnumbered all other ethnic groups, making the painting very appropriate.

The serenity and beauty of the Sacred Heart Catholic Church masked the practice of having all residents sit to the left of the altar, while guests and staff sat on the right. Additionally, Father Kelly used two chalices to administer communion.

The short landing next to the altar, where everyone would kneel to receive communion, was made of marble. Someone had taken that into account and made two large cushions in quarter round shapes that were flush to the wooden railings that surrounded the altar. One of the cushions was for the residents, and the other for staff and visitors.

This beautiful church, uniquely designed to meet the needs of the residents, also met the needs of staff unwilling to abandon the practice of segregation. Father Kelly would start communion on his left and stop at the middle of the altar where the cushion ended and then start on his left all over again until he had administered communion to all staff. Then he would change chalices and repeat the procedure to his right, where the residents sat in the pews or in their wheelchairs. Father Kelly repeated the practice that other priests had started before him, probably as requested by some hospital administrator.

On the last Sunday in February my anger compelled me to do something drastic about this archaic practice. The anger that had been brewing inside me gave me the courage to confront this unfair practice, but I was unprepared for the consequences.

Sister Jo was the first nun at Carville I learned to trust as a friend. She was the first nurse I learned to respect, as she shared my thoughts and ideas. I learned to confide in her as well as express my desire to challenge the practice of "separate but equal." She had a wonderful sense of humor and would respond to my innocent questions with answers such as: "Of course I do not shave my head," or "Yes, I can leave the order and still be allowed to have communion," and "Sure I can have kids if I leave the order."

She had volunteered to type one of my college papers while I was recuperating from a reaction. Many of my writings focused on the hospital as a community, hypothetical support groups, and general fears of mine and those of the public. Sister Jo knew my feelings about the hospital; so on the morning that I planned to challenge "the practice," I shared my intentions with her. Sister Jo smiled, shrugged her shoulders, gave me her thumbs up, and gestured as if closing a zipper on her lips. This silent support gave me the false impression that everyone else who resided or worked on the station was also screaming for change. Unfortunately I was way off base with this assessment.

Father Kelly was known for his punctuality in starting Mass, and this Sunday was no exception. I purposely arrived at 9:05 a.m., entered through the main doors, and walked along the wall to the right of the church's "T" where nuns and staff usually sat.

One of the hospital's surgeons was sitting in the front pew. As I walked toward the pew on the staff side, I sensed the razor-sharp stare of his eyes following my movement. Suddenly I felt the heat of stares coming from the front, sides, and back. Father Kelly's face started to turn colors—pink and then flush red. I took the only seat available, in the front pew. The Mass continued slowly, and so did the stares. As the Mass progressed, Father Kelly and others occasionally took a peek in my direction. As communion got closer, I wondered if I was doing the right thing. I started to perspire.

The time for communion arrived. As was customary, Father Kelly started to administer communion to the staff side using the staff chalice. Nuns on the pew to the right went to kneel at the altar as an indication that they were ready to receive the body of Christ by accepting the host offered by the priest. I followed them to the altar and also kneeled.

In the silence of the church, I heard Father Kelly slowly, very slowly, administer communion to those ahead of me: "The . . . body . . . of . . . Christ." His slow movement was obviously intentional, an attempt to give me the opportunity to flee and avoid embarrassment. He probably was wondering what to do when he arrived at my spot. Should he skip me, change the chalice, or administer communion from the staff chalice?

To my left, the hospital surgeon made sure that his wide body touched mine, expanding his arms so that I could feel his elbow in my ribs. He also kept clearing his throat, sending me messages of his disapproval of my intentions.

Father Kelly finally arrived and stared at me. He hesitated, processing in his mind what to do. Father LaFontaine, who was serving as his assistant, helped in making the decision to have me receive communion as he placed the communion paten under my chin. Father Kelly stared at Father LaFontaine, then at me, and in a reluctant manner, slowly moved his hand towards me with the host between his right thumb and index finger.

I opened my mouth, anticipating the host. Father Kelly said, "Body of Christ." I said, "Amen," and one of the decades-long practices at Carville came to an end.

Father Kelly continued with communion, using one chalice until he ran out of bread, and then he used the patient chalice. I felt victorious and afraid at the same time—victorious in that I had been an active participant in initiating change and afraid because my upbringing in Laredo emphasized status quo, not change. My fear was related to not knowing what to expect from my adopted community.

The unknown became clear to me when I exited the church through the left side of the T—the patient side. Normally, people would greet each other, discuss the weather or their plans for the remainder of the day. Hoping for some sign of support from my peers, I encountered silence. The other residents were reluctant to make eye contact with me, much less respond to my attempts to receive a greeting. The only noises in the narrow walkway were from the quick steps of feet, the fast rotation of bicycle tires, and the squeak of self-propelled wheelchairs. No human sound was heard.

My shoulders sank deep into my chest. I slowly turned back and reentered the church, by now vacated of all parishioners. I sensed the bottom of my glasses getting wet from tears. I realized that I was standing in front of the altar, feeling hollow inside. I looked up at Christ on the cross, and softly asked, "Por qué?" ("Why?"). "No ves que usando dos copas es mal?" ("Don't you realize that using two chalices is wrong?")

Suddenly, the spotlights directed at the cross came on and for an instant I thought I saw a smile on the face of Christ. Father Kelly had turned on the lights to the altar as he exited from the back room. With a gentle and compassionate look on his face, a side of him I had never seen, he said, "It's not often that he has smiled in this house," and retreated to his cottage.

Father Kelly had never articulated a word of praise or encouragement to me, but now, in the presence of God, he had complimented me. My tears stopped and as I left the church I moved slowly, lightly touching the brick that ran the length of the wall, and walked directly into the bright sunlight. I felt reenergized.

For the next month I received a mixture of angry stares, confusing questions, compliments couched in caution, and encouragement to continue with other challenges. The only commonality to the reactions was that there was no consensus on consequences for my behavior. Residents and staff alike, according to rumor, were divided on my future, which ranged from banishment to apologies; I was seen as a hero or loser, troublemaker or stupid, sinister or innocent.

Darryl was the elder chosen to deliver the verdict for my actions. He and Mary Ruth invited me to lunch after Mass approximately one month after the communion incident. During the recital of grace before we ate he said, "Lord, thank you for giving us life and happiness on this planet and forgive us when we act stupidly in your house, but continue to give us the courage to seek *new* horizons." The other guests at the table, Mary Ruth, Albert Landry, and Milton Grossenbacher, said a loud "Amen" and laughed heartily at the message.

The communion incident was never spoken about again until I mentioned it at the 1994 centennial celebration—by then it was a minor footnote in the history of this century-old lady known simply as Carville.

Darryl was not new to the battle of change. In 1953 as president of the Patients' Federation he used the Baton Rouge media and a patient boycott to oust Dr. Gordon as director of the hospital. Dr. Gordon initiated policies that restricted contact with staff and relatives, and this greatly offended and angered the residents.

Mom was so surprised with what I had done, as if I had committed a great sin against the church, that she took drastic measures to save me, *salvarte*. She understood the rigid rules of the hospital and was willing to challenge them herself, but challenging the church was equivalent to questioning her strong faith. Considering that I was now a man, *un hombre*, she could not threaten me with physical pain, but she could contribute towards my soul cleansing. So she made *una promesa*, a promise, on behalf of all my siblings to attend the 6:30 a.m. Mass, a major sacrifice for such a large family with kids of varying ages. My siblings did not learn until years later that Mom's *promesa* was related to my actions 750 miles away.

Magdalena was struggling too much with her own "extreme feelings of sadness" to respond to my actions other than to write, "I'm surprised Father Kelly did not croak." The continued isolation, uncertainty about her future after graduation, and ongoing pressures from her mom to terminate our relationship combined to have her "seriously consider" sending me a "Dear John letter." "Why," she asked, "must we punish ourselves with thousands of written words and hundreds of miles of distance?" Both of us felt the strain and challenge of love via long distance.

We exchanged letters and shared similar thoughts. We missed each other, desired each other's company, and made a pact that if we were to terminate our relationship, we would do it in person, not by letter or telephone. We learned to share the bad times along with the good, tightening the bonds of our relationship each time we communicated with each other.

Before we realized it, May was upon us and final exams stared at us. The "environmental stress" described by Dr. Bauschard months before came to knock on my door again, and resulted in a 103 degree fever and readmission to the infirmary. Unfortunately, this visit forced me to miss Rudy and Javier's graduation from high school on May 29, and Magdalena's college graduation on May 31.

Having missed Magdalena's graduation and now void of stress from finals, I was not about to skip her birthday. So I went to Laredo via Greyhound bus during the first week in August of 1970. Our reunion opened up opportunities to again rekindle our love and renew our commitment to each other. There is no substitute for face-to-face contact. Magdalena had natural beauty, a compassionate heart, a sympathetic ear, beautiful legs, a wonderful laugh, high motivation to succeed, and a unique ability to socialize with just about anyone. This gal was for me, and I knew she would one day be my wife.

Both of us were anxious to find out about her new life as a student at the University of Texas at Arlington's Graduate School of Social Work. Magdalena was the first person in either family, Santos or Ramirez, to graduate from junior college and college, and now she was ready for postgraduate studies. I was so proud of her. We were all proud of her.

My brother Rudy and I traveled to Arlington with her so I could see her new home for the next two years. She had searched and found a roommate, Ann, from Hong Kong. Ann introduced her to Asian culture, and Magdalena, in turn, taught her about Mexican American customs and values.

Magdalena was also introduced to two things she had never seen before, female students walking around braless and people drinking beer in public. She wrote to me in one of her many letters, "I don't know if I will ever have the courage to do that." We were both starting to be introduced to things we had only read about.

Magdalena additionally had the good fortune to see and hear the opinions of Mexican American leaders, something I could only dream would occur at LSU. The entire country was engaged in a rekindling of social justice and community organization. Predictably, "the establishment," viewed as anyone older than thirty, was calling for the control of "outside agitators." My own thoughts about justice had been aroused by circumstances very close to home. One such passion dealt with the labeling of persons and outright racism. My enrollment at LSU introduced me to openness about racism which frightened me.

It would be another year before I walked in the shoes of a black person and was called "nigger" while taking the infamous experimental drug called B-663, which darkened the skin. However, I had already felt the sting of being labeled "spic," "greaser," and "wetback" while doing migrant work, "alien" when registering at LSU, and "leper" when people knew of my residence or diagnosis. The sting of all those labels and others painfully resurfaced when students closely aligned with the Ku Klux Klan described those of us with leprosy as "unworthy survivors" on earth. It was difficult to recover from such wounds.

The labeling from fellow classmates at LSU came at the "Soapbox" located next to the student union. The Soapbox at one time was just that, and it was set up to allow students the opportunity to speak their views. One person frequently used this venue to speak the views of the Ku Klux Klan (KKK). The Bible was usually cited to justify the racist and discriminatory statements made by their spokesperson.

I tried, unsuccessfully, to give a rebuttal to the painful comments made. However, since I had had little practice in public speaking, my words were filled with angry emotions and were ineffective with the primarily white audience. I decided to counter the dreadful views of the KKK by speaking to other classmates about HD on an individual basis. Some day, I would say to myself, I will be able to educate large groups.

Both of our mental states took a dramatic turn for the better during the Thanksgiving holidays in 1970 when Magdalena came to Carville for five days. The initial plan was for me to travel to Dallas, but that changed when I had a minor bout with the flu, and the doctors were predicting that I would have another reaction. Magdalena flew to Baton Rouge, as she had the last time after I saved my change and bought a ticket on Trans-Texas Airways.

Magdalena, as always, made everything around her look brighter, lovelier, and more serene. She looked like a shining star, so beautiful, waving her long, delicate fingers as she deplaned. Her presence and beauty simply obscured all of the other passengers and ground personnel. I felt so lucky to be loved by a woman with her beauty, warmth, and compassion. No challenge was too great whenever she was around. My heart would ache even more for a permanent return to my beloved Texas.

The residents and the staff acknowledged Magdalena positively as she engaged them in genuine conversation. She always had the skills of a good social worker, making eye contact, listening attentively, and gently giving warm handshakes and/or *abrazos* (hugs).

Both of us were short on funds, so we had planned on spending most of our time on the hospital grounds. These plans changed as a result of an accident I had with a cow the night before her arrival. As I was returning to the hospital from LSU at around 9 p.m., a black cow ran onto the road and I hit her. The cow was killed instantly, and the car sustained substantial damage. The state trooper who investigated the accident said I was very fortunate that it was not a horse. With its longer legs, a horse would have rolled over on its side towards the windshield and possibly caused me serious injury.

I also found out from the trooper that Louisiana has one law related to animal-auto accidents, but with two different consequences. Depending on where the accident occurs, the driver can be held liable (north Louisiana). Luckily it happened in south Louisiana.

On the day that Magdalena arrived, we drove to the home of the cow's owner. He lived on the back side of the hospital in a beautiful, white, two-story home with large columns. The gentleman greeted us out front and invited us for coffee by his pool. A black woman in a black and white uniform brought us coffee on a large silver tray. We felt as if we were on a movie set and were speechless as his beautiful blond wife with her expensive jewelry came to say hi. The gentleman apologized for the accident and gave me a check to cover repairs and "other inconveniences." Magdalena and I used the extra money to visit New Orleans and treat ourselves to a nice dinner. Our carefree reunion ended when she boarded a Greyhound bus bound for Dallas.

December was a short month for both of us. The first three weeks were very intense with schoolwork. Surprisingly, even though I felt very weak, I did not get a reaction. It was the first December in five years that I had celebrated Christmas fever-free.

Julia Rivera and her five kids were going to visit her family for the first Christmas since she became the first ex-resident employed by the federal government at Carville. Considering the long drive and the stress of transporting a small army of children, she offered to give me a ride to McAllen, Texas, provided that I help with the driving. I quickly accepted her invitation and called Magdalena and my parents to inform them of my plans.

I knew her kids, and wanted to take on the big brother role I had missed while in Louisiana. So, before departure, I insisted that they all go to the bathroom because "we will not stop once we get on the road." I sounded like Mr. R. who had previously driven me to Laredo, and the kids obediently ran to the bathroom. Unfortunately, I did not empty my bladder like everyone else, so within a half hour I had to stop at the first service station that came into view. The kids could not control their giggles and said, "We will not stop." I was not amused, but eventually joined in on the laughter.

I also wanted to show my manly authority and insisted that I drive all night. We departed at approximately 8 p.m., but I did not plan on the fact that I had had an exhausting and sleepless twenty-four hours finishing up on my exams. Additionally, I had taken a double dose of thalidomide, as I was still on 400 mg daily and had missed my afternoon blue capsule. I therefore had to make another stop so that Julia could take over the driving. I woke up six hours later in Houston. I did manage to assist with the driving to McAllen. Four hours after boarding a bus in McAllen, I was in Laredo.

I was exhausted from the long trip, but the two weeks in Laredo were the best I had experienced since becoming a resident at Carville. Fortunately, I did not have any aches and pains, fevers or reactions. However, the high dose of prednisone (steroids) dramatically affected my mood swings.

During the mornings when I took my daily dose of white pills, I felt energized and happy, and was, in Magdalena's words, "warm, caring and compassionate." However, as the effects of the steroids dwindled, so did my desire to do much of anything, and, according to Magdalena, I looked "depressed" and became "cold and rude." With all the ups and downs of my medications, I wondered if I would ever escape them. It was difficult experiencing so many mood swings, especially when I was with the woman I loved.

Magdalena's shy demeanor was what originally attracted me to her, because I was challenged to use my communication skills rather than my athletic skills to have her even consider going on a date. I admired her conservative upbringing and her strength in avoiding the temptations of poverty, such as joining a gang. However, our lengthy separation and her lonely nights in an all-girl dorm had opened up opportunities for her to become more verbal. This newly discovered strength both saddened and excited me. Where, I would ask, has my Magdalena gone? But I also loved her courage to tell me what was on her mind.

I was, however, at a loss to explain why I felt so "up" one moment and then so "down" a short time later. Those ups and downs led us to discuss our future and whether it would be a joint future. Both of us wanted to experience marital harmony and financial success. However, my mood swings and the detour I was forced to take in completing my education were not adding up to a successful future. Steroids, I was convinced, would not rule my future.

Our conversations at the conclusion of the year 1970 steered more and more towards our strong faith in having dreams magically transformed into reality. Thus we entered the new year with a renewed passion for joint success.

# The Power of Motherly Love

"What short intervals we've spent together," wrote Magdalena after the holidays. "Let's highlight the happy moments over the sad ones." The "sad ones" related to still another confrontation with her mother about our relationship. Her mom had complained about being ill all through the holidays, but her one visit to a physician ruled out any type of illness that would require medication. Magdalena's aunt from Monterrey, *Tía* Maria, described her sister's illness to Magdalena as *"una enfermedad de ser madre, con dolor en el corazón,"* an illness related to being a mother, a pain of the heart. Other aunts would encourage Magdalena to listen to God for guidance, emphasizing bibilical passages that mentioned children's obedience to their parents.

Magdalena visited her bedridden mother and asked what she could do to make her feel better. Her mom responded by stating that she could never feel better as long as she worried about Magdalena's future. She did not hesitate to share with Magdalena her fear of *la enfermedad*, the illness, and what it could do to Magdalena when, not if, she contracted the disease.

Magdalena and I both felt the painful sting of loneliness. We had thought, far too many times to guess the number, that our relationship was constantly challenged because of a grossly misunderstood disease and the never-ending search for new knowledge, new experiences, and a new life that did not involve waiting. Delayed gratification had been part of most of our existence, due, somewhat, to our parents' limited incomes and hungry younger siblings. Delayed gratification, in the arena of love, was not something we wished to confront within our lives. So, we had agreed to part ways *if* we ever felt that the battle of loneliness and separation was not one we had the energy to continue fighting.

Her mother cried *con mucho sentimiento*, with much sentiment, as she lay in bed begging Magdalena to please, *por favor*, end our relationship. Magdalena, pulled by her mother's uncompromising love and my unconditional love, made a quick decision. She believed that her mom's obsession with the myths of HD would eventually negatively affect her physical health. Magdalena could not live with the thought that she might contribute to her mother's incapacitated state.

Magdalena painfully described how she, "with tears pouring out," informed her mother that we had ended our relationship. Realizing that she was forced to make such a painful statement, she felt "empty and distant" from her mother. However, she strongly believed that she had to do this, sacrifice our relationship, in order for her mom to find the strength, the motivation, to get back on her feet. My beautiful, wonderful girlfriend had symbolically slit her wrists for her "mom's sake" in order to give her life. "Please," she begged in her letters, "do not judge her like others have judged you because of HD."

I cried for most of January, reading Magdalena's letters nightly, wondering if I would ever see her again. I was angry with Magdalena's mother, but I promised not to judge her. Some of my siblings and my own mother suspected that Mrs. Santos objected to our relationship. However, they kept their thoughts secret and never spoke harshly of her.

January of 1971 was a time when Magdalena's and my emotions were flooded with confusion about what to do with our futures. We eventually concluded that God had presented us with this enormous challenge in order to appreciate the never-ending love of a mother and to see the potential of our love.

Magdalena continued to feel the pain of her words and actions, imagining death as a way to end the pain. She struggled to stay focused at school and wrote a "Dear John" letter, which she never mailed. Nevertheless, her sense of guilt was evident in her letters. She talked about "ending it all," but said, "Soy canalla para buscárla" ("I am a coward to seek it [death]"). Feeling very alone in Arlington, she sought refuge in my letters. My telephone calls and words could not console her, but my previous letters gave her the strength she needed to move forward.

There were times since my arrival at Carville that I had contemplated suicide, but had always managed to overcome such dark thoughts. Support from others, love of family, and faith in God had helped me deal with my loneliness. Magdalena slowly regained her bright outlook on life and recovered enough to start sending me intimately seductive letters. Ahh, I thought, she's back.

Magdalena came to visit me as I was starting to get my darkest color from the B-663. With predictable charm, she joked about my "tan," but never exhibited a difference in behavior. "I know the color of your skin is not important."

Well, many of Louisiana's residents did not agree with her. During a quick visit to New Orleans, I was verbally abused by some tourist-looking types at Jackson Square and refused service at a bar in the French Quarter; Magdalena was insulted when she was yelled at as a "white witch going with the nigger." We departed New Orleans, and I returned only when others were with us.

Each incident related to the color of my skin and illness generated much anger and fear. I heard from residents and black employees how they constantly faced the challenges of harsh squinting stares and assumptions that they were involved in some form of illegal activity. Wearing the shoes of a black person gave me the courage to emulate their pride and strength by not allowing hatred to drown my dreams for a better life.

Many of the older residents had their own tales of social injustice and treatment that questioned their presence on this earth. They, too, were role models for me. Their hearts were heavy with the pain caused by insensitive people, but they still encouraged me to continue my exposure to the outside world.

The stresses of school, Magdalena's ongoing battles with her mother, conducting meetings of the Sociology Club, the pending graduation of my close and special friends like Donna Bunce and Doug Burns, and my change in skin color due to B-663 forced me to stay in my room more and more.

Due to the peaks and valleys I had felt during my reactions and, at times, the need to request either an "Incomplete" or "Drop" from some classes, my graduation would not occur until August of 1971.

In April, I formally applied for admission to the graduate school of social work in the fall. Looking at Vernon Bahlinger as a role model, and dreaming that I could some day work at the hospital, I asked Vernon for a recommendation. He gave me an enthusiastic one and diplomatically described my "social actions." He wrote: "He has awareness, although sometimes subjective, of changes that need to be brought about in the hospital environment, which would attribute to the therapeutic goals of patient care. This type of social action has, at times, been in conflict with the attitudes of some of the staff, but Mr. Ramirez has handled the situation well."

At the same time that I applied to graduate school, I also requested financial assistance from Mike Garcia, my counselor at Texas Vocational Rehabilitation. My chances of funding, I was told, were "slim." A master's degree was considered a luxury by TVR; plus Mr. Garcia believed that I was close to discharge.

Funding was approved after I received my acceptance letter from LSU. However, approval came at a price. I had received a mixed blessing: projection from Dr. Bauschard that my hospitalization and ultimate cure "might not be for three to five years," and funding for one year only (the graduate program is sixty hours or two years).

The residents and staff started to congratulate me approximately six months before I graduated. The residents gave me support as if a family member had accomplished the impossible. In my opinion, they were rooting for something they might have achieved if isolation and ostracism had not been so rampant at the time of their admission to Carville. I was on my way to achieving *our* dream.

Soon after completing her first year of graduate school at the University of Texas at Arlington, Magdalena found a summer job in Wichita Falls, located in the Texas panhandle. Prior to starting her job, she decided to visit her family in Laredo and share with her mom that we had "renewed" our relationship.

Magdalena wrote that the meeting with her mom "frightened her." Her mom, without emotion, had said, "Si sigues con él, espera la terminación de apoyo del corazón" ("If you continue with him, you can expect an end to [my] emotional support"). "I can do it alone," Magdalena wrote, "with many tears."

I was not physically with Magdalena to wipe away her tears, but I mailed her a bouquet of flowers with a note saying, "Deseo que las rosas puedan iluminar tu día" ("I hope the roses can brighten your day"). Magdalena kept the rose petals as a reminder that each day is different, and pain can be diminished with love.

Even though I visited Magdalena briefly during one weekend in Wichita Falls, the crushing loneliness she felt was evident in her letters: "I feel as if I sleep in the darkest of caves and wake to find the gloom and gray of fog during the day."

I wrote words of encouragement, made telephone calls to reassure her that our future together would be bright, and mailed homemade cards. However, it was the love of and acceptance by her mother that she sought. She confessed to going on dinner dates with some male friends from work, explaining that she simply needed company. While I was not fully accepting of this, I understood her sorrow and did not complain.

"I need you there," she said, "next time I visit Mom." How tragic, I imagined, that the final days some people had with their loved one was spent arguing with their mothers as their spouse, sibling, lover was being forced to go to Carville. How horrible, I thought, that they were not able to make a choice about their lives. How shameful it would be if we, Magdalena and I, did not stay together because of her mother's misunderstanding about HD.

So, without telling Magdalena, I wrote a lengthy letter to her mom. I emphasized how well my treatment was progressing, and quoted doctors and researchers about how most people are immune to the HD bacillus. I added pictures of the hospital and facts about Louisiana in general. I also included articles on the disease translated into Spanish by fellow residents Ymelda and Julia Rivera. I closed with an invitation to my graduation, set for August 6, 1971. Mrs. Santos never responded, but she did write to Magdalena about the letter, and stated, "Entiendo un poco más" ("I understand a little better"). Magdalena was elated and mailed me "a thousand kisses." We believed that we were on our way to creating some positive change in how Mrs. Santos viewed leprosy.

Graduation from LSU was an exhilarating experience. Parents, many of my siblings, and some of my nephews came to an event that proved to be very hot and confusing.

Graduation used to be held in the Agricultural Building, affectionately known by the students as "The Cow Palace" and LSU basketball fans as "The Home of Pete Maravich." (Pete, of course, was the legendary basketball player who was elected to the NBA Hall of Fame.) The ceremonies included a lengthy procession of graduates and an even longer procession of speakers and politicians. Graduation became official when we were asked to stand up and symbolically accept our diplomas. Only those who received doctoral degrees were allowed to go on stage for a handshake from the university president.

The structured activities did not lessen my excitement or my family's enthusiasm. Dad gave a loud and lengthy whistle from the bleachers. His whistle was similar to the song of a bird. This was a whistle we had all grown to recognize as children; it had a unique emphasis, length, and pitch. He used the whistle to call us for supper, get our attention, point out something we were doing wrong, or to praise us.

Upon our return to the hospital, the compliments continued, some with a simple nod and others, as with Hiram from Cuba, including a loud yell and embrace. Collectively, the Daughters of Charity and Father Kelly, representatives of an institution that I had both sought comfort from and rebelled against, were probably the most complimentary of the diploma from LSU. This group gave me something I had never owned. They gave me a Bible.[2] I cried as soon as I realized what it was, looked at my parents and said, "Ven, esto significa que Diós no los está castigando con mi enfermedad" ("See, this signifies that God is not punishing you through my illness"). The whole family cried.

After graduation, I went to Laredo briefly prior to starting graduate school. My acceptance to graduate school was on a part-time basis, due, in large part, to my "unstable medical condition," i.e., chronic reactions. The part-time status was not an issue for me, as I knew how hard Bob Miller, Vernon Bahlinger, Mike Garcia, and others had worked on my behalf. It was up to me to turn this wonderful opportunity into a success and, I hoped, pave the road for others to follow.

Magdalena and I, as usual, spent much time together. Her pending return to school resurrected her energies, and my entrance into a new experience made me nervous. We attempted not to talk about the barriers to marriage, and chose to highlight all of the positives instead. Our discussions led to a basic conclusion; we had the love, desire, and time to seriously consider marriage. I had already decided that I would offer myself in marriage, so these talks solidified my plans.

On an August evening, not too long after her twenty-third birthday, we drove to a secluded part of Lake Casa Blanca. All young lovers in Laredo knew this lake. We had visited this site many times during our high school years. On this particular evening, we found ourselves alone on one of the highest peaks that encircle the lake, which offered us the best view of the water. There was a cool breeze blowing from the east, unusual for Laredo in hot August. The full moon was directly in front of us, and it illuminated a spectacular view.

I asked Magdalena to step outside so that we could admire the scenery. I then got on one knee and quickly fell on my side. I had placed my knee on a rock with sharp edges and cut it. A romantic moment had turned into slapstick comedy.

Magdalena obviously realized what I was attempting to do and tried very hard to keep a solemn face and not giggle. I do not recall the words of my proposal of marriage, but she tearfully accepted. "Ahora," she said, "tenemos que trabajar en cuando van a ir tus papases a pedir por mi mano" ("Now we must plan on when your parents will formally ask my parents for my hand in marriage"). We sighed, embraced, and silently thought about this precious moment, and not the future.

Upon my return to Carville, I was welcomed with a flood of appointment slips. Dr. Hull explained that TVR had requested a thorough review of my medical status. I assumed that Mike Garcia was being pressured by his supervisors in Austin to continue to justify financial assistance for me. I complied with all of the usual tests, including blood work, skin scrapings, P.T., O.T., etc.

During the last four months of 1971, our letter writing dramatically increased, as did our bouts of depression. School studies kept both of us occupied, but we still struggled to find a resolution to the fear of the illness felt by Mrs. Santos. Magdalena got to the point of refusing to call home because of the crying spells her mother would have. Magdalena felt so exasperated and "angry" at me for putting her "through hell." She wrote, "How can I love you so much? . . . The more I love you, the more pain I feel."

Life at Carville was very monotonous and predictable. My escape from the monotony was to bury myself in studies, read voraciously, and save every piece of change so that I could visit Magdalena on long weekends. Thus, the pain I caused Magdalena because she was now my fiancée was occasionally lessened by my physical presence. With me by her side, she could easily confront me about the pain I caused her, and then relieve the sting with warm embraces.

At the beginning of December, I became acutely ill with another reaction, exacerbated by dusky red lesions. Dr. Hull expressed doubts that I would ever finish my graduate studies because of the ongoing bouts with the stubborn bacillus. I was readmitted to the infirmary and encouraged to request an "Incomplete" for one of my courses. I was sleeping so much with the high fevers that I could not stay awake long enough to study. So, in consultation with Vernon, I again requested and received an "I" for one of my courses. Luckily, I recovered enough before Christmas to take a special exam and completed the course with an A.

I received a belated graduation present from the Mexican Club, one similar to another gift two years earlier—a round-trip bus ticket to Laredo, so I celebrated the New Year with family and Magdalena.

My siblings were getting older and wiser. With four sisters either married or on the edge of marriage, only two remained to face the demands of my six brothers. My exposure to the world of semi-independence and semi-institutional living had given me a different perspective on responsibility.

Mom's upbringing had been focused on meeting the needs of the head of the household, i.e., my father. The proper training of my sisters for their ascribed role involved the expectation that they were to meet the needs of their brothers. In essence, they were to pick up after them, wash and iron their clothes, cook and wash their dishes.

I felt a responsibility to lead my brothers to become a little more independent and not to rely on women to cater to them. Unfortunately, their everyday existence did not allow them the opportunity to practice independent living skills. The influence of male dominance was too strong. They did, however, listen attentively to me, with blank stares. They had no clue about the points I was attempting to make.

The evening prior to our leaving Laredo, we had been at my parents' home enjoying a *carne asada*. Since I had agreed to help Magdalena drive to Arlington, we decided to leave the party early.

After helping Magdalena drive her Chevy back to Arlington, I hopped on a plane to Baton Rouge. Darryl and Mary Ruth were patiently waiting to give me a lift back to Carville. On the ride back, Mary told me how much she enjoyed being my second mother.

Both sets of mothers were always giving me a lift somewhere or out of somewhere, as in out of debt, out of self-pity, out of depression. Both mothers made great sacrifices on my behalf. The two mothers magically appeared, spiritually if not physically, whenever Magdalena needed some assistance.

Magdalena's dad came from a family of large people and receding hairlines. He and his siblings faced many hardships and therefore were unwilling to accept any form of defeat. This attitude is probably what gave Magdalena her stubborn nature. Mr. Santos and his siblings were abandoned by their mother, but they all lived into their eighties. Mr. Santos had a limited formal education, but he was a genius when it came to growing plants and herbs used for medicinal purposes. He did not like to travel outside of Laredo; World War II travels had been enough for him (he was assigned the task of picking up dead colleagues on Normandy Beach). He built his own home even though he was criticized for his floor plan (the home still stands). Mr. Santos used humor to get him through the worst of times when others would cry their sorrows away. He was a role model for Magdalena in following her dreams, her desires, and her heart.

Magdalena's mother probably gave her the discipline she needed to succeed against all odds. As a young girl, Mrs. Santos had fallen from a tree, which resulted in a severe concussion. Nevertheless, she climbed the tree again after she recovered in order to conquer her fear of falling. Mrs. Santos dedicated months to intense training in pitching (softball) and swimming in order to participate in sports with her peers. She also finished college in three years to prove her skills as a student and later as a teacher.

Mary Ruth came from San Antonio, Texas. Prior to her admission to Carville, Mary's older sister, Kitty, was diagnosed with HD. Their parents provided them with the support they needed to confront the harsh realities of such a diagnosis. Mary Ruth always had a smile on her face, and would say "sweetie" and "honey," and would shower Magdalena with affection and lend a supportive ear. Mary Ruth never questioned Magdalena's beliefs and always complimented Mrs. Santos on "what a great job" she had done as a mother. Mary Ruth gave Magdalena a special, motherly love that had become dormant in her own mother and did not resurface until after we were married.

Survival is a marvel. We adapt. We change. We learn new skills. Ultimately, though, we follow those who can help us lessen internal pain. Mary Ruth was the person who magically appeared for Magdalena and me, to lessen our pain.

Mom, as usual, did not want me to worry about how things were going in Laredo. She would predictably start her letters with two statements, "Estamos todos bien de salud G.A.D. [Gracias a Diós]" ("We are all in good health thanks to God") and "Todo sigue la misma rutina" ("Everything is the same as always").

My sister Diana, who realized I was no fool and knew that I would worry more if I didn't know what was going on at home, would brief me on details. She informed me, for example, that another sister, Margarita, had almost died after an ovarian cyst had ruptured. She was saved only through emergency surgery. Dad still struggled to find full-time employment, so he continued doing odd jobs as a carpenter.

I had stopped asking Mom and Dad for money since my admission to Carville. In addition to the small amounts I would save to pay for trips to visit Magdalena, I also had a savings plan to send Mom money, usually five to ten dollars per month. She used this small amount, I found out later, to buy some basic food items—flour for tortillas, tomatoes for freshly made chili, and spices.

As the summer of '72 approached, Magdalena struggled with whether to seek employment in Baton Rouge after graduation. "This idea," she wrote, "may resolve the conflict of separation, but intensify the level of alienation from Mom." My preference, which I did not share with Magdalena for fear of adding to the stress of attempting to receive acceptance from her mom, was simply to elope after her graduation.

This idea would probably have created other challenges, since Carville's policy was to not allow nonpatients, other than staff, to reside at the station. Additionally, neither of us had a sufficient income to pay for rent in the community. Finally, my ongoing treatment with cocktails of thalidomide and clofazimine, and their experimental status, put a huge damper on a quick wedding.

In May of 1972, Magdalena received her master's degree from the University of Texas at Arlington Graduate School of Social Work. Neither of us wanted to have a confrontation with her mother that would detract from Magdalena's accomplishments, so we compromised, and I attended a graduation party prior to her family's arrival for the ceremonies. I was at Carville at the moment of her graduation. I should have been there, standing by her side.

Magdalena returned to Laredo and quickly realized that her employment options were very bleak. In 1972, a person with a master's degree in social work was not in great demand in Laredo. Most places where she applied which had advertised for a social worker were actually looking for people to act as bill collectors so they could "use their communication skills."

Magdalena became seriously depressed. She was a college graduate, unemployed, living at home, and she was daily reminded by her mom of her opposition to our relationship. Laredo, she wrote, "no cambia" ("does not change"), "lo mismo, siempre tierroso y un calorón" ("the same, dusty and extremely hot weather").

She continued, "Se me pasa el tiempo" ("Time flies"). "Gasto el tiempo nada más esperando" ("I waste my time simply waiting"). "Espero a ti, por un trabajo, por cambio en mamá y cambio en la vida" ("I wait for you, wait for a job offer, wait for a change in Mom's way of thinking, and wait for a change in my life").

Waiting, I reminded her, is what many of the Carville residents were forced to endure when diagnosed with HD. Waiting is what led many of my brothers and sisters in Carville to succumb to loneliness, alcohol abuse, and even death by their own hands. Refusing to wait, I added, was what eventually led Mary Ruth to confront her new life and accept love from Darryl. Refusing to wait is what led Tom to leave Carville for a new life "on the outside." Refusing to wait for innovative surgeries to correct her badly damaged hands is what gave Grace Choy the courage to become an expert at knitting and crocheting. Refusing to wait for blindness to set in is what allowed Manuel to grow beautiful orchids. Refusing to wait for staff acceptance is what led Julia and Ray to marry.

Her stubborn refusal, I emphasized, to give in to temporary barriers, such as the "fences of Carville," is what allowed me to keep my sanity and the candle of love lit. I quoted her excellent advice when I was seriously contemplating suicide. "Time is but a speck of dust on this great universe," she had written several years before, "but two specks of dust joined together will quickly ignite change." I begged her to see me as that second speck of dust and think about us in unison, not separate.

Coincidentally, Magdalena received my correspondence at the same time that she received a written job offer from Terrell State Hospital near Dallas. She tearfully embraced my advice and joyfully accepted the job offer.

Life at home continued as usual. My sister Mague married her high school boyfriend, my brother Rudy joined the army and was assigned to a tank battalion in Kentucky, and Dad took jobs anywhere he could find them.

Dad's financial limitations placed some restrictions on my siblings in terms of participating in their school's extracurricular activities. Ferny chose to secure odd jobs in order to earn spending money, giving up the opportunity to play high school baseball. Idalia opted to not even try for the Golden

Spurs dance troop at high school, as the family could not afford to buy her the required uniform.

Magdalena's mood dramatically changed once she started her job. Her primary responsibility was to provide counseling in the children's and adolescents' unit at Terrell. Her love of children made her job easy, but she despised the paperwork that came with it.

At the start of summer I applied at different places for a summer job, my first outside the hospital. The advice I received from staff and residents was evenly split between "Yes, try it" and "No, you'll only be disappointed with the rejections." I was finally interviewed and hired at Earl K. Long Charity Hospital. According to my records, there was "a great deal of hesitation" on the part of the hospital's personnel department to even consider me for an interview. Vernon Bahlinger intervened on my behalf, and Dorothy Tideman, director of social work services at the hospital, offered me a job.

Dorothy asked for my opinion on whether the social work staff should be informed about my condition. My first inclination was to say no. However, I thought about their reaction if they found out through the rumor mill, so I changed my mind. To my surprise, no one objected. In fact, Dorothy invited me to her home for dinner and asked me to "educate" her husband about HD. Our close friendship continued throughout the years, especially since Magdalena eventually would work at Earl K. Long as well.

While working at Terrell, Magdalena became friends with Roberta, who was Native American. They bonded for several reasons, but primarily because both could relate to their separation from family (Magdalena—Laredo, Roberta—Oklahoma) and impoverished upbringings (poor neighborhood and on the reservation).

Roberta invited Magdalena to a powwow on her reservation. Magdalena was so impressed with the values and traditions she saw being exhibited at the powwow that she began to wonder how our values, customs, and traditions would have to be brought to the forefront prior to our getting married.

On one of the visits to Chickashay, Oklahoma, Roberta invited me to "join the fun." I accompanied Magdalena to the powwow. We both experienced such joy and warmth that it was difficult to accept the end of the weekend.

It was a very close-knit Native American community in Oklahoma. At the powwow, Magdalena and I were quizzed about the Chicano culture and about HD. On the former, we found many similarities relating to customs of marriage, such as seeking the blessing of the bride's family and having the extended family sponsor certain parts of the marriage ceremony.

On the topic of HD, I shared all of my knowledge and they asked for more. One question that left me puzzled was "How many Native Americans have the disease?" I was mute and simply shrugged my shoulders. Actually, as of the year 2008, there was no documented evidence that any Native American in the U.S. had been diagnosed with HD.[3] They are the only homogenous group in the world who, collectively, appear to have a natural immunity to the disease; or, ironically, the discriminatory practice of placing them on reservations might have protected them from the HD bacillus.

After the return to our respective second homes, we synchronized our calendars, and I agreed to *"pedir la mano,"* ask for Magdalena's hand in marriage, on September 5, 1972.

It is our tradition to formally ask for the future bride's hand in marriage via a home visit by the groom's parents. We both dreaded the moment, silently thinking that Mrs. Santos would not consent to the visit. Even though we could get married without her consent, her blessing was critical. We believed that beginning the marriage on a dark note might also increase the possibility of starting on the road to an unhappy marriage.

Magdalena informed her dad about the plan for September 5. His approach was that the decision to marry, good or bad, was up to each individual. Without being asked, he volunteered to be the messenger to Mrs. Santos and basically guaranteed that she would be present and not boycott this important event.

On September 5, my parents and I traveled to Magdalena's home in complete silence, not knowing what to expect. My recollection of the meeting was that there was little verbal interaction. Our respective fathers did most of the talking—the asking for her hand and the acceptance. The ceremony was brief. Before long we parted company. Mrs. Santos did not voice an objection, but her rigid silence was not exactly a gesture of acceptance. Unfortunately, this visit resulted in Mr. and Mrs. Santos not talking to each other for several months, adding friction to an already stressful time for all of us.

Magdalena told me that she asked her mom to visit Guadalupe Church, talk to a priest, and attempt to set a date for the wedding, preferably during the Thanksgiving holidays. Mrs. Santos kept insisting that Magdalena never asked her to visit the church and claimed to have lost the letters in which she repeated the request.

A month prior to the meeting to ask for Magdalena's hand, one of her maternal aunts in Monterrey, Mexico, died unexpectedly. A month after the ceremony, a maternal uncle also died. The grief caused by these two deaths, plus the silent objection to the wedding, made Magdalena wonder if any of her mom's family would even attend the yet-to-be-scheduled event.

Any contact with her mom inevitably led to questions about 1) permission from medical staff for us to marry, 2) authorization from the court to grant us a marriage license, and 3) a blessing from the priest to allow us to get married in the church. Each question, repeated over and over again, hurt us deeply, but did not break our spirits.

Magdalena "felt great conflict" when she counseled the adolescents at her job to "listen to your parents," and then she would not do the same. She felt this contradiction was an attack against the cultural expectation of respecting our parents. The ultimate insult in our culture is to be disrespectful, especially to our elders. This pain of disobedience wounded us, hurt our relationship, made us question our actions, and gave rise to arguments over minor and insignificant issues.

Having a wedding date, though it was not yet set by the end of September, was critical in order for us to meet church expectations, e.g., attending Pre-Cana classes as a couple. These classes last for up to three hours each and are focused on such things as premarital sex, marital sacrifices, children, obligation to church, and financial responsibilities. The classes were once a week over a six-week period.

We were able to convince priests in Baton Rouge and Dallas to allow us to attend the classes without our respective partners. Each time we arrived for a class, we were quizzed on why we were alone and then encountered stares from the couples. We shared comical stories about the class called "The Introduction to Sex," when a priest in Baton Rouge attempted to show over one hundred couples the "proper way" (missionary position) to have sex, which he illustrated by using two large dolls on a stage.

In our culture, the family of the bride primarily coordinates wedding plans, but costs are evenly shared. Magdalena reluctantly called my mother to request that she coordinate the wedding plans. Magdalena's mom never expressed objections to her decision; however, she secretly called Mom for details of the plans. She also sought sponsors for the wedding, but did not tell Magdalena what she was doing.

Ah, sponsors. Without them, none of us in Laredo would have enjoyed such large and beautiful weddings. Sponsors, or *padrinos/madrinas*, were identified from among extended and immediate family members, family friends, friends of the bride and groom, and even politicians one had helped during elections. Mom was very knowledgeable about this ritual, having coordinated the wedding ceremonies of three of my sisters. Sponsors, some of whom volunteered, exhibited a form of familial commitment. Being a sponsor is an honor bestowed on someone who is admired and trusted. Ultimately it also means being able to financially support the marriage ceremony.

There is a great sense of pride in being a sponsor. The family name is advertised as a *padrino* in the invitation, e.g., *padrinos* of groom's cake, bride's cake, music, salon, pictures, food, church, beaded lasso (large rosaries strung together and placed over the shoulders of the bride and groom to signify commitment), cushions, *aras* (thirteen Mexican dimes signifying financial stability) and many, many other items. This ritual of *padrinos de matrimonio*, or sponsors for the marriage ceremony, is what makes it possible for even the poorest of couples to have a lavish ceremony and not start the marriage in debt. This ritual also allows the *padrinos* and their immediate families to attend the ceremonies and enjoy a good meal and wonderful live music.

Two important expenses we were responsible for were Magdalena's gown, purchased off the rack, and a matching wedding ring set purchased at Zales jewelry store for seventy-five dollars.

Mom pushed for an appointment with the monsignor at Guadalupe Church and scheduled the wedding date, on our behalf, for December 24, at the 11:00 a.m. Mass. This was the only date available. It was the last time that a priest assigned to Guadalupe Church would perform a marriage ceremony during 11 a.m. Sunday Mass.

We invited Darryl and Mary Ruth to serve as witnesses at our wedding and invited many of the residents and staff to attend. Unfortunately, no one from Carville was able to come. This was not a sign of disapproval. Residents at Carville would start planning what they would do for Christmas months before December. This was done so as to plan for medical passes, expenses, and means of travel. With that in mind, they "regretfully declined" the invitation. Complimentary comments and cards, however, were shared with us. Magdalena had managed to accomplish what four years earlier had appeared to be the impossible. She reversed the attitude of most of the residents, and they now accepted her as one of their very own.

Mrs. Santos continued to give Magdalena the impression that she was not interested in the wedding plans, but she stayed in telephone contact with Mom. Magdalena, without a job awaiting her in Louisiana, gave notice of resignation at her job effective December 15, nine days before the wedding. My, oh my, we laughed and cried at the same time. What the heck were we getting into?

School continued for me. My designated internship (two days per week) was at city hall in New Orleans during the Moon Landrieu administration. What a unique time to be part of this historical city. What a dangerous time to be sent to the Desire Housing Project to gather information on housing needs from residents who probably viewed me as a foreigner and as a part of a mistrusted bureaucracy. What an opportunity for me to use my Spanish and interview newly arrived Cubans on their housing and health care needs. What an experience to have a classmate and fellow traveler to New Orleans share with me that he was gay and then introduce me simply as "straight" at many of New Orleans's secret gay bars. What a scary time to be seen as a black "boy" at the slowly diversifying city hall.

A unique surprise I received while assigned to city hall was when the mayor's staff summoned me for a press conference. I had been collecting data on the level of transition made by the large number of Cubans moving to New Orleans. My report, "Doing Well," was carried on the evening news. The change to a new culture was going smoothly, in part because Charity Hospital had started to hire bilingual staff and have signs in Spanish, which lessened the confusion and stress involved in seeking medical assistance. I have found that recent arrivals to the U.S. are able to adjust more quickly to change when their medical needs are met. This was evident among the Cubans who were newly diagnosed with leprosy and were sent to Carville for treatment. The interviews with the Cubans in New Orleans helped me to better understand this proud group of people, and thus establish lifelong friendships with the Cubans at Carville.

The B-663 I was taking had not only affected how others saw me, but also how I felt physically. The constipation was so severe that I needed enemas almost on a weekly basis, and it also gave me painful hemorrhoids. However, the fevers were less and the reactions not very severe. So I thought maybe the name calling and pain in the rear would pay off with better long-term health and a discharge.

Magdalena applied for a number of positions in Baton Rouge. In the latter part of October, after giving notice at her job in Texas, she went to several interviews. One of them was with Dorothy Tideman at Earl K. Long Charity Hospital. Magdalena's hunger for knowledge, her friendly persona, her dream of being a medical social worker, and her bilingual skills made her a good candidate, and there was an immediate job offer, which she accepted.

November went by in a breeze. The days were filled with ongoing stomachaches from the B-663, letters from Mom about the wedding plans, anxious calls from Magdalena instructing me to find "an affordable, furnished apartment close to LSU," and plans for bridal showers at Carville and in Laredo.

Ten days before the wedding, Darryl, Milton Grossenbacher, and Albert Landry drove me to Arlington. With Magdalena's car and a U-Haul trailer, the four of us relocated her to an apartment that I had found close to the LSU campus. Darryl, Mary Ruth, and others made it a point to tell Magdalena and me that they would be monitoring my Carville departure and arrival times on a daily basis; i.e., they would not condone my spending the night at "our apartment" prior to December 24.

I scheduled a time for both of us to meet with Dr. Jacobson, hospital director at Carville. We discussed, again, that HD was not known to be transmitted via sexual intimacy and that our children would likely not get the disease but that there was also a possibility of not having children (low sperm count due to multiple and severe reactions). Dr. Jacobson congratulated us and hinted that we would "make great social workers at Carville."

Magdalena barely had enough time to complete her new employee orientation and be assigned an office before we packed for Laredo one last time as boyfriend/girlfriend. Many residents confided in me that they felt jealous of our happiness, but they did not feel angry or deprived because of their own losses in the field of love. Most still had their memories. So in isolated corners and vacant hallways, they shared with me experiences with love, tenderness, caressing faces, soft skin, gentle kisses, warm embraces, sweet smells of perfume. Each of them remembered the time, date, and type of weather when their loved ones departed from the scene. Their lonely stories would end with both of us in tears. A strong, silent embrace would follow, and we would walk away in opposite directions. The timing of my diagnosis had spared me the pain felt by almost everyone who arrived at Carville prior to 1968.

On Wednesday evening, December 21, 1972, Magdalena and I started on our twenty-hour journey to Laredo. Instead of enjoying a leisurely drive, we felt the stress of the approaching wedding and wondered aloud if her mom might change her mind and not attend. We also started to speculate on whether Dad would attend the wedding, as his traditional and valued role as head of the household, *el hombre de la casa,* had been severely blemished by his long periods of either unemployment or underemployment.

The last letter I received from Dad was on December 21. He described his embarrassment at not being able to adequately provide for the family. He had accepted another carpentry job in Pearsall, Texas, and implied that he would work throughout the weekend, missing the wedding. Our adopted families in Louisiana had embraced our marriage, but now it was our blood families who were unable to make a commitment to be present.

Magdalena dropped me off at the house at 5:30 a.m. on December 22 and drove home. Both of us went straight to bed, but by 8:00 a.m. we were faced with many minor details that were time consuming and irritating to sleep-deprived brains. Details such as flower arrangements, color of tuxedo, extra food, and time to start the ceremonies exhausted us and depleted our patience.

At 9:00 p.m. on December 23, we finally found some time to be alone. Simultaneously, we realized that we had not purchased Christmas presents for anyone. We quickly drove to the H.E.B. Food Store and bought perfumes for the women and after-shave lotion for the men. Luckily they were all prewrapped in Christmas colors. Driving in cold silence to her house, we reached out in the dark and gently caressed each other's hands. We communicated a message of yes, it has been worth it. At 10:00 p.m. I walked Magdalena to the front door and kissed her. Her mother, as she had done since we started dating at age seventeen, turned on the porch light to signal my *"adiós"* for the evening.

On Sunday, December 24, 1972, I woke up without the familiar smells of fresh flour tortillas, coffee, or sautéed chile with onions. All of the women had left the house for early morning appointments with the hairdresser. So, as each of my brothers woke up, they too noticed the strange silence in the kitchen. Dad finally woke us all to reality when he placed some bologna and white bread on the dining room table. "Coman rápido" ("Eat quickly"), he ordered. He then gave us all marching orders to the shower because "cuando lleguen las mujeres, no va haber tiempo" ("when the ladies arrive, there will not be any time to enter the bathroom"). The military routine was funny for two reasons. First, we used to have similar fun times with Dad when we were kids. Second, Dad was not expected to be home so we were all glad with the outcome.

At approximately 9:30 a.m., they arrived and went straight to the bathroom, one at a time. By 10:30 a.m., everyone was dressed and ready to board the caravan of cars to Our Lady of Guadalupe Church.

I rode with Mom and Dad. With Dad driving and Mom looking straight ahead, they started talking about how proud they were of my accomplishments and how Magdalena was going to make me *un hombre feliz,* a happy man. They reminisced about the long road to Carville and how a small bet had made it possible to pay for gas and sent me on the road to recovery. They were talking as if I were not in the car, possibly to avoid crying in my presence again.

Then he said "Ya estamos aquí, kid" ("We are here, kid"). They hugged me gently, caressed my face, and gave me thumbs up. I walked up some steps and entered the church by a side entrance. With my black tie tuxedo, the churchgoers immediately recognized me as the groom. People smiled, nodded their heads, and then glanced to the main entrance, where Magdalena was standing.

I followed suit and peeked at the beautiful bride. As I squinted to see my bride in her white gown, I noticed that her mother was moving toward her from the side. Magdalena's peripheral vision picked up the movement to her left. Her head slowly, very slowly, turned until she was face-to-face with her mom. Mrs. Santos gently caressed the right side of Magdalena's face with the back of her fingers. I could not see Mrs. Santos's face, but I could tell from Magdalena's tearful smile that her mom was relaying the long-sought message of "I approve."

They embraced as the organist started to play the wedding march. Thirty minutes later, Magdalena and I became husband and wife. Prejudices and ignorance about leprosy had made the previous four years appear to be only a bad dream. On December 24, our nightmare was transformed into a colorful, living dream. Dozens of friends, family, medical staff, and fellow residents had made many sacrifices to make our dream come true.

Mrs. Santos loved Magdalena dearly. Due to her ignorance about leprosy and the treatment available to combat this illness, she was afraid that Magdalena would become infected by me. My mother, on the other hand, would do anything to make me well again. One can never underestimate the love of a mother.

CHAPTER

11

# Life after Death

As we exited the church, hand in hand, an army of family members was waiting to greet us. Even those who were only attending Mass and not part of the wedding party greeted us warmly, sensing something special and saying, *"felicidades,"* congratulations. Our parents and siblings were crying. It was difficult to see the crowd because our eyes were swelled with tears too. Many individuals whom we did not recognize came to us and said, "Amazing, we thought you were dead, *qué milagro,"* what a miracle.

Yes, it was a miracle for us. After so many obstacles, we had finally attained what seemed to be an unattainable goal. For all of us, December 24 was like a resurrection, an opportunity to live and laugh again. And we did plenty of smiling and laughing at the wedding reception. It lasted until almost 7 p.m. and over three hundred guests attended.

To this date, my older siblings remember the wedding fondly, seeing their *hermanito,* little brother, so happy. For my younger siblings, it was the end of a torturous two months. Mom had invested all of her time, energy, and limited funds in the wedding, leaving little time for the purchase of Christmas presents.

The next day, Magdalena and I boarded a second-class bus to Mexico City. Second class meant no bathroom. Also, live chickens in boxes were allowed on the luggage carrier. We spent four days in the apartment of one of Magdalena's cousins. The walls were paper thin, and the sleeping accommodations consisted of two beds, each just large enough to fit a small teenager. We could not get the beds together because any shift in weight resulted in one of us slipping to the floor. Once we stopped laughing, we reached the conclusion that our honeymoon would consist of holding hands.

By the time we returned to Baton Rouge in January 1973, I was experiencing another of my many severe reactions. Magdalena stayed at our tiny apartment, and I went to Carville's infirmary for a week. The intermittent separations continued until November 26, 1974, when I was finally taken off thalidomide.

Four months after our marriage I received a telephone call from Jim Montgomery of the *Wall Street Journal*. Montgomery was writing an article on HD, eventually titling it "Suffering in Silence." He reported on an interview he did with Magdalena and me, but primarily focused on how many of Carville's residents were "overwhelmed by the stigma of their disease."

The courage to speak about my experiences and the many injustices suffered by my "brothers and sisters" grew gradually. My confidence increased to the point that I could address a group as small as two or as large as two thousand. I could sense how the intensity of the subject matter could transform people ignorant about HD into lifelong advocates.

Magdalena and I started taking baby steps to educate others about HD, having conversations with friends, family, colleagues; making presentations at state and national conferences; writing articles for different newsletters; and, most important, educating ourselves about HD history, myths, and facts to avoid falling into what LSU sociologist George Tracy called "self-stigma."

Part of the education came through efforts to overcome the power of ignorance. Many of my classmates joined me in group projects/research papers and were quick to accept the idea of focusing on HD-related topics. Some of my concentration was on issues related to minorities other than blacks—the school's dean appointed me to be chair of the Minorities Committee to address a greater level of diversity in the curriculum. I started to incorporate personal experiences of HD-related issues into the numerous papers required every semester, e.g., addressing such issues as minorities, social justice, spoken and unspoken feelings in a leprosarium, community organization, stress associated with HD, peer pressure, policy development, marital stress characteristics of persons diagnosed with HD, individual and group therapy.

Two of my fellow classmates who always encouraged me to write about my experiences were Robert, who introduced me to his circle of gay friends, and Ruby Guillory, who talked about the struggles of black families living in Church Point, Louisiana. Ruby and I worked on our master's theses together and became good friends.

On May 17, 1974, the labor of eighteen years of schooling finally came to an end. I was awarded my master's degree in social work. Graduation was a day filled with fun for me as I attempted to hug and thank all of the more than four hundred residents, more than one thousand employees and nuns, parents, siblings, and Magdalena. It was such a special moment, much more significant than when I received my bachelor's degree in 1971.

In the summer of 1975, I was recognized in *The Star* for my appointments to the White House Conference on Disabilities and the board of the Louisiana Conference on Social Welfare. These were honors acknowledged by my employer, Louisiana's superintendent of education. He described me in a press release as "a productive member of society."

Coincidentally, at the same time that I was described as a productive member of society, "Carville's Bill of Rights" (intended to describe rules which governed the operation of the hospital) was changed to "exclude offensive language." This language included "apprehend," "detention," "isolation," "restraint," and "menace to the public health." The offensive terminology that had been in effect since 1922 under the Public Health Service Act and Operations Manual was finally buried deep in the archives of the U.S. Library of Congress. Stanley Stein and others referred to these rights as the "Bill of Wrongs."

In an instant, with the stroke of two pens in different parts of the U.S., thousands of others and I had stopped being a threat to society and became contributing members of society. How sad that in the year 2009 society in general still has not fully understood that those of us affected by leprosy are not "lost souls" and should not be defined by the "l" word.

Magdalena and I became enamored with Louisiana as we became part of the community. During our stay there as a married couple, our list of friends grew, as did our homes, which went from an apartment to a duplex to a three-bedroom frame house.

Magdalena continued working at Earl K. Long Charity Hospital, and I worked at the Louisiana Department of Education. My job required that I visit the different parishes and evaluate programs for children with special needs. As a result, I became very familiar with state politics, and learned to speak little when stared at because of my skin color.

I was still required to "live" at Carville due to my medication; thus my travel was extensive. We used my visits back to Carville as an opportunity to invite friends to the hospital's golf course and for crawfishing—catching crawfish with a net filled with chicken livers and boiling them with plenty of spices, potatoes, and corn. Conversely, we would invite residents from Carville to come to our home for parties with plenty of salsa dancing.

Visits from my parents became less frequent as Magdalena and I made the twenty-hour trip to Laredo twice a year. Our parents continued to struggle financially, but Mr. Santos found a job at the Laredo Junior College being responsible for the maintenance of the grounds, including all of the native plants that he loved. Dad continued to do well with Kinnin Security until he encountered some problems with the IRS which prevented him from continuing to operate the business.

Return visits to the hospital allowed me the opportunity to appreciate and admire the Corinthian columns at the recreation building, where I had spent many hours attempting to emulate my father at the pool table and gazing at the stars from out on the terrace. I walked on the outside of the long corridors and looked up at the beautifully oversized garlands and swags. I walked late at night to silently appreciate the connecting corridors and archways, and looked at the intricate cast-iron work in the moonlight. But not until 1994, when I returned as an invited guest for the Carville centennial, was I allowed to enter the administration building and walk up the circular stairwell leading to the guest quarters. Carville is a beautiful place to visit . . . as a tourist. The National Hansen's Disease Museum is filled with the history of HD in the U.S.

Both of us became members of the Louisiana Office of the National Association of Social Workers (NASW) and started to briefly share our experiences as Mexican Americans living in a world of black and white attitudes. Our observations resulted in an invitation by Dr. Demetria McJulian of Southern University's Social Work Program for me to teach a class titled Community Organization. The class was composed of seniors ready to challenge the bureaucracy and system of white bosses.

On the first day of class, I was wearing my best polyester suit with wide collar shirt and platform shoes. The shoes were specially made at Carville but not yet drilled down to an acceptable height. I had not cut my hair and the weather made it look like a short afro. As I walked into the classroom, the students greeted me with low fives and "Hi, bro." As soon as I started speaking, one of the students in the back said, "Hey, you ain't no 'bro'!" After a moment of silence, the class broke out in laughter. I continued to teach the class for two years.

During a trip to Houston in 1976 to visit my brother Javier and his wife, Magdalena and I decided to apply for jobs. Our goal was to eventually return to our families in Laredo. Living in Houston would shorten the trip by three hundred miles. Luckily, our bilingual/bicultural skills were being sought by an organization called Chicano Training Center (CTC). Magdalena accepted a job offer as a clinician in the barrio working with Mexican Americans. I accepted a job as a trainer and traveled throughout the U.S. to provide information on Mexican American families, historical perspectives, and mental health issues.

Our move to Houston forced us to face new challenges. Considering that I was no longer on experimental medication but taking dapsone (DDS) and still prone to reactions and injury to insensitive hands and feet, I reluctantly agreed to a medical pass. Within a twelve-month span, after moving to Houston, I returned for follow-up treatment at Carville on three separate occasions. I was so afraid of a major relapse that I initiated a return at the slightest hint of a fever or reactions. Magdalena was supportive. However, on only one of those occasions was I admitted to the infirmary.[1]

By 1977, many residents had experienced the opportunity to "live outside," so my move to Houston was not exactly unique news. What was unique was that there were still residents at Carville who had not left the facility in over forty years and had no intention of leaving. They had become the modern-day "living dead," persons with no family outside the hospital grounds. Their stories were available only in a brief, typewritten social history in their medical charts, and, at the time, they had no legal access to their records. Their origins were buried deep in their memories.

One year after arriving in Houston, Magdalena and I discussed our future away from the world of HD. In July 1977, I requested a discharge from the U.S.P.H.S. Hospital and on August 31, 1977, I received my official discharge. We celebrated the moment quietly at home, thankful that this chapter of our lives was finally over. How wrong we were.

My association with Chicano Training Center opened up opportunities to sharpen my public speaking skills and make more presentations on HD. In 1978, two of my colleagues at CTC and I went to Carville at the invitation of the social work department to make several presentations at a one-day seminar on psychosocial aspects of the Mexican American population.[2]

The Carville staff who attended the seminar gave me mixed reactions, ranging from pats on the back to indifference, mostly the latter, possibly because they could not acknowledge that I was now a paid consultant, not a patient. I returned with less fanfare to make other presentations to staff and others from 1999 to 2004 as a consultant to the National Hansen's Disease Outpatient Program.

My employment with CTC also allowed me the opportunity to educate others about HD. *The Star* published a summary of a study I had done on HD and marital stress while attending graduate school, and identified me as a professional from Houston, not simply as an ex-resident.[3]

At the same time that I was battling the system at Carville, Bernard Punikai'a was fighting the state of Hawaii. Bernard, a native Hawaiian who was diagnosed witht HD at age six and a half, was separated from his family and isolated at Honolulu's Kalihi Hospital (later known as Hale Mohalu), where people diagnosed with HD were kept prior to being shipped to Kalaupapa Settlement on the island of Molokai, and after leaving the Kalaupapa Settlement.

This wonderful man with a poetic tongue and singing voice has often described the "great sadness" he felt on the last day he saw his mother. He spoke of the "confusing thoughts" that raced through his mind as the Japanese Zero planes zoomed by at tree level on their way to bomb Pearl Harbor, while he and others played at Kalihi Hospital. He clearly recalls the "petrified fear" that engulfed his body as he was gently shoved off the boat that took him to the remote Kalaupapa Peninsula on Molokai Island. At Kalaupapa, he experienced "dark loneliness" every night for decades after his "arrival at Father Damien's home."

The year 1969 was the year that Hawaii eliminated the mandatory isolation law for people with HD. However, no one had been forcibly sent to Kalaupapa since 1949. It was also the year that Hawaii's board of health, state legislature, and governor started to initiate steps to close Kalihi Hospital, or Hale Mohalu. Hale Mohalu was located on land that became very valuable with the increased interest in tourism. Bernard took a leadership role in getting this unjust movement stopped, but not before experiencing severe ill health, becoming homeless, being described in despicable terms by many politicians, and being arrested for simply practicing his freedom of speech.[4]

It was almost ten years before Bernard and many other residents of Kalaupapa felt victorious. Hale Mohalu is now a beautiful retirement home for persons who are elderly and disabled. He was honored for his work during the dedication of the "new" Hale Mohalu, and a mural depicting his struggles is located in the main lobby of this sensibly designed facility.

Bernard is a hero in Hawaii and has surpassed Father Damien as the most recognized figure in Honolulu. On July 3, 2008, Pope Benedict XVI approved a miracle linked to Damien while he worked at Kalaupapa, opening the door for sainthood. Bernard is *my* hero and one of the few men I can truly say that I love dearly.

In May 1978, I was informed by my employer at CTC that the National Institute of Mental Health (NIMH) grant which created my position was not going to be "renewed." Later in the month, Magdalena informed me she was pregnant.

We had thought that my many reactions and the medications I took might affect our ability to conceive. We had started talking about adoption when Magdalena announced she was pregnant.

After so many years of trying to have a child, we had given up. We were both unprepared for my unemployment as well as our foray into parenthood. The market for social workers at the time was not very good, so I worked three part-time jobs for four months until I was offered a position with Mental Health and Mental Retardation Authority (MHMRA) of Harris

County. The HD reactions had resulted in my having a very low sperm count, but God had allowed us the opportunity to become parents. The pregnancy was a mixture of wonderful exhilaration and stress. Our families in Laredo and Carville could only marvel at our good fortune, and everyone wished us well.

In December of 1978, Magdalena, eight months pregnant, and I returned to Laredo to celebrate Christmas with family. That Christmas was a joyous event at the home of one of my sisters, Diana Ortiz. After opening presents and eating heartily, we sat down to share stories and reminisce about the past. As usual, Dad led all the discussions.

One of the stories that came up in a joking way was the manner in which I had been transported to Carville—by hearse. My surprised look made everyone realize that I had no knowledge of this, as hard as it might be to believe. Everyone started to share their memory of the day we traveled to Louisiana. A sad silence permeated the Ortiz home, and I walked outside into the dark cold of the evening. By the time Magdalena reached me, I was unable to utter a word. She stroked my back and head as a way of comforting me.

Later we returned to the living room. One by one, my parents, siblings, and their spouses came to me and gave me a strong embrace. They too had felt my pain and also recalled the cold day I was lifted into the back of the hearse. The consensus among all of my siblings was that they would not see me alive. The sadness turned to laughter when Diana said, "Híjole, y aquí estás todavía" ("And darn, you are still here").

In 1979, a miracle baby, José Roberto (J. R.) Santos Ramirez was born. J. R.'s birth was cause for a big celebration in Houston, Laredo, and Carville.

Mom and Mrs. Santos both traveled to Houston for J. R.'s birth. Mrs. Santos, however, stayed for two months. She helped Magdalena recover from her cesarean surgery, took care of J. R., washed the hundreds of cloth diapers, and showered me with wonderful meals. We never spoke of our limited contact prior to my marrying her daughter. We did, however, speak of love of country, commitment to traditional family values, and unconditional love. I met a person different from the one who years earlier feared I would transmit HD to Magdalena. J. R.'s birth helped us heal our pain.

J. R. received much attention from Magdalena, as she stayed home for one year after his birth. He was taken out on walks in the neighborhood and to the few malls that were in Houston at the time. J. R. also enjoyed going to the Astrodome to see the Astros play.

After a year, Magdalena returned to work at M. D. Anderson Hospital, the foremost hospital in the treatment of cancer. She was there for three months and then found her dream job at the Houston V. A. Medical Center.

My work at MHMRA was in coordinating discharge plans for persons returning to Houston from Austin State Hospital. The labeling and disrespect encountered by these individuals awakened my desires for advocacy and stigma-busting strategies.

After one year, I decided to seek other employment, but I was asked to consider another position at MHMRA. I realized that my MSW and bilingual skills were an asset, so I continued to apply for other positions within MHMRA which resulted in promotions. The other positions were in working with persons with mental retardation, now referred to as intellectual and developmental disabilities (IDD).

## chapter 12

# The Road to Advocacy

In 1981, an effort was initiated to decrease the population at Carville, due, in large part, to the success of multiple drug therapy (MDT). Even though many of the younger residents had previously been strongly encouraged to return to their respective communities, few were convinced that treatment without fear on the part of the medical profession would be available. The federal government took some important steps in order to lessen those fears by creating ten outpatient clinics. In the beginning the clinics were fully staffed, but lacked the presence of a social worker to address the psychosocial issues associated with the disease. Contract workers staffed these clinics.

In 1982, I was contacted by the Houston Department of Health to make a presentation to their staff that addressed the impact that HD has on the way people see themselves and how others perceive them. At this time I was still employed at the Mental Health and Mental Retardation Authority Community Center as a social worker. Having others besides myself make the connection between HD, fear, stigma and its impact on one's mental health gave me a great deal of satisfaction. So, I invited a colleague at MHMRA, also a social worker, to co-present with me. I proposed to focus on the HD and she on mental health.

As the invitation intrigued her, she tentatively agreed to copresent pending a discussion with her husband. "After all," she said, "we have a two-year-old baby." Her comment did not make sense to me, but I dismissed it, thinking she might be nervous. The next day, my colleague informed me via telephone that her husband had refused to give her "permission" to present and "risk the life of the family." I recall that all I could say was "okay" as silence prevailed. I felt saddened that evening as I described the telephone call to Magdalena. "Maybe," she said, "it's for the best" and urged me to make the presentation by myself. I did and approximately fifty people attended.

Prior to this incident, I had talked about HD in general and my time at Carville if the opportunity arose. Afterward, I stopped sharing such experiences in an effort to avoid being hurt again.

In 1984, our second miracle baby was born, Erika Betzabe (Betsy in Spanish). We felt so blessed to be able to have another child. Erika was very healthy and seemed ready to conquer the world. J. R. was in the first grade when Erika was born. Unlike in my own childhood, when hospitals had many restrictions on visitors, he was allowed to visit Erika at the hospital in Magdalena's room. He serenaded her with a lullaby taught at school.

In 1986, I saw the reappearance of fear of the unknown in a two-story brick home protected from the hot sun by tall pine trees and nestled in a quiet neighborhood, within walking distance of one of the best medical centers in the world. I had seen this fear many times before. It was this fear that emanated from a fourteen-year-old individual living at a residential program operated by my employer. I had sensed it in many stares from afar and in talk about being unhealthy and unclean.

This young black man, labeled by society for his color, by the court system for his bouts with law enforcement agencies, by the educational system for not learning as quickly as others, now had another label from the medical profession. He was diagnosed as having AIDS. Not deemed suited for inclusion in the regular school curriculum but with enough street smarts that he could live independently, he was the first person any of the residential staff where I worked had known who was infected with the virus that caused AIDS.

The hospital staff where he was admitted quickly placed him in isolation and handed him food only after shrouding themselves with surgical caps, gloves, gowns, and shoes. The residential staff emulated the fear from the hospital by reacting in a negative manner. These actions resurrected my thoughts on how I was similarly treated in 1968.

The young man, with a severely weakened immune system, died within months of his diagnosis. Years later, three of my previous supervisors and two colleagues died from AIDS, but not before each of us shared our experiences of rejection. In 2009, many of us affected by HD or AIDS are now sharing something else—the drug thalidomide for treatment of both diseases. Thalidomide, which caused so much grief to unsuspecting mothers and their unborn children almost a half century ago, is now a "miracle drug" that has brought smiles to a group of people usually devoid of such simple pleasures when informed of their diagnosis.

In 1987, my youngest brother, Gerardo, applied to become an officer with the Laredo Police Department, following in our father's footsteps. Gerardo was one of my siblings diagnosed with a "mild case of HD" during a routine examination at the health department while I was still at Carville.

My brother met all of the requirements for the job. However, the chief of police decided to disqualify him based on his history with HD. I urged Gerardo to challenge the chief, and I assisted by writing a letter, as did Carville's director of training and the editor of *The Star*. He also went to the two physicians who had collaborated in discovering my diagnosis. Everyone wrote on the same theme—HD is considered only mildly communicable and Gerardo's treatment with dapsone made him HD free. Knowledge won over ignorance, and the chief reversed his decision. Gerardo has been on the police force for over twenty years and has served as a mentor for many rookies.

I always discussed my Carville days with J. R. and Erika so that they would not be afraid of HD. Also Magdalena and I wanted to rule out the possibility that they might carry the HD bacillus. So, in December of 1989, I took both of them on their first trip to Carville so they could experience firsthand the uniqueness of the facility. The kids were thoroughly examined with hand and foot screens, skin scrapings of ear lobes, elbows, knees, and blood work. The results showed that neither had the bacillus.

They ate in the cafeteria with the other residents. They rode bicycles through the walkways and walked the lonely halls at night. They visited with my surrogate parents in their one-bedroom home.

The drive back to Houston went by quickly as they asked me many questions. After receiving a huge and warm embrace from Magdalena, they overwhelmed her with sentences that started, "Mom, did you know that at Carville . . ." They learned a great deal about HD and about life. Magdalena, who did not accompany us on this trip, was happy with the outcome.

The following year, J. R. was required to do a science project for his fifth-grade class. After discussing many ideas he finally settled on doing a questionnaire designed to rank fear, and his subjects were his classmates. He developed nine questions on topics such as fear of failure and fear of the dark. For his tenth question, he decided to include fear of leprosy.

This simple project gave him some interesting results. Fear of leprosy was ranked number one by his peers. His teacher was so impressed with the results that he suggested J. R. conduct a similar survey with adults. Again, he had questions related to, for example, fear of failure, fear of divorce, etc. His tenth question involved fear of leprosy. Surprisingly, this last one was also ranked number one by adults as the thing they feared the most.

We concluded that their responses were linked to the religious education received at an early age at home, with references to leprosy in Leviticus. J. R. won third place in a countywide science fair. Unfortunately, his certificate of award, poster, and data were all lost in 2001 when our home was flooded by Tropical Storm Allison.

In July of 1994, Julia Elwood invited me to copresent with James Carville and four other current or former residents at Carville's centennial celebration on November 30. James is the son of Chester Carville, who ran the Carville store—thus the routine reference to the hospital as Carville. Having been disillusioned in 1982 by a co-worker, I had silently vowed not to make any more presentations on HD. My initial urge was to decline the invitation, but that meant I would have to wait another hundred years before I might be asked to speak at a similar celebration!

I nervously worked on my presentation almost nightly, sharing my words with Magdalena. My presentation, which was supposed to last five minutes, went closer to twenty. It ended up serving as a rough outline for this book.

Not fully comprehending the significance of the celebration, neither my parents nor Magdalena attended. Darryl and Mary Ruth, however, were there for support. Darryl, who was in a wheelchair, was one of the speakers. On the morning of November 30 I picked him and Mary Ruth up at their home. Darryl was the celebrity of the moment, being acknowledged by the keynote speaker James Carville (who was President Clinton's senior political advisor) as his "father's best friend." Mary Matalin, his bride of one year, explained to me that one of their first dates was on a tour of Carville.

"James," said Mary, "wanted to show me the roots of his passion and love . . . how he learned about commitments to friends." Mary added that during the presidential campaign between the first President Bush and Governor Clinton, she finally capitulated to James's courting efforts. They sneaked out of their respective hotels while both candidates were in New Orleans for campaign speeches. The tour of the hospital was conducted by a childhood friend and culminated with a visit to Darryl and Mary Ruth.

The event proved to be emotionally draining and therapeutic for me. In the middle of the presentation, as I reflected on the love and support I had received from my family and Magdalena, I sobbed uncontrollably. The pain I had felt since being diagnosed twenty-five years earlier surfaced in front of over five hundred people. I recall attempting to continue with the speech, but could not. I looked up at the audience, hoping to see a familiar face, a face that could help me lessen the flow of tears that rolled down my face.

I looked at Mary Ruth, who was sitting in the front row. I could see in Mary Ruth's angelic face my own mother's tears, the caress of Magdalena's hands, the understanding eyes of my sister Diana, and the anguish felt by all who had come before me to Carville. I felt a sigh of relief and a flood of love filling my heart. I could cry openly, and others could join me and rejoice in being educated about this misunderstood disease and how it could wreak havoc on the body.

I finished my speech with a *"gracias."* As I walked back to my chair, I could only hear my heartbeat, but as Louisiana's secretary of state, Mary Landrieu, and James gave me a thumbs up, I heard the congratulating applause from Mary Ruth, Darryl, Betty Martin, Johnny Harmon, and Julia Elwood. Immediately following James's uplifting and powerful speech, he and Mary dashed out to catch a plane. The rest of us simply cried some more and hugged each other. People from all over the world and from different international organizations came to the stage and congratulated all of us, many handing out business cards.

One lady I met, Anwei Law, encouraged me to become "a full-time advocate for persons with HD." This brief encounter was with a lady well known in the world of HD. She was the daughter of a famous leprologist, Dr. Skinsnes, and lived at Kalaupapa Settlement on Molokai Island with her husband. He was the superintendent of Kalaupapa National Historic Park. She had written numerous articles on HD and filmed a documentary of two people affected by the stigmas of HIV and HD. She had also produced and written a documentary with residents at Carville on the hospital's history that was shown as part of the centennial celebration. Our chance encounter blossomed into a partnership on HD education.

By the time I arrived home in Houston on the evening of November 30, Magdalena and the kids were waiting with open arms. Several people had called and described my "crying spell" and blamed her for loving me so much. While it was difficult to explain my emotions, the renewal of tears helped Magdalena and the kids understand that my visit to Carville had been very unique and special.

In April of 1996, Anwei called to invite me to Washington, D.C., to meet with leaders of HD fund-raising organizations. My "assignment" was to discuss the importance of addressing the mental as well as the physical cure of HD. Much of the pain, which had been resurrected at the centennial, was still fresh in my mind.

My message to the group was simple, as I challenged the audience to make the light of knowledge brighter so as to avoid falls on the road to inclusion and education. The group, meeting in executive session, voted to include Dr. G. K. Gopal of India as part of their medical-social commission. Dr. Gopal is a social worker like me, but with a Ph.D. Also, like me, he was cured of HD.

I was amazed to find how many leprosy organizations exist throughout the world that provide valuable services and funding for research. However, few, if any, of them had people affected by leprosy on their boards.

U.S. Senator Bill Frist of Tennessee, a physician by training, hosted a dinner in the famous caucus room of the Russell Senate Office Building for the D.C. meeting. He told me that the goal set in 1991 by the World Health Organization (WHO) to "eliminate" HD as a public health problem by the year 2000 was "not reachable" because data collected internationally showed an upward trend in cases being diagnosed. This was the first time I had heard about this lofty goal. Many others as well as I became vocal critics of the WHO goal, as it became associated with the analogy of putting the cart before the horse. Two major things occurred as a result of this poorly planned goal: funding for HD research decreased, and endemic countries lessened their priorities for the treatment of HD. WHO was forced to set a new goal, the year 2005, for the elimination of HD. In the year 2003, most people working in the field conducting research or associated with leprosy-related fund-raising organizations did not believe WHO's goal was attainable. Many of the doubts were publicly debated at an international conference on HD in Brazil in 2002.

On my forty-eighth birthday in 1996, I visited my father at the same hospital where I had been originally diagnosed with HD. He had been admitted for continuing problems with congestive heart failure. As always, Mom was by his bedside.

Dad was weak and unreceptive to even eating some of Mom's homemade tortillas. His eyes had a glazed look, but he recognized all visitors. He remembered my birthday and asked if I still wore the gold chain and medal with the Virgin of Guadalupe he and Mom had given me before traveling to Carville. I showed him the chain and medal, and he whispered that he had never figured out why God had punished him through me.

Five days later, Dad passed away after my siblings had treated him with a trio, singing Mexican songs from his era. "His life ended," I said during the eulogy at the funeral, "but the memories of his strength will always be alive." Erika, age twelve, made a few remarks on behalf of her cousins, and emphasized how his magic with the guitar had inspired her to play the violin from kindergarten to the fourth grade.

Four months after my father died, my daughter brought our lives to a sudden stop. On a Friday evening in June while waiting for relatives to arrive for a weekend visit, Erika had what can best be described as a severe seizure. Her breathing became erratic as her body went limp. The ambulance arrived and she was taken to Texas Children's Hospital. However, the doctors could not determine what was wrong and discharged her.

The next afternoon she had a similar episode, but I did not wait for the ambulance and instead rushed her in my car to the hospital. Erika was only partially conscious when I carried her into the emergency room, still wearing the hospital band issued the night before. This time she was admitted and thoroughly examined by a team of specialists. Their diagnosis was "multiple strokes with partial paralysis."

Erika was in the hospital for two weeks and, with excellent treatment and therapy, recovered. A major impact on us was that, as parents, we realized the pain my parents probably felt watching a child come close to losing his life. Even though I was never in any danger of dying when diagnosed with HD, my parents did not know that.

Another significant occurrence was when Erika's softball coaches, Larry Sams and Bob Dyer, and her all-star teammates surprised her with a visit. Dyer, a large man with a huge heart, brought a tiny pot of miniature roses, making Erika cry and smile at the same time. At that moment, we all knew she would play softball again.

During her hospitalization, Erika received visits that boosted her spirits. These were from her aunts, uncles, cousins, schoolmates, and colleagues from Magdalena's and my jobs. Erika demanded more time from the physical therapist in order to regain her ability to walk.

Erika's doctors were never able to identify a cause for the strokes, and added that minors rarely have strokes, thus making diagnosis difficult.

Erika recovered and returned to the baseball diamond to be introduced with her teammates at the all-star game, though she could not play. Her introduction at the game also served as a springboard into a life full of increased energy and motivation.

In August of 1996, I traveled to several places in Japan with Dr. G. K. Gopal of India. We flew to this unique and beautiful country at the invitation of the Sasakawa Memorial Health Foundation as a way of introducing IDEA (the International Association for Integration, Dignity and Economic Advancement), a twenty-thousand-member organization whose leadership is primarily made up of persons affected by leprosy. The speech at Carville had resulted in my being described as an advocate for persons with disabilities. I was not sure I was capable of playing such a role, but I gratefully accepted the invitation.

Earlier that year, the government of Japan had abolished their ninety-seven-year-old leprosy prevention law.[1] This extremely harsh law basically imprisoned people diagnosed with leprosy in one of thirteen government-run sanatoria. They were segregated from their families. Sterilization and late-term abortions ensured that no children would be born to people with leprosy. The new freedom was so exhilarating that the Japanese Patients' Union demanded and received an apology from Japan's minister of health for the past injustices of this law. Additionally, the group collected enough donations to build a first-class museum with artifacts, pictures, and written stories of their hardships.

Mr. Jujiro Takase, president of Japan's Union of Residents in the sanatoria openly told anyone willing to listen that "nothing has changed that is obvious to the naked eye, but psychologically, we are much healthier. . . ."

Dr. Gopal and I traveled throughout Japan with Sasakawa representatives and Dr. Due from Vietnam to visit several HD sanatoria. We traveled by train, plane, bus, taxi, and boat. At each visit, Dr. Due would be welcomed with bows, an honor bestowed upon a world-renowned leprologist and hero of Vietnam. Dr. Gopal, Dr. Due, and I delivered a message of community involvement, cooperation with education efforts, and continued fighting for dignity and respect. Dr. Gopal and I were warmly received, especially after the residents of the sanatoria recognized our scars. The disease affected Dr. Gopal in his hands and feet. I literally was in a position whereby I had to raise my trouser legs for the Japanese to see the damage caused by the disease. Some of the older residents could not understand how leprosy had spared me of deformities of the face and hands.

After we spoke, we would close the meetings with toasts of saki and strong embraces. Japan, still a firm believer in male dominance, oftentimes excluded women from our meetings.

Dr. Due, soft-spoken and short but very tall in the world of leprosy, walked with a cane. His limp was due to an infection from a cut to his leg. He explained that he had fallen and cut his leg on a bamboo shoot while practicing evacuation drills during the Vietnam War, known in Vietnam as the "American War." As "one of the few trained physicians" in North Vietnam, Dr. Due reflected on how he was directed to treat wounded soldiers and American pilots. He recalled meeting Ho Chi Minh and being "mesmerized by his powerful words in leading us to battle and his soulful poetry in soothing our pain." His stories intrigued me because of my lost dreams of serving in the military, and also because he told the following story, which I have not been able to confirm.

"In the middle of the war," he said, "I was director of the Quynh Lâp Leprosarium with over twenty-five hundred patients in Nghê An Province on the coast south of Hanoi." He added that the "U.S. offensive strategy was to use psychological warfare." He claimed that one of these examples was when U.S. planes "bombed [my] leprosarium ten times, in spite of having a large red cross on one of the buildings.

"The U.S. intent," Dr. Due explained, "was to force the relocation of the leprosy patients, much feared and ostracized by the community, to surrounding villages." This strategy, he believed, was to create anger and fear among the people and make them "rebel against the North Vietnam government. The strategy," he beamed, "backfired, as the villagers built a new hospital."

Dr. Due's story sounds logical considering the fear most societies have of leprosy. The U.S. military might have initiated such a plan without issuing direct orders in writing. Nevertheless, we may never find out if the bombing of his leprosarium was designed to "create anger and fear," or if there was such a bombing.

Approximately two months after returning from Japan, I was asked to be a major speaker at the American Leprosy Missions' ninetieth anniversary fund-raising luncheon. The keynote speaker, Tony Campole, had been one of President Clinton's religious advisors during the Monica Lewinsky affair.

During my twelve-minute presentation, I spoke about the challenges faced by persons diagnosed with HD and the inevitable labeling with the "l" word. I stated my preference to be seen as a human being, with a name, even a person affected by HD, but not as a patient, no longer hospitalized, nor referred to as a "leper."

Campolo mesmerized the audience with his knowledge and eloquence. However, I lost my appetite for listening when he kept referring to me by the "l" word. As he concluded his presentation, the lights were dimmed and Tony magically exited the ballroom. I managed to quietly congratulate him on the speech and reminded him that the "l" word was inappropriate for describing others and me with HD. All he was able to say as he was gently pushed out of the room by one of the organizers was "oh." I followed up with a letter, and, two months later, Tony sent me a written apology and made a commitment to educate others, especially those at his church, Mount Carmel Baptist Church in Pennsylvania, "to use right terminology."

The more I traveled, the more I learned, and the more I realized how far removed society was from the injustices and pain felt by persons affected by HD. My desire to educate became stronger and more focused.

In April of 1997, Magdalena accompanied me on a trip to Spain, experiencing firsthand the victories felt by persons long isolated from the general populace. The trip to Spain was to attend a three-day conference cosponsored by IDEA and several other organizations. The theme was "The Last Leprosy Hospitals and the People Who Call Them Home." Many people from throughout the world affected by HD attended.

The trip was a unique experience for everyone. Nine different languages were spoken, and since Magdalena, Irma Guerra (staff at Carville), and I spoke both English and Spanish fluently, we served as primary interpreters.

The group was composed of numerous individuals, many of whom were elderly. Some were in wheelchairs, others had lost their vision, and still others had prostheses. However, everyone refused to be limited by his or her disability. For the elderly and disabled, managing a walk on thousand-year-old cobblestone streets or boarding trains at stations where porters are nonexistent proved to be a unique challenge. Negotiating cab fares and prices from vendors became our constant task. Many joining the chaos were individuals who had never traveled outside of their country or even their residence.

Our ultimate destination was the HD hospital known as Fontilles. Our trip took us through Valencia. One day's experience gave me the inspiration to write an article that was published in the *Houston Chronicle*. The article was in a section titled "Among Friends."

Sunday, April 13, 1997, was a beautiful day in Valencia, Spain, with a bright blue sky and a gentle but chilly breeze. The caressing wind was dispersing the sweet smell of orange blossoms flourishing all over the city. As is the custom throughout their country, Spaniards of all ages and socioeconomic backgrounds were leisurely enjoying the sunny day in the historic city's central plaza.

The place was crowded with enterprising vendors, smartly dressed churchgoers, young couples clinging to each other, black-clad beggars, creative mimes and a few tourists with well-worn backpacks. Mixed into this potpourri of people was a small group of first-time visitors to Spain, six individuals brought together by a common cause.

The old section of Valencia was obviously not built to accommodate wheelchairs, which made our wandering difficult. This, along with some of our physical disabilities, attracted some stares.

Two in our group, both in their 70's, maneuvered their wheelchairs through the large crowd. Their feet had either been lost to amputation or dramatically weakened after decades of poor circulation, slow-healing ulcers, and a lack of sensation to physical touch. Their hands had been twisted by the constant pounding of knuckles on hard surfaces in completing the most routine tasks, such as turning a doorknob.

One of the wheelchair riders was a gentle woman from Louisiana in a dark pantsuit, red blouse and matching earrings, with light makeup that accentuated her high cheekbones and salt-and-pepper hair. The other, a man from Hawaii, wore a gray Hawaiian T-shirt, dark trousers and a Houston Rockets cap.

Three others in our group had walked into the most crowded of the narrow cobblestone streets seeking bargains from vendors who looked forward to quick, intensely negotiated sales. I stayed with my friends in their wheelchairs.

Being stared at was nothing new to our group. The woman in the wheelchair, who had lost her sight to the disease that had bonded our group, reassured me that she was not offended by stares.

Being young enough, at 49, to be their adult child, I reacted like an overly protective son and stared back at the crowd. My friend in the Rockets cap sensed my growing anger and said, "Look, I can't change the way I look, but maybe I can use this cap to ask for donations." The three of us laughed uncontrollably.

A handsome old man was standing in front of us, holding hands with his spouse. He was staring at us. Slowly he pulled out 15 pesetas (the equivalent of 11 cents) and somberly and gently placed the three small coins in the remnants of my Hawaiian friend's hand. My friend, being much wiser than I, looked at the donor with genuine warmth, tipped his head and said, *"Gracias, señor."* The gentleman, without speaking a word, acknowledged the gratitude and vanished into the crowd.

My other friend said maybe I should lend her my Houston Astros cap so she could get her "share of the loot." We laughed so hard that the brakes on the wheelchairs became dislodged and my friends almost rolled into the busy street.

Our laughter, of course, only served to escalate the staring. One lady, about 4 feet tall, probably in her 80's, nicely dressed with matching shoes and purse, seemed startled to see us laughing. She admonished us for being so "carefree" and urged us to move to another location that she had "scouted" for us.

"You can make more money over there," she said. She gently touched each of our faces, made the sign of the cross, wished us well, smiled broadly and quickly walked away.

The article briefly described the common bond among those in the group—Hansen's disease and our unending friendship.

The group traveled from Valencia to Fontilles by bus. Fontilles, established in 1909 by Jesuit priests, is located in the province of Alicante close to a small town called Valle de Loguart. The hospital, built to accommodate 420 residents, was designed to be self-sufficient. It is nestled on jagged cliffs and surrounded by a ten-foot wall of rock reminiscent of the Great Wall of China. I was told that the "little wall" was built in the 1950s after residents in surrounding communities sounded an alarm that "they might escape and contaminate the community."

Realizing that leprosy was not a health issue in Spain, the government initiated a plan to convert Fontilles into an assisted living type facility, opening up eligibility to anyone in the community who was "elderly." This redesign of a leprosarium to a multipurpose facility, with appropriate supports, is what most of us affected by leprosy have been advocating. The closure of such a hospital, however, should not be done simply to decrease costs, or without proper supports to address treatment, public education, and psychosocial issues.

Magdalena and I would return to Spain on three other occasions. One was to make a presentation on stigma at the annual meeting of the International Federation of Anti-Leprosy Associations (ILEP) in Valencia. Another was to conduct interviews of residents at Fontilles for an oral history project. Finally, we went to Madrid to address the national press corps on World Leprosy Day in 2005. The last trip was made on behalf of the ILEP member Amigos de Fontilles. This was the first time they had invited a person affected by HD to be their representative on this unique day—always the last Sunday in January.

Individuals who have stayed in hospitals for decades have either been forced to do so via legislation or public pressure, resulting in loss of job and family. Research has shown that the events in one's life that can trigger the highest levels of depression include divorce, loss of job, and loss of home. Going to a leprosarium for treatment causes great trauma to the mind, as all three losses may be experienced simultaneously. And, for elderly people to lose yet another home, a hospital, which is the only home they know, without the essential supports, is inhumane.

On October 30, 1997, IDEA, in association with the World Health Organization and the Nippon Foundation, successfully launched an exhibit titled Quest for Dignity: A Victory over Leprosy/Hansen's Disease. This exhibit was on display at the United Nations in New York City for three weeks. Secretary-General Kofi Annan opened the exhibit in front of a crowd that exceeded three hundred people from all over the world. Presidential advisor and political consultant James Carville served as master of ceremonies at the dinner after the opening.

The exhibit, composed of portraits of individuals affected by leprosy, personal thoughts articulated by many throughout the world who have been attacked by the HD bacillus, maps showing the prevalence of HD, and drawings depicting the history of the disease was designed to educate as well as reflect human dignity.

Numerous dignitaries, including President Clinton and President Carter, recognized this event, the first of its kind. President Carter has some knowledge of leprosy, as his mother, Miss Lillian, volunteered at a leprosy hospital in India during his administration. The international media, especially in Japan, where the coverage lasted for over a week, also reported it. This had an extraspecial significance in Japan because, just one year earlier, the government had repealed the leprosy prevention law.

Mr. Yohei Sasakawa, president of the Nippon Foundation, honored invited guests and twenty-five people affected by leprosy from all over the world. Mr. Sasakawa surprised the attendees by presenting the *Kan Toh Shoh*—Fighting Spirit Award—to me. He further honored me by asking that I introduce the other recipients of this first-of-its-kind award.

Mr. Sasakawa explained that sumo wrestling is a highly respected sport in Japan, and the challenges faced by these unique athletes require a special "fighting spirit," a spirit common among those of us who have become advocates for persons affected by HD.

The award was a large gold medal with profiles of a Greek warrior (wrestler) and educator, inscribed on the back with the name of the award, date, and location. I accepted the award in honor of my wife, Magdalena, who was so influential in my recovery, and thanked my family in Laredo for their emotional support. I introduced each of the recipients as Mr. Sasakawa presented them with their award. The award was anchored with a large red, white, and blue ribbon that made the medal rest over the heart of each person. Each was introduced as follows:

Antonio Oliviera Borges, Jr., and Ana Maria Borges—from Brazil. A couple who have been long-time fighters on behalf of others with HD and are active members of Morhan, a national organization on HD.

Olivia Breitha—from Hawaii. She has written her autobiography and demands to be on the driver's side when it comes to dispelling myths about leprosy.

C. S. Cheriyan—from India. This honoree has fought long and hard against the prejudices of leprosy that have been painful to him, such as when his fiancée was abandoned by her family after she accepted his proposal of marriage.

Mamadou Coulibaly—from Mali, Africa. He refused to be ostracized at age seventeen when diagnosed with leprosy and was at that time president of the Leprosy Association. He worked at a radio station, and was happily married with four children.

Uche 'M Ekekezie—from Nigeria. This lady has fought forces of nature and ignorance of the mind to help those affected by HD.

Julia Elwood—originally from Elsa, Texas. She was a cheerleader in high school when diagnosed with leprosy and has regularly led the cheers to permanently document our struggles and accomplishments through the HD Museum at the Gillis Long Center in Carville, Louisiana.

Precious Etuokwu—from Nigeria. This beautiful woman, the youngest recipient, has started her climb to physical and mental recovery.

Dr. P. K. Gopal—from India. His dedication to accuracy about leprosy has resulted in his appointment to an international committee addressing social issues related to leprosy.

Geraldo Lourenco—from Washington, D.C. He is multilingual and will verbalize, in any language, that the fear others may have of leprosy will not deter his efforts to be a good husband, father, and friend.

Makia Malo—from Hawaii. This gentleman, who awoke our spirits through a Hawaiian chant at the reception, persistently touches our lives with riveting and accurate "storytelling" about leprosy.

Richard Marks—from Hawaii. He is the second person diagnosed with leprosy to receive the Damien-Dutton award and is owner and chief guide of the Damien Tours at Kalaupapa, hypnotizing visitors with his eloquence and transporting them to "Damien times."

Miyoji and Mieko Morimoto—from Japan. This angelic and charitable couple have been role models in donating invaluable time and economic resources to organizations that assist other persons with HD throughout the world.

Les Parker—from Britain. A shy person when discussing his accomplishments, he is a fierce warrior when it comes to educating others about the pejorative meaning of the "l" word. Les pointed out to all of us that the "l" word spelled backwards is "repel."

Sam and Theresa Wilson—originally from Trinidad. This beautiful and classy couple constantly teach those of us who allegedly have sight not to be blinded by those ignorant about leprosy.

Arega Kassa Zelelew—from Ethiopia. He is chairman of the ten-thousand-member Ethiopian National Association of Persons Affected by Leprosy.

Jack and Rachael Pendleton—from Arizona and Texas, respectively. They are a feisty twosome, fearless of the bureaucracy, and have been teachers of empowerment, serving as leaders for many.

Francisco Faustino Pinto—from Brazil. He represents a new and younger type of battleship ready to go to war against the evils of stereotyping.

Catherine Puahala—from Hawaii. She has been a long-term instructor on hand-to-hand battles with stigmas, a feat her deceased husband was very proud of.

Bernard Punikai'a—from Hawaii. He has lived a unique life of contradiction, labeled a "criminal" by Honolulu police when arrested for fighting for the rights of the disabled and called a "saint" when chosen by the Vatican to receive Holy Communion from Pope John Paul.

There were many others deserving of this award who are now deceased or because of illness or lack of funding were unable to travel to New York.

# Change Is Good

The success of the opening of the exhibit produced an exhilaration that was in contrast to our sadness at the death of two world-known advocates for people with leprosy. The tragic deaths of Princess Diana and Mother Teresa, within months of each other, generated much publicity on the living conditions of many individuals with leprosy, along with the disabilities that can occur after years of misdiagnosis and/or inappropriate treatment. Regrettably, their deaths also resurrected the use of the "l" word and its alleged association with sin and unclean souls. Many of us in IDEA mailed dozens of letters to the media attempting to correct the damage caused by their ignorant use of the "l" word. I succeeded in getting an article printed in the *Houston Chronicle*. The editor chose to title the article "Hansen's Disease sufferers are not 'lepers.'"

While I was in New York for the exhibit, word spread quickly about the signing of House Resolution 2264, Section 211 by President Clinton. This legislative action allowed persons who met complex criteria of residency at Carville—being on the rolls since 1986 or being of a certain age—to receive a yearly stipend of thirty-three thousand dollars if they chose to relocate and live in the community. The legislation, unfortunately, did not address the sacrifices made by many when they left Carville prior to 1986 to live a life of secrecy.

Additionally, those people deciding not to leave were told that they could remain at the Carville complex as long as they wished. Those in need of constant medical care could remain as patients of the Gillis W. Long Center, but relocate to another site in Baton Rouge. The resolution also included another strange twist: the Carville facility would be given to the state of Louisiana for the National Guard to use in operating a boot camp for at-risk kids.

The signing of the resolution was not a surprise. The sting that resulted in numbness was how much of the HRSA News (HHS's Human Resources and Services Administration) was focused on employee rights and how little on the future of the hospital's residents. The media quickly read the press release as the imminent closing of Carville; thus reporters, news crews, and documentary scriptwriters converged on the hospital grounds.

For years, or at least since I was a resident of Carville, rumors had abounded concerning the possible closing of the hospital. A rumor in the 1970s was that U.S. Senator Russell Long would initiate legislation to award large one-time payments for "pain and suffering" to anyone having been admitted to Carville. Another was the possible declaration of the facility as a national monument similar to President Carter's executive order that declared Kalaupapa Settlement on Molokai Island a national historical park. Nevertheless, residents became jaded with other rumors concerning the closing of Carville, and dismissed any further talk about similar discussions.

In 1994, when Carville celebrated its centennial with a weeklong schedule of activities and the presence of many former residents, friends, dignitaries, and government officials, the rumors about closings and stipends were again resurrected. When Carville's centennial was being held, activities behind the scenes resulted in the relocation of most of the facility at Carville to Baton Rouge.

These activities became newsworthy in 1995, and coverage by the press intensified. By then, Mary Landrieu had lost the governor's race to a political unknown, Mike Foster. U.S. Congressman Cleo Fields was on the verge of losing his seat due to redistricting. An individual who was a strong advocate of persons receiving lifetime stipends and closing the hospital led the Patients' Federation at Carville. Carville employees, recipients for decades of 25 percent hazard pay, became concerned not only that their paychecks would be the same as all other federal employees at equal grades, but also that their jobs would eventually be eliminated. Still another piece to this political puzzle was that federal judge Frank Polozola had been advocating for a highly concentrated education/vocational program, or "boot camp," for teenagers in the southern part of the state who were at risk of becoming habitual criminals. He hoped to emulate the kinds of programs already operating in Pineville and Alexandria and administered by the Louisiana National Guard.

After Mary Landrieu was elected senator by a narrow margin, the focus on who would control the operation of Carville turned to Louisiana State University's Graduate School of Social Work, School of Education, and School of Medicine. The university reacted with surprise at this plan, and the chancellor responded to one of my letters by stating that "this is a congressional matter" and "LSU does not wish to force patients at Carville to be left homeless." Reportedly, the plan was to have graduate social work students provide therapeutic services, education interns handle classroom instruction, and medical interns address medical needs of the teenage students identified for placement at Carville.

Wasey Daigle, a.k.a. Darryl Broussard, #1325, died on March 22, 1998. My surrogate father, who had spent decades in Carville's seven-foot-by-eleven-foot post office delivering good news, bad news, and news of indifference, took his last breath. His only surviving sister was notified. She expressed regret to Mary Ruth that the Daigle family had declared Wasey dead upon his diagnosis with HD. There were many at Carville with families on the "outside" who experienced similar regrets after their deaths.

In September of 1998, as the debate continued on the future of the Carville complex, Magdalena and I traveled to Beijing, China, for the 15th International Leprosy Congress. The closest the congress had come to collectively addressing the subject of psychosocial issues was in 1948 at their meeting in Cuba, where they unanimously agreed to stop using the word "leper," and to educate the public about their decision. Unfortunately, sixty years later, their resolution has had little impact on attitudes among the congress members; i.e., the "l" word is still used by many.

The purpose of the trip to China for IDEA was threefold. It was to ensure that psychosocial issues were discussed in focus groups (Dr. Gopal and I were keynote speakers), educate conference participants about dignity and respect via the exhibit originally shown at the United Nations, and travel to Guanghou to visit several HD hospitals and villages.

In addition to Magdalena, I was usually in the company of Bernard Punikai'a and pushed his wheelchair. As we were walking through the huge exhibit hall that had been the location of the Asian Games and International Women's Conference years before, I noticed several conference participants staring at Bernard. The rude stares turned to words—"Look at that one"—followed by facial gestures expressing disgust. My immediate reaction was to mirror their behaviors and say, "Look at those two," as I pointed my finger towards them. Regrettably, this scene was repeated several times throughout the day.

One unique walk we took while in China was on the Great Wall. The trip to the top involves steep, narrow walkways, rides on several cable cars, and a climb of hundreds of uneven, tiny stairs made of stone. In spite of all of the disabilities of many in the group, they were determined to reach the top. So, with a group of individuals in wheelchairs and with sight impairments, canes, weak limbs, and hand deformities, we accomplished this marvelous climb.

As we sat exhausted at the top, absorbing the beautiful view, Bernard said, "My climb today has been easy, compared to my daily climb out of bed since age six," when he had been diagnosed with HD.

The exhibit and numerous presentations made by IDEA members, some of whom had never spoken before about their personal experiences, were considered a huge success. Grace Choy, born in China but raised in the U.S., has spent all of her adult life at Carville, and "felt courage from her motherland to speak." Grace took a handful of Chinese dirt to spread around Carville.

The immense size of China impressed the twenty-eight in the group who took the thirty-two-hour train ride to Guangzhou. The others, primarily those with severe disabilities, flew from Beijing. Because of China's size and large population, we were told that "over six hundred leprosy hospitals" exist, most built in remote areas during Mao's regime.

Prior to the congress, none of us affected by leprosy would have been allowed into the country. Special negotiations had to be worked out with the ministry of health to relax this exclusion and allow our entry.

During our four days in Guangzhou, we visited the HANDA/IDEA Sewing School and three HD hospitals. Being diagnosed with HD in China, regardless of the level of disability, often results in losing the opportunities for education and employment. Young women in particular can lose their value as a potential wife and income-generating spouse. Training received at the school, which encompasses all daily living skills and a professional skill, allows the young women to be more positively received by the community. We could see the major difference between the new arrivals, unsmiling and refusing eye contact, and those nearing graduation, with enthusiasm in their voices and upright postures. We were all jubilant about the wonderful success of our advocacy work.

The three leprosy hospitals we visited had an older population divorced from their families and the community at large. They received limited medical support during the day and none at night. Most of the residents had lost limbs through amputation, but were still required to be self-sufficient. The medical staff was shrouded in caps, gowns, masks, and gloves. Most of the buildings, some in disrepair, had been built in the 1950s. Some of the residents wore archaic prostheses made of bamboo or metal, and others had built bicycles from scrap that they drove with one leg or hand. The hospitals, built in rural areas away from large communities, on isolated islands or in the country surrounded by rice paddies with high bushes, did not have public access for visitors. We were received with caution. However, when they saw our HD-related scars, their mood shifted to exuberance, and it became difficult to leave our brothers and sisters.

One person who stood out at the leprosy hospital built on an island was a young woman eighteen years old. She was the youngest of all the residents and stood quietly on the margins of the group. Because of her dark complexion, we suspected she was taking clofazimine. We found out from our guide that she had been abandoned by her family after diagnosis. In order to survive and have food, she had turned to prostitution within the hospital, and thus was not liked by the other women.

Having heard that a number of young women in China were taking clofazimine, Magdalena had packed a large supply of Mary Kay cosmetics for use with residents. As a part-time sales consultant for this product, she knew how to effectively hide blemishes. Magdalena used her wares with the young ladies at the sewing school, assisted by one of the congress participants, Mien Peltier. Mien, a pretty former resident of Carville and a Vietnamese refugee, had been on clofazimine, as were the Chinese teenagers. With the makeup, all of the ladies became radiant with their beauty, and encouraged Magdalena to continue spreading her special touch.

Mien knew about rejection, as her family had sold her to a military officer as a servant during the Vietnam War, and then her "adopted" family in the U.S. abandoned her when she was diagnosed with leprosy.

Upon hearing the story of the young girl at the hospital on the island, Magdalena and Mien quietly took her aside and convinced her to try the beauty products. Within an hour, she returned to join the group, smiling and with her head held high. The young lady had been magically transformed. The residents of the hospital stared at her new appearance. It was as if everyone at once became aware of her innocence. Magdalena left the young lady all of the Mary Kay products she had. Regrettably, she was unsuccessful in convincing the makers of Mary Kay to donate some of their products to China.

Prior to leaving China, the Executive Committee of IDEA, representing seven different countries, elected me as USA coordinator for the organization. I have held many positions on a paid and voluntary basis; however, this is the one I am most proud of.

The euphoria of the trip to China soon diminished as word spread of a meeting at Carville's once-elegant auditorium/theater, the same place where courageous residents had volunteered to start the "miracle at Carville." This was the place where residents had bonded together to exhibit their political power. It was also where residents were informed that their right to vote had been resurrected, and where the 1994 centennial had been held. This grand place was now the site where residents were formally told that their home was being converted into a boot camp. With this decision, the only hospital of its kind in the continental United States was declared to be in critical condition, and its continued existence deemed questionable. During its 105-year history, a U.S. president had never visited.

Magdalena's father, as well as my dad, enjoyed listening to our stories of traveling to Europe and Asia, as they had had their share of travels during World War II. Magdalena shared her last story with Mr. Santos before he died on December 23, 1998. He always supported the idea that it was Magdalena's choice to live any way she wished—he had done his job teaching her about work, love, and family values.

In an effort to attack past injustices and address the pending loss of support systems for Carville residents, I worked with IDEA to declare March 11, 1999, as the 1st International Day of Dignity and Respect. The day before, March 10, was also the fifty-eighth anniversary of that day when the miracle drug promin was first administered to volunteers at Carville, leading to a cure.

The residents were mistrustful of the conflicting messages being delivered by different groups. The U.S. Department of Health and Human Services press releases continued to focus on employee rights and to ignore resident issues. U.S. Congressman Richard Baker had previously promised in a newsletter that residents "will never have to leave Carville."

My belief, and IDEA's, was that Resolution 2264 did not adequately address the desire of some to remain at Carville, nor the availability of community resources, including psychosocial services, for those leaving and others yet to be diagnosed. When I relayed this concern via telephone to an aide of Congressman Baker, I received a return call. The aide informed me that Congressman Baker was "very angry" that I was not assisting with the "smooth transition" and yelled over the phone that "you and IDEA are just a bunch of outside agitators." I never thought that I would be considered an "outside agitator," especially after having been resident #2855 for 3,476 days.

According to some hospital employees, one of the hospital administrators had allegedly threatened staff with termination if they participated in the March 11 protest. The Daughters of Charity and the hospital priest criticized the event. The staff was afraid to participate. The National Guard, already on the premises, was rumored to have requested assistance from the sheriff's department and state police for crowd control. The large media corps composed of news agencies, journalists, TV crews, and documentary filmmakers from all over the world converged on this tiny community. Many of us believed that this perceived chaos, and the video cameras, might frighten the residents about participating in this special event. The plan was to march from the hospital's administration building to the cemetery to honor those who had previously fought for basic human rights.

The day before the march, the residents signed a petition to President Clinton addressing their concerns about choice, dignity, respect, and support from a government that historically had been unsupportive. The president, who had become known for making apologies regarding injustices that had occurred in the U.S. throughout the twentieth century, never offered an apology to those who had been considered dead simply because they were diagnosed with HD. U.S. senators John Breaux and Mary Landrieu were our lone support from the elected community.

On the morning of March 11, almost all of the residents who usually avoided the media, those who refused to leave the sanctuary of the enclosed walkways, those in wheelchairs, and those admitted to the infirmary because they were too ill to walk came out for the march. They made colorful signs and posters in various languages that described their feelings, such as "Why have you lied to us?" "Heck no, we won't go," and "You are stealing our home." The march was completed by some in electric wheelchairs, on bicycles, in golf carts and push wheelchairs, with canes or crutches, and by others who simply walked.

After our arrival at the cemetery, a prayer was said in different languages, and Betty Martin declared, "This day is a beautiful day for victory." A small hole was dug next to the grave of Harry Martin, and I symbolically buried prejudices, stigma, labeling, the "l" word, unfounded fear, and emotional pain. Many of us lingered, gently caressing every tombstone, long after the media, dignitaries, and "police protection" had vanished from sight. The "victory" referred to by Betty was measured in tears, and a wonderful sense of accomplishment, of telling the world that we were united. We were not "outside agitators." The 1st International Day of Dignity and Respect was also celebrated at HD hospitals throughout the world.

Without fanfare, the property's deed was returned to the state of Louisiana twenty-eight days after the march, on April 8, 1999.

One month after the deed passed hands, I joined up with a group long known for its work in the field of HD—the American Leprosy Missions (ALM). One of my previous physicians (Lee Yoder) had recommended me to the board. I also joined another physician (Margaret Brand) on the board who had been at Carville for many years and was affectionately known as the "eye doctor." I was able to get "afflicted by" and the "l" word deleted from written policy and substituted with "person affected by leprosy." My nine-year term ended in 2007.

Four and a half months later, one day after IDEA opened The Quest for Dignity Exhibit at the Presidio in San Francisco, the U.S. Department of Health and Human Services ceremoniously presented the Carville deed to Louisiana's Governor Foster. The governor then gave the key to the facility's front gate to the National Guard. August 19, 1999, was a sad day for all of us affected by leprosy.

During the 105 years that the facility was operated as a leprosarium, thousands of persons were affected by stigma, labeling, lives lost, identities changed, rights denied, and unjust practices. I also felt sad about the ongoing resistance by the federal government to provide adequate psychosocial services to those diagnosed with HD and living in the community.

The changing of the guard did not erase the unforgettable friendships, remarkable memories, achievements in research, and attacks on myths. We still felt joy in knowing that the need for a leprosarium and institutionalization had finally come to an end—there would not be any new admissions, but those declining the stipend could stay for life. Many still chose to remain in Carville, as they had no other home.

The event in San Francisco made my moods swing from peaks to valleys. I felt somber reading about the missed ceremonies at Carville, but I experienced special warmth when a family member, brother-in-law Glenn Skates, attended the San Francisco activities. Other than Magdalena and Erika, no other family member had ever seen the exhibit. I felt overjoyed that the opening ceremonies for the exhibit presented another opportunity to dispel myths about HD.

In January of 2000, Magdalena and I traveled with good friends Willie and Gloria Quintanilla to Turkey and Greece. Prior to the trip, we communicated with three Turkish friends we had met at the Spain conference. Dr. Türkan Saylan (famous leprologist), Dr. Ayse Yuksel, and Hatice Erdogan invited us to attend an event to celebrate World Leprosy Day at the University of Istanbul where all three served on the faculty. I was presented with a unique surprise, the Etem Utku Medal for outstanding international advocacy work in the field of leprosy. People in the audience and recipients of other awards congratulated me as photos were taken. The surprise had an even bigger impact as we discovered our picture and accompanying story in one of Istanbul's newspapers.

The next day, Dr. Yuksel gave me a personal tour of their leprosy hospital. The hospital is located on a hill and was built at a time when this area was considered to be on the outskirts of Istanbul, past the ancient walls of Constantinople. The hospital complex did not have fortresslike walls, but visitors did have to pass a security gate. The facility, at the time with fewer than forty residents, was in the middle of two other institutions. One was a large enclosed complex for the chronically mentally ill and the other was an even larger facility with twenty-foot walls, razor wire, and armed sentries—"a military hospital for dangerous criminals." The hospital was an island, surrounded not by water but by other people traditionally ostracized by society.

The residents had different levels of disabilities, and unlike in many other hospitals throughout the world, were a varied age group, ranging from people in their twenties to those in their eighties. I greeted each of my brothers and sisters with a hello, or *"merhaba,"* and facial embrace on both cheeks.

We had the opportunity to visit with many of my brothers and sisters, some of whom had had similar experiences with their mothers-in-law. So, with many wonderful memories, a beautiful medal, and newly made friends, we boarded a ship and left Turkey after getting information about other HD hospitals in the Mediterranean area.

The next four days gave me additional insights into how past and present societies have had similar views on people with leprosy. On the first day of our ride on the ship, we viewed a promotional video, which focused on the different tours. These included a visit to the ancient port city of Ephesus on the island of Kusadasi, and Spinalonga was the "last leper colony in Europe" according to the video narrator.

According to numerous historians and medical researchers, leprosy arrived in the Aegean Sea area through slaves transported by Alexander the Great, the Romans, and the Crusaders.

Our ship passed many of the islands previously used as places to isolate persons affected by leprosy, including the islands of Mt. Athos, Samos, and Leros, off the coast of Turkey. The "outcasts" were forced to live on their own as best they could, in abandoned fortresses or in monasteries as unpaid laborers. Greece also had similar places on a small cape on the northwest corner of the island of Rhodes and the better known Spinalonga off the coast of Crete.

The ship's first stop on the island of Kusadasi gave us the opportunity to visit the home where Mary, the mother of Jesus, allegedly lived after her son's crucifixion. This was an exhilarating sight until we were told by the tour guide that the fountain of Saint Mary was said to be "healing water, except for [persons with leprosy]." The tour guide explained that because the disease was so feared even today by the locals, persons suspected of having leprosy were barred from the fountain of Saint Mary.

Ironically, I was wearing IDEA's Quest for Dignity cap (international tour of the HD exhibit). During this walking tour, I was asked by a fellow tourist what it meant. When I explained the significance, she was aghast to hear that leprosy still existed, especially since all of the tours implied that this disease had been extinct for many years. This chance encounter with the pretty lady from California opened up opportunities for me to educate others in the group about HD.

The ancient port city of Ephesus was one of the most modern cities of its time. It possessed a huge library, jewelry stores, a well-stocked market, running water, public toilets, large stadiums and theaters, exquisite statues such as *Nike, the Goddess of Victory*, and a large hospital. In spite of its modern ambiance, the leaders of Ephesus still "refused to treat persons affected by leprosy," and they were instead banished to one of the islands previously mentioned.[1] Even though the biblical person with leprosy asked Jesus "if you will, please heal me," the populace of Ephesus was not accepting of this grossly misunderstood disease.

We left this beautiful community shrouded in a cold rain, feeling not only exhilaration in viewing a place we had previously seen only through our imaginations, but also sadness because of the fear that has always followed the leprosy bacillus.

Our next stop was at a large island located farther south in Rhodes. Rhodes is commonly known for its mink, the old fortress now known as Old Town, and Lindos, the site of the Temple of Athena, with over 250 steps which "lead to the heavens." Lesser known to the tourist is the monastery once used to house persons affected with leprosy. Lesser known still is the small Bay of Hippocrates where the father of medicine used to go to bathe and experiment with the plants growing in the area, which were used for medicinal purposes.

One of the plants he reportedly experimented with was the fruit from the karobe (*sic*) tree. According to the tour guide, Hippocrates used the karobe fruit to make tea to treat what is now known as diabetes. The residents of outcast communities knew that Hippocrates experimented with this fruit. The men who completed their medical studies bathed in the Bay of Hippocrates and drank tea made from the karobe tree. Reportedly, the outcasts grew this tree on their usually barren islands, hoping and praying that it would be their miracle medicine to cure them of leprosy.

The next island on our tour was Crete, the largest island in the Aegean Sea. The Venetians built a fortress and defended their occupation of Crete until ousted by the Turks. Eventually, the Cretan Republic passed a resolution to convert Spinalonga to a place for the isolation of persons with leprosy in 1903. Hundreds of people from throughout Greece eventually were "sentenced for life" to Spinalonga, and many of the "inmates" died of secondary infections due to the dearth of medical care.

The law of 1903 continued to be honored throughout World War II by the Axis powers and later the Allies. In 1957, the government of Greece finally closed the facility and moved twenty-eight of the residents to a newly built center on the grounds of a general hospital in Athens.

Prior to the residents of Spinalonga being moved to Athens, the government built a modern facility with readily available medical care. The facility, named the Center for the Rehabilitation of Leprosy Patients, was in the rear of the spacious acreage designated for the West Attica General Hospital, was colored differently from other buildings, and was encircled with a cyclone fence.

The residents continue to receive a small stipend from the government, but the original center is now abandoned, and residents live in a more modern building approximately forty yards from their "first home" in Athens. The average age of the residents is seventy-five; all have HD-related disabilities, and their rooms are filled with religious icons.

Our final stop on the tour of the "Land of Myth" was Athens, where I visited the only HD hospital in Greece. I had the privilege of meeting with Dr. K. P. Kyriakis, Dr. George Kontochristopolis, and Dr. Demetrius Panteleos.

Dr. K. P. Kyriakis of the West Attica General Hospital and Leprosy Center in Athens has many diaries of residents which chronicled the horrible conditions of their existence on Spinalonga. According to Dr. Kyriakis, the Greek government is currently excavating the island for archeological purposes and plans to restore the Venetian fortress to museum quality.

The medical staff noted that the incidence of leprosy in Greece has declined to almost negligible percentages during the twentieth century, even though the country has not initiated any eradication programs. The biggest problem appeared to be with persons effectively treated with MDT who neglected to comply with instructions for follow-up examinations. Additionally, persons living in rural areas do not consistently follow treatment requirements, and thus may be "required" to become inpatients at the center until after they have repeated negative tests. Their stay at the hospital is designed to emulate their natural home as much as possible, and many bring such things as gardening tools and chickens.

Maria Vacenaki is an eighty-year-old who lived at the center in Athens and had resided at Spinalonga from 1948 to 1957. She was twenty-eight years old when diagnosed after a doctor in her village in Crete noticed that she had lost her eyebrows, a common trait among those with HD. She eventually married a young man she had previously admired from afar—"a young man from a neighboring village also forced to go to Spinalonga."

Ms. Vacenaki described life on Spinalonga as "pleasant," even though everyone worked hard to survive, many were sick, and families were separated; she lived a "decent life with only my clothes and two wooden chairs as possessions." She did not feel bitterness about her "imprisonment" and emphasized that "leprosy is not hereditary because many women had children and none of the children became ill." She added that her experiences were "as God wills."

She and her husband declined Greece's invitation in 1957 to move to Athens and instead returned to her village on the island of Crete. She described finding her home in the same condition as when she has been "escorted to Spinalonga." The villagers initially had expressed fear and then felt that a miracle had occurred and welcomed her back to the community and her church.

Currently, Greece has approximately one thousand individuals who have or are being treated for HD, with three to five new cases per year. However, there is still so much fear of the disease, with physicians expressing little interest in this specialty, that those newly diagnosed are "still placed in isolation and the staff cover their bodies with caps, gloves, gowns, etc." The three physicians added that the Greek Orthodox Church has been very supportive of persons with HD.

Later that evening after visiting Ms. Vacenaki, we boarded a plane for our return trip to the U.S. Thinking that I was through hearing the "l" word, I watched a movie titled *Music of the Heart* with Meryl Streep. In the movie, Ms. Streep's character has a conversation with a friend who describes the Bronx in New York City as "a leper colony." My newfound friends, sitting in front and to the side of me, booed and gave the thumbs down—telling me, with a big smile, that *they* knew better.

We arrived home on the evening of February 11. Realizing that on Sunday, February 13, all Catholic churches were scheduled to have a reading relating to persons affected by leprosy, I had written to my bishop and pastor months before. I had encouraged them to use this time to educate parishioners about the severe and unjust negative connotations surrounding the "l" word.

I was rewarded with compassion and understanding the day after the reading from Leviticus. Many of my friends and colleagues excitedly talked to me about the sermons at their respective churches. The sermons included accurate information about HD. They praised their church leaders for their willingness to educate the community about leprosy, and all encouraged me to continue my role as advocate on behalf of other persons affected by leprosy. In a short time, the organization IDEA and I had become synonymous with advocacy.

In May of 2000, I traveled to Italy at the invitation of AIFO (International Association for Friends of Raoul Follereau). Follereau was a French journalist who became a passionate advocate in the 1950s for persons affected by leprosy. He was a flamboyant man and always did things with much gusto. His enthusiasm lives on through the organizations named after him.

AIFO awarded IDEA the 2000 Raoul Follereau Award for "courageous work in impacting change in the field of leprosy." AIFO invited Anwei Law, international coordinator for IDEA, Dr. Gopal, IDEA's president for international relations, and me, IDEA's USA coordinator, to accept the award on behalf of IDEA. The three of us, along with Anwei's eight-year-old daughter, Lian, traveled to several leprosy hospitals and met with numerous residents, most of whom were seventy years and older. The first one we visited was San Marino Leprosy Hospital in Genova, home of Christopher Columbus. The hospital was established in 1150, making it the oldest one of its kind. The administrator, Dr. Nuñez, had kept a site that was over a hundred years old and that "used to be home for many patients" as a living museum.

The second was called Caserta Leprosy Hospital. It was situated far from the main highway, as with most leprosy hospitals, and was hugged by large trees. Even some of the natives in the area were unaware of its location. The residents at Caserta were primarily elderly women, each assigned a room with a tiny kitchen so that she could cook her own meals if she wished. One of the women told us a fascinating story about being diagnosed as a young girl and sent to the hospital, meeting her "lost" childhood friend at the hospital, and eventually marrying him.

The trip to Italy brought me full circle from a tearful moment with Mom in 1968. Dad had died believing that God was punishing him through me for some horrible sins he had allegedly committed. Mom had told me she did not want to die with the same thought, but did not know how to cleanse her soul. With the assistance of my parish pastor in Houston, I started on a journey to help open the gates of heaven for Mom.

Monsignor James Jamail of St. Vincent's Catholic Church and Monsignor Frank Rossi of the Houston-Galveston Catholic Diocese intervened in getting me a special audience with Pope John Paul II on May 31 after I informed them of my trip to Italy and the award. Up to forty thousand persons can receive a pass for an audience with the pope in St. Peter's Square. However, a special audience meant joining approximately one hundred individuals for a personal, one-on-one blessing from the pope.

Unfortunately, the special audience did not occur because an official at the U.S. Vatican Office became upset that AIFO, unbeknownst to me, had also made a request to "a high official" that I get "an extra special audience." The monsignor assigned to the U.S Vatican Office was very clear with his message—"AIFO went over my head, so now you can go to the Vatican and plead your case to get a pass for a special audience." The harshness of his words left me speechless and puzzled about the gravity of his action. After so many years of hoping to find a way to ease my mother's guilt, and having an opportunity to be blessed by the pope, politics got in the way. It was so unreal.

Georgio Trevisan, an eighty-year-old resident of Tivoli and avid volunteer with AIFO, was my guide and interpreter. His white face turned red in response to the monsignor's pettiness and his refusal to allow me the special audience. Mr. Trevisan grabbed my hand and rushed me out of the office, explaining that as a "very good Catholic [he] could not punch a priest."

I was denied the opportunity to get a special blessing from the pope, but Mr. Trevisan still managed to get me within five feet of His Holiness. I had purchased a number of rosaries made by friars assigned to the Basilica of San Antonio in Padova. When the pope and I made brief eye contact, he raised his right hand and made the sign of the cross as I held up the rosaries. One of the rosaries was made of rosewood, and I got it for Mom, whose name is Rosa.

At precisely 11:30 a.m., the pope was whisked out of St. Peter's Square and May 31, 2000, became a very special day for me. I left with a great sense of accomplishment, of warmth, tenderness, and cleanliness, no longer feeling "unclean."

So much doubt about my existence was wiped away by a simple blessing from the pope—even if it was done from five feet away. Thirty-two years of silently crying to relieve the pain of having been removed from my family were relieved in an instant, resurrecting a new me. Mr. Trevisan caressed my arm and gave me a warm smile as he slowly nodded his head.

Paola Springhetti of AIFO had shared with me words spoken by the pope related to HD. Pope John Paul II said, "I . . . join the worldwide journey of people with leprosy . . . following the examples of Christ . . . [and] . . . embrace all my brothers and sisters who suffer from this disease called Hansen's . . . [and] . . . renew my promise . . . that . . . you will feel the solidarity of healing." To my knowledge, no other pope had ever addressed this topic in such a compassionate manner. I felt especially touched by his comments, as I have, on occasion, been criticized for referring to other persons with HD throughout the world as my "brothers and sisters." I returned to the States with a renewed vigor in my faith.

Three months after my return from Italy, I went to Laredo on a work-related visit. Even though I was occupied with work during the day, I spent evenings at my sister's home, also home to Mom at the time.

Mom had been experiencing serious lapses in memory, but on a warm, clear day in September 2000, her mind was lucid and her eyes focused. On this day I shared with her Pope John Paul's words in Spanish. She stared at me, her lips became tight, her chin started to quiver, and large tears started to slowly move down her cheeks. Mom hugged me tightly and whispered, "Ya puedo morir con mi alma limpia" ("Now I can die with a clean soul").

Mom reluctantly confirmed that she had packed only a small suitcase for my trip to Carville. Deep down, she said, she wanted to believe that I would recover. However, her ignorance about the illness and the deep-rooted belief about sin and punishment being links to leprosy forced her to consider that she might never see me alive again after leaving me at Carville. I still have the small suitcase, made of green canvas and earth-tone vinyl with my name on the side. She asked for forgiveness, but I reassured her that my love for her was unconditional. We hugged tightly and silently sobbed. I saved all of my letters in this suitcase.

The next day I flew out of Laredo, and, as the plane lifted into the sky, I squinted hard to take a good look at the land that might have been the cause of my disease. I saw Laredo, the town that did not know whether to comfort me or fear me. In the distance was the home that served as the center, where my values were rooted. I sensed the presence of the mother who sacrificed so much for her son. Mom's guilt that God was punishing her through me for unknown sins she had committed was erased from her mind forever.

# Living with a Clean Soul

Within one month after my reunion with Mom, I felt a new level of energy as I embarked on another journey of discovery. Many of the emotions I felt while at Carville and the physical pain I endured had become somewhat easier to describe to others. My view of life was definitely not colored gray, as when I was initially diagnosed with HD.

By recalling many intimate meetings with the leprosy bacillus, I was able to develop a presentation titled "The Power of Ignorance." This topic was a tool I could use to describe the manner in which injustices, stigma, and segregation were interconnected. Unfortunately, those blinded by fear of the unknown have given these three words life. As a social worker, ex-resident of Carville, and person of Mexican ancestry, I was able to talk passionately about these issues and, in the process, heighten the knowledge base of many laypersons, physicians, researchers, and social workers.

My experience addressing issues related to leprosy prepared me for other presentations, such as when a co-worker, Donna Olson-Salas, and I became instructors at the Houston Police Academy. For nearly two decades, I have been a part of the presentation of general information regarding mental disabilities through law enforcement agencies in Houston. However, with a focus on mental retardation, Donna and I were able to infuse some new knowledge about stigma. The recipients of this information were seasoned police officers, men and women who had already confronted dangerous situations involving people with cognitive disabilities. Stigma does not restrict itself to one group or a specific disability.

In May of 2001, the social work unit in El Paso, Texas, invited me to make a presentation titled "Surviving the Stigma of Disabilities." I once again took a step toward healing as a result of my diagnosis and institutionalization. One of the attendees at the presentation had just been confronted with what she described as "an unbearable burden"—how to help a person newly diagnosed with leprosy. We worked collaboratively in linking the person with appropriate resources and helped to defuse the unfounded fear expressed by the family.

The rest of 2001 placed me in a position of experiencing a great range of emotions, from exhilaration at one end to frightful sorrow at the other. On June 6, I was attending a meeting at the Houston chapter of the American Red Cross when pagers started to go off for some of the attendees at the meeting: law enforcement and the emergency medical department for the Houston Fire Department. The alarm was that the National Weather Service was issuing a "severe weather alert"—Tropical Storm Allison was heading straight for Houston.

Allison, whose name has since been removed from the list of future storms, lingered throughout the greater Houston area. She dropped a bomb of water during a four-day period and transformed Houston into a lake. A total of thirty-eight inches of rain accumulated, causing twenty-two deaths and billions of dollars in damage. At the time, it was deemed the most costly natural disaster in the United States (Katrina would surpass Allison in cost).

On June 9, when most of the rain fell, Magdalena's mother arrived at our home for a three-month stay. Magdalena's brother, Bobby, had driven her from Laredo. Her arrival, as usual, was a joyous occasion for both families, one receiving their mother and the other bidding a temporary farewell. Mrs. Santos's self-prescribed regimen was a challenge to all of the siblings. Nevertheless, her arrival was anticipated and well planned for, and we looked forward to the next three months.

We spent the evening of June 9 watching the movie *Molokai: The Story of Father Damien* with Kris Kristofferson. It had been filmed on location at Kalaupapa Settlement on Molokai Island with most of the residents playing themselves, but with makeup designed to mimic advanced stages of the disease prevalent during the days of yesteryear when treatment was not available. It was exciting to watch the movie, as Magdalena and I knew many of the characters living at the settlement, but the movie itself was very disappointing; the acting was flat and the lack of a dramatic musical soundtrack did not help the viewer stay focused on the story. In fact, when the tape finally ended at 11 p.m., my kids, Bobby, and his wife had fallen asleep on the couch.

Once I turned the movie off and everyone went to bed, I decided to watch a "special weather report" on one of the local TV channels. I was surprised to hear that major flooding was occurring throughout the greater Houston area and that several people had reportedly drowned. As I switched channels,

I could sense a great urgency on the part of the newscasters to warn viewers about the dangers created by Allison. My sleepiness disappeared instantly and I peeked outside. Luckily we had driven all of the cars up the driveway. Others were not as fortunate, and I saw my neighbor's commercial pickup and much debris from other homes floating on the water. Our street and hundreds of others became raging rivers removing everything not firmly tied down.

The rain was falling with such intensity that I could not see more than two feet in front of me. Also, once I woke up Magdalena, we had difficulty hearing each other. It felt as if we were standing next to a huge waterfall. The dangerous flow of the water reminded me of the similarly dangerous muddy water of the Mississippi River as it raced past the levy which protected Carville.

As the water continued to inch toward the house, I wondered about the damage about to occur. I could visualize my parents' feeling of hopelessness and despair when they could not find a cause for my illness. I could now understand their fears, as I felt helpless to save my own family from the pain of facing the destructive power of water. I had never bothered to secure flood insurance, placing our home in a vulnerable position.

In vain, I tried to hold the water back by placing a cardboard box by the front door. Finally, as the water started to come in, bubbling through the wooden floors, we all stood in stunned silence, admiring the crystal-clear flow. The water, however, was not so "clear," as it was a thousand times more toxic than a dirty swimming pool. The rising water also forced many animals, such as snakes and rats, to seek refuge in our home. We discouraged their entry by pushing them out of the house with a broomstick.

The rain did not lessen until 3:30 a.m., and the streets were not passable until 10 a.m. However, without having had any sleep, at daybreak we started the backbreaking task of removing clothing, furniture, and pictures from the house. The worst job was tearing out the saturated carpet. In time, we realized that the most valuable items we had lost were pictures, J. R.'s certificates and awards, and our respective yearbooks. I was fortunate to be able to save the thousands of letters mailed to me while at Carville.

The scorching heat followed once the sun broke through the clouds, along with large sewer flies, fire ants, a sea of mosquitoes inflicting up to one hundred bites per hour, and the mold now so well known to insurance companies. The severe damage to our home was compounded by the collapse of the community's infrastructure. The building where I worked was completely destroyed, and hundreds of Magdalena's co-workers were affected by Allison.

What followed for us was an introduction to the bureaucracy of the recovery process and the realization that there was no rescue unit en route to make everything right again. Like thousands of others in Houston, we were confronted with community meetings conducted by elected officials from every level of office and with mountains of paperwork in applying for assistance through the Red Cross, FEMA, and SBA (the Small Business Administration provides loans for rebuilding of homes after natural disasters).

Magdalena and I also faced the challenges of work. The field of social work is a helping profession; thus we still needed to address staff and consumer issues. Both of our employers, MHMRA of Harris County and the VA hospital, operate on a 24/7 basis, so there was little time for self-pity. Instead, we focused on helping others and relished the support given to us by family and neighbors. Regarding the latter, we received assistance for electrical work, boxes for storage, cleaning detergents, and food. Boxes, however, can be a bad omen, as storing any flood-damaged materials in them can dramatically heighten the growth of mold.

In tabulating the damage done to our home, we estimated losing two-thirds of all our furniture and personal effects. The costs of repairs were as much as building a new home; thus we chose the latter. We did not realize the value of having made the last payment of our mortgage on the day of the flood until such time that we needed collateral on the loan to rebuild.

The rebuilding process took twenty-one months as we struggled through the frightening experiences of dealing with contractors, deed restrictions, designs, permits, lawyers, and much more. During the time that our house was being rebuilt, we stayed at a 1940s home on the property of the VA hospital. The hospital administrators had offered to help the hundreds of VA employees affected by the flood by offering free hotel accommodations and VA foreclosed homes. When Magdalena's name came up, one of the three homes on the hospital grounds was available. We accepted the administration's offer of paying a competitive rent and lived in a two-story home with a bomb shelter for twenty-one months.

The house reminded me of similar structures found on the grounds of Carville. How ironic that I was again residing on federal property, but the second time around, I was not restricted from entering the family homes or moving around the property.

Approximately one month after the devastating flood, the Texas Chapter of the National Association of Social Workers (NASW) chose Magdalena as Texas Social Worker of the Year. The material losses seemed so trivial when Magdalena's thirty years of service was recognized by peers. The award was a culmination of her work in the community and contributions to social work in general. The best parts were having J. R. and Erika receive the award on her behalf before an audience of one thousand social workers and receiving a congratulatory letter from President George W. Bush.

Magdalena was unable to go to the luncheon in Austin, Texas, on October 12, 2001, to receive her social work award because she was at home recovering from surgery. The day of the flood from Tropical Storm Allison, she was scheduled to have a mammogram. She rescheduled because of the flooding and did not receive her examination until September. Within weeks of the exam, she underwent surgery for breast cancer.

Two months or so after being notified of her award, Magdalena was wondering out loud, and silently, about my love for "half a woman." Feeling branded with her diagnosis and anticipating rejection, she pleaded that I not judge her for having only one breast. She became very despondent, usually cried herself to sleep, anticipated death, and felt stigmatized by the situation. My words were not strong enough to console her, so I let my actions of support and prayer guide her in recognizing my eternal love.

Her first surgery resulted in serious infections, as the skin flap did not heal and became necrotic. I purchased a shower chair and would gently bathe her each morning, providing dressings for her reddish-looking wound, which gradually turned black. As the healing process took longer than anticipated, visiting nurses would care for the infection. On occasion, a nun or priest from our church would visit and administer communion.

Most of her recovery time was spent either at the hospital or on the second floor of our rented home. Her doctor had issued specific instructions for her to avoid climbing stairs; thus our bedroom became her miniprison.

J. R. and Erika insulated their pain by not asking questions and established heavy schedules so that their activities would be away from home. Magdalena and I misinterpreted their actions and started to believe that they were insensitive to her physical and emotional pain. In time, the four of us started to articulate our fears. We realized that our love for each other had not diminished, but rather had actually become stronger.

Magdalena eventually required two additional surgeries, one of which I thought might be fatal. She was away from work for three months. During this time she had occasions when she would perk up and feel so well that she ventured to come down from the second floor to stand by the front door and smell the fresh air. Later, we found out that her perky demeanor was linked to times when friends and family members had organized prayer groups for her health.

After many months, Magdalena received the doctor's okay to return to work. She requested that I escort her to her favorite beauty shop, which she exited with a new look—red hair. She then directed me to take her to purchase a red dress. Later, on the evening of January 22, 2002, Magdalena accompanied me to the MHMRA Employee Recognition Dinner where I served as master of ceremonies. I was happy to recognize the more than one hundred employees being honored; however, I was also silently recognizing Magdalena as a survivor of breast cancer.

As the months passed, Magdalena regained her confidence to lead in the workplace. With the purchase of a prosthesis, which balanced her appearance, she became active in a support group and submitted an abstract for presentation at a social work conference. Even though the abstract was not accepted for presentation because the reviewers did not deem this topic important at the time, she used the time to write about her experiences. This was one of many stepping stones toward her emotional recovery. Her beauty and vigor returned in full force.

Magdalena was reenergized even more as J.R. started his final exams in preparation for his graduation from the University of Houston. His graduation was due, in part, to the discipline he had acquired while playing baseball at Bellaire High School. His coach, Rocky Manuel, had instilled in J. R. a desire to succeed. Even though he was never a starter on a team full of players being recruited to play Division I ball or sign professional contracts, he blossomed into a star in the classroom. At graduation, I gave him the same whistle of pride my own father had given me at my graduation from LSU.

Three months after Tropical Storm Allison and the occurrence of four major events in our lives, a different type of bomb disrupted our security.

September 11, 2001, was a devastating day for all U.S. residents. I recall the serenity of the day, the beautiful blue skies. It was the first time since Erika started driving that I had not offered her hints on how to improve. She acknowledged such as we swapped seats after arriving at Bellaire High School. "What can possibly ruin such a wonderful day?" I thought. Well, the answer was obvious, as millions witnessed the collapse of the Twin Towers in New York City.

The first-year anniversary of the attack on America included many commemorative events throughout the country. In Houston, I was invited by my employer to read a statement to fellow workers about my thoughts on 9/11. Additionally, the *Houston Chronicle* printed an excerpt of my statement, and the local CBS affiliate recorded my words: "I recall hugging everyone around me and calling my wife at work. I realized that the same extreme sadness I felt as a high school student learning of President Kennedy's assassination was resurrected when human bombs were thrown at our country."

For almost twelve months after September 11, the VA compound where we lived became one of the most secure places in the city as federal police and military personnel monitored the three entrances to the property.

On June 14, 2002, one year after the flood, Magdalena and I were witnesses to an extraordinary event, which occurred in Auburn, New York, at the home of Harriet Tubman. Ms. Tubman had been a leader of the Underground Railroad during the Civil War. She had risked her life to guide three hundred slaves to freedom.

On June 14, Ms. Tubman's great-grandniece, who serves as guide in the great liberator's home, now a museum, met two women from Ghana. Ironically, these two ladies, in traditional dress, had come to the United States to talk about their stigma, a stigma created when they were diagnosed with HD. The women were visiting Seneca Falls, minutes away from Auburn, to participate in the First International Conference on Women Affected by Leprosy hosted by IDEA.

Magdalena presented the keynote address at the conference, titled "The Spirit of Women." She focused her presentation on the kaleidoscope of emotions she had experienced when diagnosed with breast cancer. She equated her emotions with the challenges she faced when I was diagnosed with leprosy and acknowledged two women from Texas diagnosed with leprosy who have served as her role models. These women were Mary Ruth Daigle and Julia Elwood.

Many of the conference attendees spoke about their gut-wrenching experiences at the First Presbyterian Church where another social worker, Alice Paul, had proposed the first Equal Rights Amendment. The ladies celebrated their newfound courage to speak against the injustices they were forced to endure by embracing seven women from the U.S. honored at the National Women's Hall of Fame, where the first inductee had also been a social worker, Jane Addams. Finally, the women slept in homes around Seneca Falls that Harriet Tubman had used in her network to freedom.

Women at this first-of-its-kind conference made history by voicing their pain and by passing a resolution declaring their empowerment. Some of their declarations included:

• The World Health Organization should recognize the harm resulting from past practices which condoned the separation of women diagnosed with leprosy from their children, and sponsor:
Workshops to address healing and conciliation between mothers and their children.
Workshops to address healing for parents deprived of their right to have children.
• All religious faiths should work collaboratively to change gross misconceptions that leprosy is synonymous with "sin."

- Medical schools should initiate curricula which address the psychosocial aspects of being diagnosed with leprosy or other misunderstood diseases.
- Governments should make funding available for women affected by leprosy to record their experiences in oral histories so that this documentary of injustices is not repeated by other generations.

Seneca Falls, New York, the town Frank Capra used as the model for Bedford Falls in the movie *It's a Wonderful Life*, was touched by women affected by leprosy. These courageous women were ready to fight with words and education to end the painful sting of stigma.

Two months after the women's conference, I visited the land of Brazil as the U.S. representative for IDEA. This country is rich with a unique history, a diverse population composed of many who migrated to Brazil seeking better lives. As a result, there are many Japanese, for example, who do not speak their native language but practice many of their customs, and Japanese restaurants flourish throughout the country. There are also many descendents of people who resided in the American South during the pre–Civil War era. Many of them have English names but speak no English; however, they sing "Dixie" and display the Confederate flag at their jobs and homes.[1]

The trip to Salvador, Brazil, located on the Atlantic coast and oftentimes visited by Brazilians during their vacations, was for the purpose of attending the 16th International Leprosy Congress/Hansen's Disease. The title of the conference included "Hansen's disease" as a compromise to the Brazilian government because the word leprosy is banned from their vocabulary. This is one of the many efforts initiated by ex-residents of HD hospitals to reduce the stigma of the disease.

Besides those making an attack on terminology, there is a powerful group of individuals who formed the organization called MORHAN (Movement for the Reintegration of People Affected by HD). MORHAN has support from one of Brazil's most respected poets, Maria Leda. Additionally, the country's best-known soap opera star, Solange Couto, convinced her director to incorporate several HD-related scenes into one of the program's stories, enhancing the country's knowledge of HD. In real life, Ms. Couto has an intimate knowledge of the illness, as her mother was once treated for the disease.

MORHAN also has secured funding from the Ministry of Health to use billboards throughout the country to educate the public about HD. The goal is to encourage individuals who suspect they have HD to seek treatment, and, in the long run, create a more accepting attitude about the disease, thus reducing stigma.

One of the members of MORHAN, Christiano Torres, has completed a fascinating history of the more than four hundred leprosy villages that had been constructed by humans and then devoured by the Brazilian jungles. Few people in Brazil, much less the rest of the world, have an understanding of how widespread the forces of isolation have been when the term "Hansen's disease" has been introduced to a community.

The congress in Brazil was the third such meeting I had attended and the one I felt most energized by, primarily because I knew many of the attendees. The host group and I had the opportunity to make presentations on stigma, women's issues, and advocacy.

For the first time since the congress started meeting, the topic of stigma was discussed at length. The first congress, held in Berlin in 1897, excluded the participation of nonphysicians. The oral presentations and papers were so focused on the HD bacilli that a review of the literature, even into the twenty-first century, couldn't determine whether the author is referencing the bacillus or a person. Additionally, pictures in publications have included only slides of body parts, never the person. This "scientific" approach has only strengthened the public's perception of HD, i.e., individuals affected by leprosy are nonpersons.

The organizers planned a two-day pre-congress session on stigma. Even though this was part of the formal program, only fifty persons attended. References were commonly made to Erving Goffman's definition of stigma; however, none of the attendees had a universal way to measure stigma. While I am a firm believer in scholarly and well-researched materials, I also believe that stigma needs to be gauged based on what people articulate about their feelings, e.g., fear, divorce, isolation, guilt, uncleanness, etc. However, stigma can also be defused with intervention from helping professionals who can validate their fears and redirect those fears with accurate information about leprosy.

The presentation on advocacy generated the most interest, with over four hundred in attendance. Part of it, I like to believe, was because of my presence, and the discussion on how public ignorance about HD can result in social stigma and isolation. However, the real attraction was soap opera star Solange Couto. Another star was the president of Brazil's Prostitute Association, who addressed the double stigma when those of their lifestyle are diagnosed with HD.

One of the comments I made about advocacy is that without the appropriate support resources when someone is first diagnosed with HD, the person can easily become entrapped in a deep cavern of depression. I described my own periods of depression and how suicide, at the time, seemed like the only route to take as a means to eliminate the emotional pain. Surprisingly, during the question and answer period, three of the attendees vividly described how they too had fallen prey to depression and suicide ideation. Like me, they were lucky to have had someone intervene and prevent a fatality from occurring. Many of the physicians and researchers present commented to me later that they were shocked at the statements about suicide. They finally realized how HD could affect the mind as well as the body.

One of the most unique actions taken by members of the congress was to develop a list of recommendations designed to counter decisions made by the World Health Organization (WHO). The congress struggled for over a decade before publicly voicing an opinion which ran contrary to views presented by WHO.

In 1985, WHO identified 122 countries where leprosy was endemic. Endemicity was and continues to be defined in terms of numbers, i.e., prevalence of one HD case per ten thousand population. Six years later, in 1991, the World Health Assembly adopted as an objective "the elimination of leprosy as a public health problem by the year 2000," the goal being to decrease the number of leprosy cases to fewer than one per ten thousand.

Additionally, WHO developed a grading system to identify levels of disability of persons affected by HD. The grading system was intended for use as a tool for the development of treatment and/or rehabilitation centers. Grade 1, for example, identifies persons with a high degree of disability (amputation and severe sensory loss) as also being at serious risk of other impairments. Higher grades refer to persons with lesser disabilities.

Third, WHO created guidelines for diagnosis of leprosy by field staff. The guidelines focused on the visible signs and anesthetic patches common to this disease. However, it excludes others who are ill but with few obvious signs. These are the individuals who can ultimately end up with serious nerve damage and face obvious stigma.

The recommendations approved by the congress included:

• Abolish the goal of "prevalence," as this is not a good indicator of HD control, i.e., data from the field indicates that HD cases will continue to rise up through the year 2025.
• Focus on a system to educate professionals and the public about HD, and not on a grading system of disability, i.e., integrate HD control programs into general health services.
• Train all levels of staff involved in HD control, e.g., communication targeted at general public and students in medical schools.

My return flight from Brazil was uneventful, as I traveled at night and slept most of the trip. However, I had a rude awakening in my homeland.

I deplaned in Houston at approximately 6 a.m. and proceeded through the usual checkpoints for reentry into the U.S. Upon arriving at one of the customs checks, I was quizzed by an official who told me to declare everything I had bought in Brazil. She assumed that I was a physician after learning of my attendance at the congress. When pressed for more information, I simply explained that I had been previously treated for HD and attended the congress as a paid member and speaker. The lady slowly moved two steps back, extended her fingers outwards while keeping her arms glued to her body and whispered, "You are a leper!" Her next words were "move on . . . quickly."

As I passed, she continued to keep her distance. I could sense her staring but I was too tired from the flight to stare back and did not wish to be detained further if I remotely appeared to be argumentative. Ah, my welcomes after leprosy-related trips have been unpredictable and memorable.

Within weeks after I returned from Brazil, on August 30, 2002, all of the Ramirez siblings and some of their children met at Gerardo's house in Laredo to celebrate Mom's eightieth birthday. She was able to recognize all of her children; however, she appeared puzzled at being hugged and kissed "by strangers" who were actually her grandchildren. Alzheimer's had started to affect her memory.

The event included a cake, many presents, music, food, and a piñata. In years past, Mom would have been the first to take a whack at the piñata, but not this time. She explained about being *cansada*, tired, and asked to be taken home. By midnight, Mom was on her way to bed.

August 30 was a special occasion for me in a different sense, as it was the day before my twenty-fifth anniversary of being discharged from Carville. It was also the day that I chose to cease taking dapsone (DDS). I felt a sense of freedom and slept very soundly that evening.

One month after my return from Brazil, I was in Baton Rouge, Louisiana, attending an HD seminar while our home was being bulldozed to the ground because of the flood. At the seminar, I presented on the psychosocial issues which affect someone newly diagnosed with HD. It is a topic that I have become well versed in, and the physicians and nurses in attendance were, according to the evaluations, appreciative of the content. The National Hansen's Disease Outpatient Program hosted the seminar.

While in Baton Rouge, I also visited my other family, at Carville, twenty-four elderly residents. One of them, of course, was Mary Ruth Daigle. Thirty-four years after I met Mary for the first time, she still greeted me with the same friendly disposition of a new acquaintance. In 2002, she was eighty-five years old, self-sufficient in her one-room apartment, going to appointments in her electric wheelchair, and working two jobs.

The toppling of the home Magdalena and I had lived in for twenty-six years countered my exhilaration from having had a successful trip to Louisiana. We saved the decorative wrought-iron column from the front porch and took a deep breath as we moved on to another chapter in our lives. Moving into our new home did not occur for another seven months.

By the time the house was demolished, Erika had started her senior year at Bellaire High School. By December 24, when Magdalena and I celebrated our thirtieth wedding anniversary, Erika had some unique accomplishments. She was voted senior class president and homecoming queen, celebrated her eighteenth birthday, worked at a popular restaurant and used her earnings to pay the $150 note on a used red Mustang, was voted Miss Bellaire, was chosen for varsity girls' softball, and was honored as a National Hispanic Scholar.

Erika and her middle school friends had, almost magically overnight, become young men and women.

Mom's illness from Alzheimer's worsened rapidly after her birthday. By December of 2002, she would shuffle her feet in a stationary position when asked to move to another location. After eating, she would discard any leftover food or drink on the floor, making my sister and her husband cringe as the carpet stains grew. My siblings had hired a lady to stay with Mom during the day and alternated caring for her on weekends. However, she had become verbally abusive and would "borrow" things that were shiny or new, like jewelry, table ornaments, and clothing. She would complain of pain when touched and her bowel and urinary habits became extremely irregular.

Mom's illness made us all cry and laugh at the same time. There were times when her mind and stare would wander, making us believe that she was only physically with us but not mentally. On one occasion, while in Laredo visiting her family, Magdalena went with her sister and mother to a popular cafeteria and by chance met up with Lety, my brother Rene's wife, and Mom. Lety was caring for her that day. While venting about the pressures of caring for Mom and worried about her ill father, she described her emotions by stating the challenges of having so many brothers- and sisters-in-law and said to Magdalena, "Ya sabes cómo son los Ramirez" ("You know how the Ramirez clan is"). According to Lety and Magdalena, Mom suddenly jumped back into reality, lifted her head up high, stared at both of them, and proudly declared, "Son muy buenos!" ("They are very good!"). Everyone at the table laughed hysterically.

On another occasion, Mom surprised everyone with her demand for attention. On Christmas day of 2002, my siblings and their children met at

Diana's home for the ongoing tradition of sharing food and gifts. Rudy, who had inherited the role Dad used to play in the distribution of presents, tried to call out names of adults and children in an effort to share the wealth and attention. On this day, Mom's name was not called in a manner consistent to her liking. So, during an unusual moment of silence, Mom said, "¿Con una chingada, cuando me van a dar a mi un regalo?" ("Damn it, when am I going to get a present?"). Everyone paused and embarrassedly urged Rudy to find a gift in the huge pile under the Christmas tree. Rudy made it a point to call out her name more frequently, resorting to even giving her the same gift twice. Alzheimer's can play cruel jokes on a family.

Rosalinda shared another memorable moment. At one time Mom was crying uncontrollably, saying that she had done something horribly wrong. Rosalinda, wishing to console her but unwilling to hear Mom's confession, reluctantly provided comfort by agreeing to listen to her. Mom, with a big sigh, said, "Tantos hijos y nadie me quiere" ("So many children and none of them love me"). Rosalinda gasped but quickly realized that it was the illness talking, not Mom.

Within a three-week period after Christmas, Mom had two falls. Neither resulted in broken bones but she required six stitches after the first fall and seventeen after the second. She was then afraid to walk and became bedridden. Her falls were attributed to ministrokes.

During the first week in February 2003, Mom was admitted to Mercy Hospital in Laredo where Dad had died and I had been originally diagnosed with HD. Her condition rapidly deteriorated, and the siblings in Laredo took turns to ensure twenty-four-hour care while she was hospitalized. Magdalena and I went to visit on February 8 and 9, the same dates on which I had visited Dad before he died on Valentine's Day, years earlier. We all sensed that Mom was ready to join Dad in heaven.

On the morning of February 9th, my birthday, I thanked Mom for giving me life fifty-five years earlier. She was incoherent, but I kissed her on the cheek and whispered for "una bendición," a sign of the cross. This was her trademark, a sign of going with God whenever any of us were ready to embark on a journey, and at the time I was returning to Houston. Unable to raise her right arm, she softly said, "No puedo" ("I can't"). She then lifted her left hand, gently stroked my hair, and said, as only a mother can, "Necesitas un corte" ("You need a haircut").

I cried and left her hospital room realizing I would not see her alive again.

Two days later, my siblings gathered in her hospital room to recite a rosary. Everyone described the moment as very uplifting, with Mom participating in the rosary and even responding to some good-natured ribbing. At approximately 5:48 a.m. on February 12, 2003, Mom took her last breaths by calling out my name and moved on to meet Dad, her parents, cousins, and *comadres*.

Everyone in the family became an active participant in celebrating Mom's life. Gerardo published a picture in the *Laredo Times*. Rudy wrote a beautiful poem, and Javier wrote an obituary with the theme "Who would have believed . . ." Yolanda and Rudy ordered the pink casket chosen by Mom. Idalia cleaned her fiftieth wedding anniversary dress. Rosalinda agreed to use her house as a gathering place after the funeral. Raquel and Diana donated the chairs and tables for the family get-together. Erika gave a eulogy on behalf of all the grandkids, and I gave a eulogy in Spanish.

Mom had a full house at the funeral home chapel and received hundreds of flowers. The priest at the funeral Mass acknowledged how much we loved her, and the funeral service concluded with a guitarist playing her favorite melodies. Afterwards, the family retreated to Rosalinda's home, and for hours we reminisced about our special moments with Mom. I was elated to have complied with her request to get a haircut.

Two other ladies who affected my life died on March 8, 2004 (Mary Ruth Daigle) and on February 18, 2007 (Margarita Ramirez Cuellar). Mague died from breast cancer. She took her last breath as I held her left hand and Magdalena her right and her children (Cynthia, Raul, and Cristy) rubbed her feet.

As I have reflected back on the sensation of drowning I felt when told of the diagnosis of leprosy, I have sensed that the lifeguard missing in 1968 was actually all around me in concrete and spiritual ways. The lack of colors evident at the moment of my diagnosis had, over a thirty-five-year period, been transformed into meaningful colors, as in the dark hair of our baby boy J. R., the wonderfully tan and talented hands of Erika, who painted her room to reflect the ocean, the brightly painted fingernails and toenails of Magdalena, the wonderful gray hair of my parents and siblings, and the bright smiles of all who supported and prayed for my recovery.

With much luck, and love, I avoided the anguish of drowning and instead was pulled out of a treacherous body of dirty water to enjoy the life of a person with a clean soul. Mom also started her new life in heaven with a soul as clear and clean as a beautiful diamond.

Time, science, and much tenacity in fighting the stigma associated with HD have presented me with a unique opportunity to receive emotional support and love from many individuals. Collectively, the support and love have strengthened my faith, and allowed me to overcome many fears.

## chapter 15

# Commonly Asked Questions

As I have expanded my horizons by traveling, I have met many individuals who have questions about Hansen's disease. I now feel comfortable enough with the history and treatment of the disease that I can provide ready responses. However, the responses do not always answer the questions. For example, whoever comes up with the correct answer to the question "How is HD transmitted?" will probably receive the Nobel Prize for Medicine. There are theories, but no concrete evidence on how HD is transmitted. Poor hygiene, as with other diseases, may be a factor in transmittal.

My response to inquiries about the disease always includes the medical term for the illness, Hansen's disease. However, this is usually followed by "more commonly known as leprosy." I use both terms, as neither perpetuates stigma. It is the "l" word that allows stigma to flourish.

Therefore it is best to simply list responses from experts provided by IDEA, Dr. Felton Ross, Dr. Wayne Meyers, Dr. Robert Jacobson, Dr. Margaret Brand, Dr. Paul Brand, and Dr. David Scollard.

*Does HD still exist?*

In June 2007, the World Health Organization (WHO) reported a "steady declining trend" of HD. WHO has had a goal, with changing time frames, to "eliminate leprosy as a public health problem" (defined as having a registered prevalence rate of < 1 case/10,000 population). Data provided by WHO for a thirteen-year period reflects a remarkable decrease in cases in India by 70 percent, although leprosy cases in India for 1993 represented 77 percent of the world total. India's education program does not adequately explain the dramatic decrease in cases. WHO claimed that the total number of "detected cases" for 2006 worldwide was 259,017, a 56.18 percent decrease in a thirteen-year period.[1]

Currently there is no standardized way to count each new diagnosis in the world.

There are several million individuals who are cured but whose lives are still affected by their physical disabilities and by social injustice.

Leprosy is endemic in fifteen countries, with the largest number of people affected residing in India, Brazil, Indonesia, Bangladesh, and Nepal.

*What is leprosy?*

HD is a chronic infectious disease caused by a bacillus, *Mycobacterium leprae*, which was discovered by Dr. Gerhard H. A. Hansen in Norway in 1873. This disproved theories that the disease was hereditary and made it possible to search for a cure.

HD primarily involves the nerves, skin, and mucous membranes. If untreated, there can be progressive and permanent damage to the skin, limbs, and eyes.

*How do you get leprosy?*

Only about 3 percent of the world's population is susceptible to HD. Leprosy is very difficult to contract.

*What is the source of infection?*

There is no universal answer to this difficult question. Depending on the source, some researchers claim that the bacillus is in the air, the soil, armadillos, the mangabey monkey.

*Can leprosy be cured?*

Yes.

In 1941, Dr. Guy Faget first used a sulfone drug, promin, in the treatment of leprosy at the U.S. Public Health Service Hospital in Carville, Louisiana. Additional sulfone drugs were then developed, including diasone, later called dapsone. These "miracle drugs" produced changes practically overnight, and individuals were increasingly able to participate in sports and other activities.

In 1981, the use of a "cocktail" of three drugs, dapsone, rifampicin, and clofazimine, known as multidrug therapy (MDT), made it possible to cure the disease more rapidly. Leaders in the field of leprosy agree that even the most ill individual becomes noninfectious within nine to twelve months of treatment as the bacillus has been eliminated from the body by this time. Thalidomide has also been used successfully to attack the bacillus.

Early diagnosis and treatment can prevent the disabilities traditionally associated with leprosy. Unfortunately, in many parts of the world, fear, ignorance, and persistent social stigma prevent many from seeking treatment or feeling completely cured.

In the United States, the National Hansen's Disease Program, under the federal Health Resources and Services Administration (HRSA), contract for the provision of HD treatment on an outpatient basis. These clinics are located in:[2]

Boston, Massachusetts
Chicago, Illinois
Los Angeles, California
Martinez, California
Miami Beach, Florida
New York, New York
Phoenix, Arizona
San Diego, California
San Juan, Puerto Rico
Seattle, Washington
Texas (several clinics)

*Can leprosy be eliminated?*

With new cases every year, this has been a difficult thing to accomplish.

The incubation period can be as long as twenty years, resulting in many untreated cases.

With the "elimination campaign" started by the World Health Organization, there are now fewer physicians specializing in the study and treatment of leprosy; i.e., the expertise in leprosy has declined.

*Does leprosy occur only in warm climates?*

No. Leprosy has been found historically in all the inhabited continents and in all major ethnic groups except the Native American (no recorded cases). The prevalence of leprosy seems to have more to do with the standard of living in an area than its climate.

*Is leprosy fatal?*

Only in very rare instances. However, according to Dr. David Scollard, chief of pathology at the National Hansen's Disease Center, individuals with advanced cases of leprosy have been known to die from secondary infections or from larynx involvement (the larynx slowly becomes swollen, cutting off air).

*How do disabilities in hands and feet occur?*

Nerve injury leads to a loss of feeling in hands and feet, rendering them more vulnerable to repeated injury and infection.

Nerve injury also causes muscle weakness and paralysis.

Due to infection and other changes, bones are reabsorbed and fingers and toes become shortened.

None of these disabilities need occur with early diagnosis and treatment.

*If leprosy is curable, why is there such a stigma attached to the disease?*

The stigma associated with leprosy has been present since some of the earliest suspected cases of the disease were documented more than three thousand years ago, long before there was any treatment or hope for those affected by it.

The stigma has been handed down from generation to generation in all parts of the world in many cultural ways—through figures of speech, art, religion, and, more recently, movies and television.

The origins of the stigma are, therefore, based on the disease as it appeared hundreds of years ago; stigma has no place in modern society.

The impact of stigma on a person's life continues long after the leprosy bacillus has been declared inactive.

Public education about HD is grossly lacking.

The author's definition of stigma is: an act of labeling, rejection, or unexplained fear of a person.

In 2005, over thirty members of IDEA made presentations at the Conference on Stigma, Identity and Human Rights on Robben Island, South Africa. Prior to Robben Island becoming a symbol of overcoming apartheid, this cold and barren place was used to isolate persons with leprosy. Other copresentations involved South Africans affected by AIDS and also facing the stigma historically reserved for persons affected by leprosy.

In January 2008, the 17th International Leprosy Congress was held in Hyderabad, India. Up to 30 percent of the sessions were on psychosocial issues. I made five presentations.

*What is the correct terminology?*

The strong negative associations with the word "leprosy" and subsequent use of the derogatory word "leper" have resulted in some advocating that the name be changed from leprosy to Hansen's disease. This has been officially done in some countries, including Brazil and Japan.

Terms like "leper," "Hansenite," and "Hanseniano" are inappropriate. These words define individuals solely on the basis of their disease and conjure up old images that have nothing to do with modern realities.

*What is the future of leprosy?*
The resources, though not currently coordinated, may be available to make vaccines for the diagnosis, prevention, and treatment of HD.

The World Health Organization (WHO) has changed its prediction that HD can be "eliminated" on several occasions. However, in 2008, WHO accepted the recommendaion of the Technical Advisory Group (TAG) that "leprosy is not an eradicable disease."

IDEA will continue to advocate for the rights of individuals affected by leprosy.

In 2003, Magdalena and I and three other members of IDEA from India, Philippines, and Ethiopia presented topics on rights to the United Nations Commission on Human Rights in Geneva, Switzerland. The trip was sponsored by the Sasakawa Memorial Health Foundation in Japan.

In January 2007, I joined fifteen of my brothers and sisters from throughout the world in signing the Global Appeal to End Stigma and Discrimination against People Affected by Leprosy. The appeal was initiated by Yohei Sasakawa, WHO Goodwill Ambassador for the Elimination of Leprosy.

In January 2008, Erika traveled with me to London; I presented "Stigma Hurts" at the Royal Society of Medicine, where the Global Appeal to Eliminate Stigma and Discrimination was launched for 2008.

The Nippon Foundation has provided funding to the International Leprosy Association's Global Project on the History of Leprosy. As a result, over 250 oral histories have been completed, along with still pictures and videos. My son, José Roberto, and I traveled to Ukraine in March 2007 and documented how during World War II the Nazis actively sought persons residing in leprosariums and killed them, simply because they had HD or worked with persons affected by leprosy.

Dr. Richard Truman, research scientist at the National Hansen's Disease Center, has predicted that by 2013 scientists will be able to prove or disprove the link between humans and armadillos in the transmittal of the HD bacillus.

*Where can readers get more information on leprosy?*
There are twenty-seven museums worldwide that have artifacts and historical information on HD. Seven of special significance are:
Acworth Leprosy Hospital and Museum, Mumbai, India
Culion Museum, Culion, Philippines
Damien Museum, Honolulu, Hawaii (USA)
Leprosy Museum (Lepra Muselt), Bergen, Norway
National Hansen's Disease Museum, Carville, Louisiana (USA)
Robben Island Museum, Robben Island, South Africa
Takamutso Memorial Museum of Hansen's Disease, Tokyo, Japan
Other information is available through:
www.idealeprosy.dignity.org
www.leprosy.org
www.nippon.foundation.or.jp
http:bphc.hrsa.gov/nhdp/NHD-MUSEUM.HISTORY.HTM>

*How do ex-residents remember Carville?*
Fondly, as sensitively described in a poem by Ymelda Rivera Beauchamp.[3]

## To Carville—The Hospital
Ymelda Beauchamp

*I want to go back to that place*
*That sits amid the willows and old oak trees*
*That beautiful place that has history*
*And a connection to many memories*
*I'm told that big house is still standing*
*Near Old Man River and the lake*
*This place that was a refuge to the sick and rejected*
*Now houses soldiers wearing green berets*
*I remember the forlorn whistles at dawn*
*Of the barges and big boats*
*Moving swiftly down the Mississippi*
*Live river ghosts dancing in the fog*

*I long to walk the corridors once again*
*Of this home so far away*
*Of that shelter that protects me, healed my body*
*And still haunts my nights and days*

*Love, do you remember that ardor of jasmine*
*And the smell of honeysuckle after rain*
*The clamor of the wheelchairs in the hallways*
*And our laughter after pain?*

*Remember the movie theater*
*And all the people in the canteen*
*The strong smell of coffee and chicory*
*And the song you always sang to me?*

*Remember love, when we cuddled*
*In that place away from prying eyes?*
*We talked about our life, hopes and dreams*
*And everything under that sultry southern sky.*

*Remember the thunder that pierced the silence*
*In the stillness of our lonely nights?*
*And muffled our secret yearnings*
*For a better life on the outside.*

*Remember all the angels dressed in their white gowns*
*That understood our fears*
*They held us in their bosom*
*And dried up all our tears?*
*I want to see the infirmary once again*
*Where I spent so many days*
*This home that nurtured and sustained my early years*
*And still beckons me today*

*I want to look back at the reflection*
*Of the young girl I used to be*
*A girl ablaze with love and passion*
*For all things that would never be.*

*Please take me back to walk those hallways,*
*Hallways covered with white walls,*
*Walls that heard so many secrets*
*Some they kept some they told and some I know . . .*
*I want to see Carville, my sweet home away from home*

*The beautiful place that witnessed suffering and profound hopes.*
*I want to go back to that home again that I left so long ago*
*Where people lived, cried and loved and now everyone is gone . . .*

# NOTES

## Chapter 1. No One Told You?

The author's response to inquiries about the disease always includes the medical term for the illness, Hansen's disease (HD). However, oftentimes this must be followed by "more commonly known as leprosy." The author uses both terms throughout the book, as neither perpetuates stigma. In the opinion of the author, it is "leper," the "l" word, that allows stigma to flourish.

1. John R. Trautman, "A Brief History of Hansen's Disease," *The Star*, vol. 45, no. 7 (November–December, 1985), p. 20.
2. "Leviticus," *The Jerusalem Bible* (Garden City, New York: Doubleday and Company, 1966) pp. 142–152.
3. Raymond McPhearson, "Biblical Leprosy vs. Present Day Hansen's Disease: A Pastoral Perspective," *The Star*, vol. 47, no. 2 (November–December, 1987), p. 8.
4. Robert C. Hastings, ed., *Leprosy* (New York: Churchhill Livingstone, 1985), p. 6.
5. "Parashas Tuzrio," *Living Each Week*, 1996, p. 225.
6. Ari Kiev, *Curanderismo* (New York: The Free Press, 1968), p. 28.
7. Richard Vara, "The Lady of Guadalupe," *Houston Chronicle*, December 9, 2000, religion section, p. 1.
8. Electronic communication with Tony Ramirez on November 25, 2000.
9. Kiev, *Curanderismo*, p. 82.
10. Hastings, *Leprosy*, p. 31.
11. Stanley Green, *Laredo 1755–1920: An Overview* (Laredo: Santander Museum Complex, 1985), p. 16.
12. A. Muzur, A. Skrobonja, V. Rotschild, and A. Skrobonja, Jr., "Saints Protectors from Leprosy: Historical Hints of Suggestive Therapy?" *International Journal of Leprosy*, vol. 70, no. 4 (2002), pp. 269–273.
13. Jim Krane, "Azteca: A Diamond in the Rough," *The Laredo Times*, August 9, 2002, section D, p. 1.

## Chapter 2. The Journey

1. McPhearson, "Biblical Leprosy," p. 9.
2. Hastings, ed., *Leprosy*, p. 6.
3. Ibid., pp. 1–4.
4. Ibid., p. 24.
5. S. J. Lerro, "Texas Leprosy Program Begins Rehabilitation," *The Star*, vol. 29, no. 1 (September–October 1969), p. 61.
6. Stanley Stein, *Alone No Longer* (New York: Funk and Wagnalls, 1964), p. 61.
7. Hastings, ed., *Leprosy*, p. 18.

## Chapter 3. Treatment at Last

1. Hastings, ed., *Leprosy*, p. 45.
2. Betty Martin, *Miracle at Carville* (Garden City, New York: Doubleday and Company, Inc., 1963).
3. Hastings, ed., *Leprosy*, p. 9.
4. Interview with Elizabeth Schexnyder, curator at the National Hansen's Disease Museum, Carville, Louisiana, July 13, 2007.

## Chapter 4. Learning about Carville

1. Leprosy Registry Department, Clinical Branch, United States Public Health Service Hospital, Carville, Louisiana, 1968.
2. Hastings, ed., *Leprosy*, p. 46.
3. Patrick Feeney, *Fight Against Leprosy* (London, N. 1: Elek Books, Limited 1964), p. 131.
4. Original manuscript at the National Hansen's Disease Museum, Carville, Louisiana.
5. "Rules for Inmates" (Louisiana Leper Board, 1913).
6. I. Thomas Buckley, *Penikese: Island of Hope* (North Chatham, Massachusetts: Stony Brook Publishing & Productions, 1997), p. 42.
7. Letter dated September 23, 1997, from Marjorie Hershey of the Texas Comptroller of Public Accounts.
8. Leprosy Registry Department.

## Chapter 5. Life at Carville

1. During my hospitalization, I received over five thousand letters and cards from my parents, siblings, other relatives, Magdalena, and high school friends. I do not know how many I wrote.
2. Stein, *Alone No Longer*, p. 75.
3. Motto for *The Star*.

## Chapter 6. Four Months and Counting

1. Berton Roueché, *Eleven Blue Men* (New York: Berkley Publishing Company, 1967), p. 112.
2. Hastings, ed., *Leprosy*, p. 49.
3. Ibid., p. 12.
4. Margaret E. Brand, with James L. Jost, *Vision for God* (Grand Rapids, Michigan: Discovery House Publishers, 2006), p. 168.
5. Greene, *Laredo*, p. 16.
6. This bell is by the front door to the National Hansen's Disease Museum in Carville, Louisiana, greeting all guests to my old home.

## Chapter 7. First Visit to Laredo

1. "Hot on the Trail," *The Laredo News*, June 3, 1984, section C, p. 1.
2. My Lions vest was donated to the National Hansen's Disease Museum.
3. Information on policy change is in my medical records.

## Chapter 8. Manhood and Beyond

1. Rob Walsh, "Mama's Got a Brand New Bag," *Houston Press*, September 28–October 4, 2000, p. 63.
2. Erving Goffman, *Stigma* (Englewood Cliffs, New Jersey: Prentice Hall, Inc., 1943), p. 8.

## Chapter 9. The Magic of Dreaming

1. Jons G. Anderson, "The Mediaeval Leper," *The Star*, vol. 50, no. 6, July–August 1991, p. 8.

## Chapter 10. The Power of Motherly Love

1. Ymelda Rivera, traductor, "Observaciones De La Lepra en 1970," *Condensaciónes de la Estrella* (Edición de Mayo–Junio 1970).
2. Mom believed that her Bible was the rosary, and thus had never bought a Bible for the family.
3. Dr. Robert Jacobson, ex-director of the hospital at Carville, oftentimes mentioned this information in his presentations.

## Chapter 11. Life after Death

1. The lasting memory of painful reactions taught all of the residents at Carville to seek medical treatment quickly. Conversely, insensitivity to pain in the hands and feet could result in an avoidance of medical care, leading to further injury.

2.    Emanuel Faria, "People," *The Star*, vol. 37, no. 5, May–June 1978, p. 9.
3.    Emanuel Faria, "HD and Marital Stress," *The Star*, vol. 36, no. 3, January–February 1977, p. 11.
4.    Emanuel Faria, op. cit., p. 1.

## Chapter 12

1.    Yasuji Hirasawa, *No Despair in Life* (Seneca Falls, New York: IDEA Center for the Voices of Humanity, 2006), p. 2.

## Chapter 13. Change Is Good

1.    Statement made by tour guide.

## Chapter 14. Living with a Clean Soul

1.    Tom Frist, *The Descendant* (Lincoln, Nebraska: Writer's Showcase, 2002), p. 8.

## Chapter 15. Commonly Asked Questions

1.    "Weekly Epidemiological Record," *World Health Organization Report* (Geneva, Switzerland: June 2007), pp. 225–232.
2.    "Outpatient HD Clinic," *Diagnosis and Treatment of Hansen's Disease in the United States* (Baton Rouge, Louisiana: National Hansen's Disease Program, 2004), p. 25.
3.    Ymelda Rivera Beauchamp, poem titled "To Carville—The Hospital," 2000.

# BIBLIOGRAPHY

Anderson, Jons G. "The Mediaeval Leper." *The Star*, vol. 50, no. 6, July–August 1991.

Beauchamp, Ymelda Rivera. "To Carville—The Hospital." 2000.

Brand, Margaret E., with James L. Jost. *Vision for God*. Rapids, MI: Discovery House Publications, 2006.

Buckley, I. Thomas. *Penikese: Island of Hope*. Chatham, MA: Stony Brook Publishing & Productions, 1997.

Daws, Goven. *Holy Man: Father Damien of Molokai*. Honolulu: Hawaii Press, 1973.

DeMers, John. "Cinco Tortillas." *Houston Chronicle*, May 2, 2001.

Faria, Emanuel. "HD and Marital Stress." *The Star*, vol. 36, no. 3, January–February 1977.

———. "People." *The Star*, vol. 37, no. 5, May–June 1978.

Feeney, Patrick. *Fight Against Leprosy*. London, N. 1: Elek Books Limited, 1964.

Frist, Tom. *The Descendant*. Lincoln, NE: Writer's Showcase, 2002.

Goffman, Erving. *Stigma*. Englewood Cliffs, NJ: Prentice Hall, Inc.,1943.

Green, Stanley. *Laredo 1755–1920: An Overview*. Laredo: Santander Museum Complex, 1985.

Gussow, Zachary, and George S. Tracy. "Status, Ideology and Adaptation to Stigmatized Illness: A Study of Leprosy." *Human Organizations*, 1970.

Hastings, Robert C., ed. *Leprosy*. New York: Churchill Livingstone, 1985.

Hirasawa, Yasuji. *No Despair in Life*. New York: IDEA Center for the Voices of Humanity, 2006.

"Hot on the Trail." *Laredo News*, June 3, 1984.

Kiev, Ari. *Curanderismo*. New York: The Free Press, 1968.

Krane, Jim. "Azteca: A Diamond in the Rough." *Laredo Times*, August 9, 1992.

Leprosy Registry Department, United States Public Health Service Hospital, Carville, Lousiana, 1968.

Lerro, S. J. "Texas Leprosy Program Begins Rehabilitation." *The Star*, vol. 29, no.1, September–October 1969.

"Leviticus." *The Jerusalem Bible*. New York: Doubleday and Company, 1966.

Martin, Betty. *Miracle at Carville*. New York: Doubleday and Company, 1963.

McPhearson, Raymond. "Biblical Leprosy vs. Present Day Hansen's Disease." *The Star*, vol. 45, no. 2, November–December 1987.

Muzur, A., A. Skrobonja, V. Rothschild, and A. Skronbonja, Jr. "Saints Protectors from Leprosy: Historical Hints of Suggestive Therapy." *International Journal of Leprosy*, vol. 70, no. 4, 2002.

"Outpatient HD Clinics." *Diagnosis and Treatment of Hansen's Disease in the United States*. National Hansen's Disease Program, Baton Rouge, Louisiana, 2004.

"Parashas, Tuzrio." *Living Each Week*, 1996.

Rivera, Ymelda, traductor. "Observaciones De La Lepra en 1970." *Estrella*, Edición de Mayo–Junio 1970.

Roueché, Berton. *Eleven Blue Men*. New York: Berkley Publishing Company, 1967.

"Rules For Inmates." Lousiana Leper Board, 1913.

Stein, Stanley. *Alone No Longer*. New York: Funk and Wagnalls, 1964.

Walsh, Rob. "Mama's Got a Brand New Bag." *Houston Press*, September 28–October 4, 2000.

Weekly Epidemiological Record. Geneva, Switzerland: *World Health Organization Report*, no. 24, June 2007.